Dignity, Degrading Treatment and Torture in Human Rights Law

Although scholars have shown longstanding interest in the boundaries of interpretation of the right not to be subjected to torture and other prohibited harm, the existing body of work does not sufficiently reflect the significance of the interpretive scope of degrading treatment. This book argues that the degrading treatment element of the right is a crucial site of analysis, in itself and for understanding the parameters of the right as a whole. It addresses how, methodologically, the scope of meaning and application of the right not to be subjected to degrading treatment should best be identified and considers the implications thereof. It systematically examines the diverse aspects of degrading treatment's scope, from foundations of legal interpretation to the drivers of humiliation. It draws on wide-ranging literature and extensive analysis of more than 1,500 judgments of the European Court of Human Rights, which has pioneered the right's interpretive growth. The book aims to explore how the interpretive possibilities, and limits, of the right not to be subjected to degrading treatment turn upon the axes of human dignity and state responsibility, and aims to show how this right's protection can be achieved as well as limited through processes of interpretation.

Dignity, Degrading Treatment and Torture in Human Rights Law provides interpreters with analytical tools to advance the application of the right not to be subjected to torture, cruel, inhuman or degrading treatment or punishment in international, regional and domestic human rights law. It will appeal to all who have an interest in understanding the right's meaning, development, and potential scope of application, as well as those with an interest in methodologies of human rights interpretation.

Elaine Webster is a lecturer in law at the University of Strathclyde, UK.

Routledge Research in Human Rights Law

For a full list of titles in this series, please visit www.routledge.com/Routledge-Research-in-Human-Rights-Law/book-series/HUMRIGHTSLAW

Available titles in this series include:

Freedom from Religion and Human Rights Law
Strengthening the Right to Freedom of Religion and Belief for Non-Religious and Atheist Rights-Holders
Marika McAdam

Freedom of Expression and Religious Hate Speech in Europe
Erica Howard

The Protection of Vulnerable Groups under International Human Rights Law
Ingrid Nifosi-Sutton

Children's Rights Law in the Global Human Rights Landscape
Isolation, Inspiration, Integration?
Edited by Eva Brems, Ellen Desmet and Wouter Vandenhole

The Istanbul Convention, Domestic Violence and Human Rights
Ronagh J. A. McQuigg

Human Rights Education and the Politics of Knowledge
Joanne Coysh

Resolving Conflicts between Human Rights
The Judge's Dilemma
Stijn Smet

The ECHR and Human Rights Theory
Reconciling the Moral and the Political Conceptions
Alain Zysset

Developing the Right to Social Security – A Gender Perspective
Beth Goldblatt

Dignity, Degrading Treatment and Torture in Human Rights Law

The Ends of Article 3 of the European Convention on Human Rights

Elaine Webster

Routledge
Taylor & Francis Group
LONDON AND NEW YORK

First published 2018
by Routledge

2 Park Square, Milton Park, Abingdon, Oxfordshire OX14 4RN
52 Vanderbilt Avenue, New York, NY 10017

Routledge is an imprint of the Taylor & Francis Group, an informa business

First issued in paperback 2019

British Library Cataloguing in Publication Data
A catalogue record for this book is available from the British Library

Library of Congress Cataloging in Publication Data
Names: Webster, Elaine, author.
Title: Dignity, degrading treatment and torture in human rights law : the ends of Article 3 of the European Convention on Human Rights / Elaine Webster.
Description: New York : Routledge, 2018. | Series: Routledge research in human rights law | Includes bibliographical references and index.
Identifiers: LCCN 2017054058 | ISBN 9781138856639 (hardback) |
ISBN 9781317516002 (epub) |
ISBN 9781317516019 (web pdf) | ISBN 9781317515999 (mobipocket)
Subjects: LCSH: Human rights–Europe. | Respect for persons–Law and legislation–Europe. | Dignity. | Cruelty. | Torture (International law) | Convention for the Protection of Human Rights and Fundamental Freedoms (1950 November 5)
Classification: LCC KJC5141 .W43 2018 | DDC 342.2408/5–dc23
LC record available at https://lccn.loc.gov/2017054058

ISBN: 978-1-138-85663-9 (hbk)
ISBN: 978-0-367-89429-0 (pbk)

Typeset in Galliard
by Taylor & Francis Books

Contents

Preface and acknowledgements

I have been intrigued by the meaning of the right not to be subjected to torture, cruel, inhuman or degrading treatment or punishment since I was a postgraduate student listening to Professor Paul Lemmens giving a lecture about the European Convention system. He talked about the case of *Yankov v. Bulgaria*, in which guards shaved a prisoner's head and placed him in solitary confinement, and in which the European Court of Human Rights arrived at a finding of degrading treatment. This book is a reflection of my thinking about this right and the other paths that have stemmed from that initial interest.

One such path relates to the idea of human dignity. This is a path that, at first, I willingly pursued. I then tried to backtrack upon it as it became clear that it was leading down a rabbit hole, overflowing with competing perspectives from multiple disciplinary and practice-based viewpoints. However, I realised that if I wanted to unpack a rationale for the right not to be subjected to torture, cruel, inhuman or degrading treatment or punishment I was going to have to embrace the dignity idea and its related field of scholarship. In hindsight I am thankful, as this path provided the foundation for my own approach to understanding human rights law and discourse more broadly – as one mechanism for protecting human dignity as a moral value, following scholars like Jack Donnelly. My interest in the dignity idea has allowed me to learn from some inspiring academic debates, notably reflected in the work of Jeremy Waldron, and it has allowed me to be part of passionate conversations, in particular with my colleague Mary Neal. I have been inspired by this focus on the dignity idea to explore it in new areas, from its role in health professional education to its place in human rights-based approaches to policy delivery.

I came to realise that all the research questions that have intrigued me have reflected a concern with interpretation. Who should we see as having the authority to interpret human rights laws, which are declared to promote empowerment of individual rights-holders in local contexts? What are the limits of interpretation, both in judicial and extra-judicial contexts? What are the pivotal moments in interpretive engagements and how do they lead (more or less directly) to advances in practical protection? How do such questions, which have long been asked in legal theoretical and socio-legal perspectives, play out within the unique vertical, individual-versus-state framework of human rights law? These questions about interpretation led me back full circle to the *Yankov* case and the then-unarticulated questions underlying it: How does a judicial interpretation of a legal text reflect the bi-directional permeability of legal interpretations, which take in and give out new meanings? How does this impact on recognition of individual demands for dignity protection and how does it filter into the way that the business of the state is conducted (through public policy practices or individual professional commitments)? To what extent does the proclaimed absolute nature of the right not to be subjected to torture and associated harm provide an observatory for both the expansive possibilities and the limits of human rights law in protecting individuals' dignity?

This book builds upon doctoral research at the University of Edinburgh, for which I am very grateful to have received funding from the Arts and Humanities Research Council. There are many people I would like to thank: the Routledge editorial team, the anonymous reviewers of the proposal for this book, and those who kindly agreed to provide feedback on individual chapters: Stewart Cunningham, Mary Neal, Sophie Oliver, Stephen Riley, Peter Robson, and Emily Rose. I am grateful to have received permission to use material previously published in E Webster, 'Degradation: A Human Rights Law Perspective' in P Kaufmann et al. (eds), *Humiliation, Degradation, Dehumanization: Human Dignity Violated* (Springer 2011). I would like to thank the Strathclyde students who have ably assisted me with various aspects of the research that has fed into this book: Elio Ajmone, Jacob Hay, Conor Hill, Natalia Lungu, and Rebecca McGregor. I would also like to acknowledge the Royal Society of Edinburgh/Caledonian Research Foundation for funding a Visiting Fellowship to the Catholic University Leuven, Belgium. This allowed time to undertake research on human dignity, to meet Professor Paul Lemmens again, and to undertake research at the library of the European Court of Human Rights. I would also like to thank, in particular, my friend the above-mentioned Sophie Oliver, whose impressive critical thinking inspired me during our postgraduate studies together; Stephen Tierney, my trusted PhD supervisor who continued to provide much-appreciated support over the years; Jane Scoular, my office mate, who has always given advice with encouragement; my friend Michelle Smith, who helped me to draw together the insights from my case-law database; and Anne de la Croix, fellow dedicated mother, academic and weekly cheerleader. I thank my family and my husband, Michaël, who provided invaluable logistical support. Finally, I thank my daughters, Margaux and Esmée, who brought me happily down to earth every day during the process of writing this book.

Additional sources

Websites

The Telegraph, 'Home Secretary: scrap the Human Rights Act', 1 October 2011, available at: <www.telegraph.co.uk/news/politics/8801651/Home-Secretary-scrap-the-Human-Rights-Act.html> (accessed 27 October 2017)

Conventions/General Comments:

Council of Europe Committee for the Prevention of Torture, *Report to the French Government on the visit to France carried out by the European Committee for the Prevention of Torture and Inhuman or Degrading Treatment or Punishment from 11 to 17 June 2003*, CPT/Inf (2004) 6

Council of Europe Committee for the Prevention of Torture, *Report to the Government of the Netherlands on the visit to the Netherlands carried out by the European Committee for the Prevention of Torture and Inhuman or Degrading Treatment or Punishment from 2 to 13 May 2016*, CPT/Inf (2017) 1

Council of Europe Committee for the Prevention of Torture, *Report to the United Kingdom Government on the visit to the United Kingdom carried out by the European Committee for the Prevention of Torture and Inhuman or Degrading Treatment or Punishment from 29 July to 10 August 1990*, CPT/Inf (91) 15

Council of Europe, *European Convention for the Prevention of Torture and Inhuman or Degrading Treatment or Punishment* (adopted 26 November 1987, entered into force 1 February 1989) ETS 126

Council of Europe, *European Convention for the Protection of Human Rights and Fundamental Freedoms*, as amended by Protocols Nos 11 and 14 (adopted 4 November 1950, entered into force 3 September 1953) ETS 5

Organisation of American States, *Inter-American Convention to Prevent and Punish Torture* (adopted 9 December 1985, entered into force 28 February 1987), 67 OASTS

Report of the Drafting Committee [on an International Bill of Rights] to the Commission on Human Rights, UN DOC E/CN.4/95, 21 May 1948, p. 6)

United Nations, Commission on Human Rights, Third Session, 54th Meeting, UN DOC E/CN.4/SR.54, 1 June 1948

United Nations, *Convention Against Torture and Other Cruel, Inhuman or Degrading Treatment or Punishment* (adopted 10 December 1984, entered into force 26 June 1987) 1465 UNTS 85

United Nations General Assembly, *International Covenant on Civil and Political Rights* (adopted 16 December 1966, entered into force 23 March 1976) 999 UNTS 171

United Nations General Assembly, *Universal Declaration of Human Rights* (10 December 1948) 217 A (III)

United Nations Human Rights Committee, *General Comment No. 20, Replaces General Comment 7 Concerning Prohibition of Torture and Cruel Treatment or Punishment* (Art. 7), 10 March 1992

United Nations, *Vienna Convention on the Law of Treaties* (adopted 23 May 1969, entered into force 27 January 1980) 1155 UNTS 331

Miscellaneous

Dignity International, 'Strategic Plan 2014–2016', May 2013, available at: <http://dignityinternational.org/v3/about-us/0> (accessed 5 March 2018)

Harvard Human Rights Journal, 'Michael Bochenek Interview, Part I', 15 May 2012, available at: <http://harvardhrj.com/2012/05/michael-bochenek-interview-part-i/> (accessed 20 October 2017)

Human Rights Watch, 'A Move to Restore Dignity to Syria's Victims', 15 September 2017, available at: <www.hrw.org/news/2017/09/15/move-restore-dignity-syrias-victims> (accessed 20 October 2017)

United Nations General Assembly, *Annotations on the Text of the Draft International Covenants on Human Rights*, A/2929, 1 July 1955 (Chapter 5)

Table of cases

Abdi Mahamud v. Malta, no. 56796/13, 3 May 2016.
Abdulaziz, Cabales and Balkandali v. UK, judgment of 28 May 1985, Series A, no. 94.
Afanasyev v. Ukraine, no. 38722/02, 5 April 2005.
Ahmed v. Austria, judgment of 17 December 1996, *Reports* 1996–VI.
Ahmet Özkan and Others v. Turkey, no. 21689/93, 6 April 2004.
Airey v. Ireland, judgement of 9 October 1979, Series A, no. 32.
Akdeniz v. Turkey, no. 25165/94, 31 May 2005.
Akkoyunlu v. Turkey, no. 7505/06, 13 October 2015.
Akkum and Others v. Turkey, no. 21894/93, 24 March 2005.
Aksoy v. Turkey, no. 21987/93, *Reports* 1996–IV.
Al Nashiri v. Poland, no. 28761/11, 24 July 2014.
Al-Saadoon and Mufdhi v. UK, no. 61498/08, ECHR 2010.
AL.K. v. Greece, no. 63542/11, 11 December 2014.
Albert et Le Compte v. Belgium, judgment of 10 February 1983, Series A, no. 58.
Aleksandr Vladimirovich Smirnov v. Ukraine, no. 69250/11, 13 March 2014.
Altun v. Turkey, no. 24561/94, 1 June 2004.
Apostu v. Romania, no. 22765/12, 3 February 2015.
Barbu Anghelescu v. Romania, no. 46430/99, 5 October 2004.
Bataliny v. Russia, no. 10060/07, 23 July 2015.
Bazorkina v. Russia, no. 69481/01, 27 July 2006.
Becciev v. Moldova, no. 9190/03, 4 October 2005.
Benzer and Others v. Turkey, no. 23502/06, 12 November 2013.
Berktay v. Turkey, no. 22493/93, 1 March 2001.
Bilgin v. Turkey, no. 23819/94, 16 November 2000.
Bouyid v. Belgium [GC], no. 23380/09, ECHR 2015.
Buldu and Others v. Turkey, no. 14017/08, 3 June 2014.
Büyükdağ v. Turkey, no. 28340/95, 21 December 2000.
Çakıcı v. Turkey [GC], 8 July 1999, *Reports of Judgments and Decisions* 1999–IV.
Čalovskis v. Latvia, no. 22205/13, 24 July 2014.
Campbell and Cosans v. UK, judgment of 25 February 1982, Series A, no. 48.
Chahal v. UK, no. 22414/93, *Reports* 1996–V.
Ciorap v. The Republic of Moldova (No. 4), no. 14092/06, 8 July 2014.

Costello-Roberts v. UK, judgment of 25 March 1993, Series A, no. 247–C.
D. v. UK, judgment of 2 May 1997, *Reports* 1997–III.
Davydov And Others v. Ukraine, 17674/02, 39081/02, 1 July 2010.
Denis Vasilyev v. Russia, no. 32704/04, 17 December 2009.
Đorđević v. Croatia, no. 41526/10, ECHR 2012.
Dougoz v. Greece, no. 40907/98, ECHR 2001–II.
Drăgan v. Romania, no. 65158/09, 2 February 2016.
Dulaş v. Turkey, no. 25801/94, 30 January 2001.
Duval v. France, no. 19868/08, 26 May 2011.
E. and Others v. UK, no. 33218/96, 26 November 2002.
E. and Others v. UK, no. 33218/96, 26 November 2002.
El-Masri v. The Former Yugoslav Republic of Macedonia, no. 39630/09, 13 December 2012.
Elberte v. Latvia, no. 61243/08, ECHR 2015.
Engel v. Hungary, no. 46857/06, 20 May 2010.
F.H. v. Greece, no. 78456/11, 31 July 2014.
Farbtuhs v. Latvia, no. 4672/02, 2 December 2004.
Frérot v. France, no. 70204/01, 12 June 2007.
Gafgen v. Germany, no. 22978/05, ECHR 2010.
Ghorbanov and Others v. Turkey, no. 28127/09, 3 December 2013.
Gongadze v. Ukraine, no. 34056/02, 8 November 2005.
Gorobet v. Moldova, no. 30951/10, 11 October 2011.
Gorodnitchev v. Russia, no. 52058/99, 24 May 2007.
Govedarski v. Bulgaria, no. 34957/12, 6 February 2016.
Gül v. Switzerland, no. 23218/94, *Reports* 1996–I.
Guzzardi v. Italy, judgment of 6 November 1980, Series A, no. 39.
H.L.R. v. France [GC], judgment of 29 April 1997, *Reports* 1997–III.
Helhal v. France, no. 10401/12, 19 February 2015.
Hénaf v. France, no. 65436/01, ECHR 2003–XI.
Hristozov and Others v. Bulgaria, no. 47039/11; 358/12, ECHR 2012 (extracts).
Iacov Stanciu v. Romania, no. 35972/05, 24 July 2012.
Ilievska v. The Former Yugoslav Republic of Macedonia, no. 20136/11, 7 May 2015.
Iljina and Sarulienė v. Lithuania, no. 32293/05, 15 March 2011.
Ioan Pop et Autres v. Romania, no. 52924/09, 6 December 2016.
Ireland v. UK, judgment of 18 January 1978, Series A, no. 25.
Iwańczuk v. Poland, no. 25196/94, 15 November 2001.
Jabari v. Turkey, no. 40035/98, ECHR 2000–VIII.
Jaeger v. Estonia, no. 1574/13, 31 July 2014.
Jalloh v. Germany, no. 54810/00, ECHR 2006–IX.
Janowiec and Others v. Russia, no. 55508/07; 29520/09, ECHR 2012.
Kalashnikov v. Russia, no. 47095/99, ECHR 2002–VI.
Karalevičius v. Lithuania, no. 53254/99, 7 April 2005.
Karayiğit v. Turkey, no. 63181/00, 20 September 2005.
Keenan v. UK, no. 27229/95, ECHR 2001–III.

Khodzhayev v. Russia, no. 52466/08, 12 May 2010.
Kitanovski v. The Former Yugoslav Republic of Macedonia, no. 15191/12, 22 January 2015.
Kurt v. Turkey, judgment of 25 May 1998, *Reports* 1998–III.
Kuruçay v. Turkey, no. 24040/04, 10 November 2005.
Kuznetsov v. Ukraine, no. 39042/97, 29 April 2003.
L. v. Lithuania, no. 27527/03.
Labzov v. Russia, no. 62208/00, 16 June 2005.
Lakatoš and Others v. Serbia, no. 3363/08, 7 January 2014.
Lindström and Mässeli v. Finland, no. 24630/10, 14 January 2014.
López Ostra v. Spain, judgment of 9 December 1994, Series A, no. 303–C.
Lyalyakin v. Russia, no. 31305/09, 12 March 2015.
M.S. V. UK, no. 24527/08, 3 May 2012.
M.S.S. v. Belgium and Greece [GC], no. 30696/09, ECHR 2011.
Mahmut Kaya v. Turkey, no. 22535/93, ECHR 2000–III.
Malika Yusupova and Others v. Russia, no. 14705/09, 15 January 2015.
Marckx v. Belgium, judgment of 13 June 1979, Series A, no. 31.
Marian Chiriţă v. Romania, no. 9443/10, 21 October 2014.
Mayzit v. Russia, no. 63378/00, 20 January 2005.
McGlinchey and Others v. UK, no. 50390/99, ECHR 2003–V.
Mehmet Emin Yüksel v. Turkey, no. 40154/98, 20 July 2004.
Members of the Gldani Congregation of Jehovah's Witnesses and Others v. Georgia, no. 71156/01, 03 May 2007.
Mircea Dumitrescu v. Romania, no. 14609/10, 30 July 2013.
Mogoş v. Romania, no. 20420/02, 13 October 2005.
Moisejevs v. Latvia, no. 64846/01, 15 June 2006.
Moldovan and Others v. Romania (No. 2), no. 41138/98; 64320/01, 12 July 2005.
Mouisel v. France, no. 67263/01, ECHR 2002–IX.
Mubilanzila Mayeka and Kaniki Mitunga v. Belgium, no. 13178/03, *Reports* 2006–XI.
N. v. Sweden, no. 23505/09, 20 July 2010.
N. v. United Kingdom, no. 26565/05, ECHR 2008.
Naumenko v. Ukraine, no. 42023/98, 10 February 2004.
Nazarenko v. Ukraine, no. 39483/98, 29 April 2003.
Nevmerzhitsky v. Ukraine, no. 54825/00, 5 April 2005.
Nicolae Augustin Rădulescu v. Romania, no. 17295/10, 11 February 2014.
Nikitenko v. Ukraine, no. 62609/00, 16 July 2009.
Nogin v. Russia, no. 58530/08, 15 January 2015.
Nsona v. The Netherlands, judgment of 28 November 1996, *Reports* 1996–V.
O'Keeffe v. Ireland, no. 35810/09ECHR 2014 (extracts).
Ognyanova and Choban v. Bulgaria, no. 46317/99, 23 February 2006.
Orhan v. Turkey, no. 25656/94, 18 June 2002.
Osman v. UK, no. 23452/94, ECHR 1998–VIII.

Pantea v. Romania, no. 33343/96, ECHR 2003-VI.
Paposhvili v. Belgium, no. 41738/10, ECHR 2016.
Peers v. Greece, no. 28524/95, ECHR 2001-III.
Petyo Petkov v. Bulgaria, no. 32130/03, 7 January 2010.
Piechowicz v. Poland, no. 20071/07, 7 April 2012.
Pitsayeva and Others v. Russia, no. 53036/08, 9 January 2014.
Plattform Ärzte für das Leben v. Austria, judgment of 21 June 1988, Series A, no. 139.
Pretty v. UK, no. 2346/02, ECHR 2002-III.
Price v. UK, no. 33394/96, ECHR 2001-VII.
Pugžlys v. Poland, no. 446/10, 14 June 2016.
R.L. and M.-J.D. v. France, no. 44568/98, 19 May 2004.
R.R. v. Poland, no. 27617/04, 26 May 2011.
Radkov and Sabev v. Bulgaria, no. 18938/07, 36069/09, 27 May 2014.
Ramishvili and Kokhreidze v. Georgia, no. 1704/06, 27 January 2009.
Raninen v. Finland, judgment of 16 December 1997, *Reports* 1997-VIII.
Rehbock v. Slovenia, no. 29462/95, ECHR 2000-XII.
Ribitsch v. Austria, judgment of 4 December 1995, Series A, no. 336.
Rohde v. Denmark, no. 69332/01, 21 July 2005.
Romanov v. Russia, no. 63993/02, 20 October 2005.
S.W. v. UK, no. 20166/92, Judgment of 22 November 1995, Series A, no. 335-B.
Saadi v. Italy [GC], no. 37201/06, ECHR 2008.
Saba v. Italy, no. 36629/10, 1 July 2014.
Salah Sheekh v. The Netherlands, no. 1948/04, 11 January 2007.
Salakhov and Islyamova v. Ukraine, no. 28005/08, 14 March 2013.
Salikhov v. Russia, no. 23880/05, 3 May 2012.
Sarban v. Moldova, no. 3456/05, 4 October 2005.
Selçuk and Asker v. Turkey, judgment of 24 April 1998, *Reports* 1998-II.
Selmouni v. France [GC], no. 25803/94, ECHR 1999-V.
Shioshvili and Others v. Russia, no. 19356/07, 20 December 2016.
Shishkov v. Russia, no. 26746/05, 20 February 2014.
Slavov and Others v. Bulgaria, no. 58500/10, 10 November 2015.
Slyusarev v. Russia, no. 60333/00, 20 April 2010.
Smith and Grady v. UK, no. 33985/96; 33986/96, ECHR 1999-VI.
Sochichiu v. Moldova, no. 28698/09, 15 May 2012.
Soering v. UK, judgment of 7 July 1989, Series A, no. 161.
Stanev v. Bulgaria, no. 36760/06, ECHR 2012.
Stefan Stankov v. Bulgaria, no. 25820/07, 17 March 2015.
Subaşı and Çoban v. Turkey, no. 20129/07, 9 July 2013.
Sufi and Elmi v. UK, nos 8319/07 and 11449/07, 28 June 2011.
Sultygov and Others v. Russia, no. 42575/07, 9 December 2014.
Svinarenko and Slyadnev v. Russia, no. 32541/08 and 43441/08, 17 July 2014.
T. v. UK [GC], no. 24724/94, 16 December 1999.
Tarhan v. Turkey, no. 9078/06, 17 July 2012.
Taş v. Turkey, no. 24396/94, 14 November 2000.

Taştan v. Turkey, no. 63748/00, 4 March 2008.
Taylan v. Turkey, no. 32051/09, 3 July 2012.
Tekin v. Turkey, judgment of 9 June 1998, *Reports* 1998–IV.
Timurtaş v. Turkey, no. 23531/94, ECHR 2000–VI.
Tomasi v. France, judgment of 27 August 1992, Series A, no. 241–A.
Toteva v. Bulgaria, no. 42027/98, 19 May 2004.
Tremblay v. France, no. 37194/02, 11 December 2007.
Tyrer v. UK, judgment of 25 April 1978, Series A, no. 26.
Uçar v. Turkey, no. 52392/99, 11 April 2006.
Ülke v. Turkey, no. 39437/98, 24 January 2006.
V.M. and Others v. Belgium, no. 60125/11, 7 July 2015.
Valasinas v. Lithuania, no. 44558/98, ECHR 2001–VIII.
Van der Ven v. the Netherlands, no. 50901/99, ECHR 2003–II.
Vidish v. Russia, no. 53120/08, 15 March 2016.
Vincent v. France, no. 6253/03, 24 October 2006.
Vinter and Others v. UK, nos 66069/09, 130/10 and 3896/10, 9 July 2013.
Wainwright v. UK, no. 12350/04, ECHR 2006–X.
Weiser v. Austria, no. 2293/03, 22 February 2007.
X. v. The Federal Republic of Germany, no. 1628/62, 12 December 1963, Collection 12, 61–69.
Yankov v. Bulgaria, no. 39084/97, 11 December 2003.
Yazgül Yılmaz v. Turkey, no. 36369/06, 1 February 2011.
Yöyler v. Turkey, no. 26973/95, 24 July 2003.
Z. and Others v. UK [GC], no. 29392/95, ECHR 2001–V.

Other ECHR judgments, decisions and reports

Budina v. Russia, no. 45603/05, 18 June 2009.
East African Asians Case, no. 4403/70, et al., Commission Report of 14 December 1973, Decisions and Reports 78.
The Greek case, Commission Report, 5 November 1969, Yearbook of the European Convention on Human Rights XII (1969) at 186, para. 2.
Golder v. UK, no. 4451/70, Commission Report of 1 June 1973, Series B, no. 16.
Golder v. UK, no. 4451/70, judgment of 21 February 1975, Series A, no. 18.
Handyside v. UK, no. 5493/72, judgment of 7 December 1976, Series A, no. 24.
Ireland v. UK, no. 5310/71, Commission Report of 25 January 1976, Series B, no. 23.
Marckx v. Belgium, no. 6833/74, Commission Decision of 29 September 1975, Decisions and Reports 3.
O'Rourke v. UK (dec.), no. 39022/97, 26 June 2001.
Plattform "Arzte für das Leben" v. Austria, judgment of 21 June 1988, Series A, no. 139.
Van Volsem v. Belgium, no. 14641/89, Commission Decision of 9 May 1990.

UK cases

R (Munjaz) v. Mersey care NHS Trust [2005] 3 WLR 793.
R (Pretty) v. Director of Public Prosecutions [2001] 3 WLR 1598.

Other jurisdiction cases

Inter-American Court of Human Rights, *Bámaca-Velásquez v. Guatemala*, Mertis, Inter-American Court of Human Rights Series C No. 70 (25 November 2000).
African Commission on Human and Peoples' Rights, *Gabriel Shumba v. Zimbabwe*, 51st Ordinary Session, Communication No. 288/04 (2 May 2012).
African Commission on Human and Peoples' Rights, *Sudan Human Rights Organisation & Centre on Housing Rights and Evictions (COHRE) v. Sudan*, 45th Ordinary Session, Communication No. 279/03–296/05 (27 May 2009).
UN Committee Against Torture, *Kwami Mopongo and Ors v. Morocco* (7 November 2014) Communication No. 321/2007 CAT/C/53/D/321/2007.
UN Committee Against Torture, *Déogratias Niyonzima v. Burundi* (21 November 2014) Communication No. 514/2012 CAT/C/53/D/514/2012.
UN Committee Against Torture, *Abdulrahman Kabura v. Burundi* (11 November 2016) Communication No. 549/2013 CAT/C/59/D/549/2013.
UN Committee Against Torture, *Ennaâma Asfari v. Morocco* (15 November 2016) Communication No. 606/2014 CAT/C/59/D/606/2014.
UN Human Rights Committee, *Young v. Jamaica* (4 November 1997) Communication No. 615/1995 CCPR/C/61/D/615/1995.
The Prosecutor v. Dražen Erdemović, no. IT–96–22–T, 29 November 1996 (International Criminal Tribunal for the former Yugoslavia).
UN Committee Against Torture, *Taoufik Elaïba v. Tunisia* (6 May 2016) Communication No. 551/2013 CAT/C/57/D/551/2013.
UN Committee Against Torture, *Kirsanov v. Russia* (14 May 2014) Communication No. 478/2011 CAT/C/52/D/478/2011.
UN Committee Against Torture, *F.K. v. Denmark* (23 November 2015) Communication No. 580/2014 CAT/C/56/D/580/2014.
UN Committee Against Torture, *D.I.S. v. Denmark* (8 December 2015) Communication No. 671/2015 CAT/C/56/D/671/2015.
UN Human Rights Committee, *Mellet v. Ireland* (31 March 2016) Communication No. 2324/2013 CCPR/C/116/D/.
UN Committee Against Torture, *B.R. v. Italy* (29 Apr 2016) Communication No. 598/2014 CAT/C/57/D/598/2014.
UN Human Rights Committee, *T.V. and A.G. v. Uzbekistan* (11 March 2016) Communication No. 2044/2011 CCPR/C/116/D/2044/2011.
UN Committee Against Torture, *Guerrero Larez v. Venezuela* (15 May 2015) Communication No. 456/2011 CAT/C/54/D/456/2011.

1 Introduction

Through interpretation of the texts of international human rights law, courts, monitoring bodies, legal practitioners, and scholars have pushed the boundaries of human rights protection. The question of the boundaries of human rights protection has come to take on particular symbolic force through interpretation of the right not to be subjected to torture, cruel, inhuman or degrading treatment or punishment. Interpreters of this right have translated its categorical expression in human rights instruments into an 'absolute' guarantee to which no legitimate limitations are permitted, and have identified it most strongly with the ideal of protecting human dignity. These unusual characteristics mean that interpretations of the terms 'torture', 'cruel', 'inhuman', 'degrading', 'treatment' and 'punishment' have special significance. When interpreters deem a particular harm to fall within the scope of these terms they recognise that an individual has experienced, or risks experiencing, a grave and intolerable kind of suffering. At the same time, they declare that if the state has perpetrated, facilitated or failed to reasonably prevent such harm it *will* be held responsible. The desire of human rights law to protect persons from grave harm, and the limits of what can reasonably be expected of states, are brought into tension, both real and emblematic, by interpretations that push the boundaries of the right not to be subjected to torture and other prohibited harm.[1]

1 One example of such tension is found in UK Government responses to the perceived restrictive impact of this right upon the Government's ability to expel foreign nationals suspected of involvement in terrorism. Former and current leaders, and senior government ministers, have criticised the *non-refoulement* rule established in *Soering v. UK* (judgment of 7 July 1989, Series A, no. 161) because it has infringed the state's freedom of action. See, e.g., *The Telegraph*, 'Home Secretary: scrap the Human Rights Act', 1 October 2011, available at: <www.telegraph.co.uk/news/politics/8801651/Home-Secretary-scrap-the-Human-Rights-Act.html> (accessed 27 October 2017). These particular tensions are now longstanding: former Prime Minister Tony Blair, in the charged wake of the London bombings in July 2005, openly referred to the restrictions imposed by Article 3 of the European Convention on Human Rights. For this and other examples see Francesca Klug, 'A Bill of Rights: Do we need one or do we already have one?' (2007) Win *Public Law* 701, 714–715. A further example of tension is found in political and academic discussion of exceptions to the prohibition

Interpretations that confront the parameters of this right bring to light questions about the limits of state responsibility and the nature of the harm at stake, in particular when such harm takes place in non-classic settings or is inflicted by non-traditional actors. Should we understand, for example, the victims of domestic violence to be victims of torture, even if the harm itself is inflicted in private places by private persons, in apparent contradiction to the international legal definition?[2] For many years feminist scholars have challenged the boundaries of interpretation of the right not to be subjected to torture, challenging us to see torture not only as something that takes place in an interrogation room by state officials, but in 'everyday' contexts.[3] It is not only in critical scholarship that such challenges occur. They permeate legal claims and decisions. Interpreters of the right have argued that it should be applied in a range of situations – spanning assisted dying contexts, situations of generalised violence in conflict zones, and situations of socio-economic destitution.[4] Such interpretations move the right beyond the traditional confines of direct state power and physical powerlessness of the individual. They expose the borderlines of state responsibility for suffering and challenge the way we perceive the nature of that suffering.

The focus for such legal claims has most often been not torture but cruel, inhuman or degrading treatment or punishment, in combination or occurring separately as distinct forms of harm. In international prohibition-of-torture discourse the 'other' forms of harm have tended to be in the background. The reason for this is a combination of historical evolution and socio-political context. The approach of the UN *Convention Against Torture and Other Cruel, Inhuman or Degrading Treatment or Punishment* (UNCAT) has undoubtedly been influential. The way that this treaty evolved led to a focus on torture; this was partly a reflection of perceptions amongst the drafters that the other forms of harm were more difficult to define,[5] partly a reflection of a focus on detention

of torture and the definitions of the 'lesser' forms of ill-treatment; for a critique see Colin Dayan, *The Story of Cruel and Unusual* (MIT Press 2007).

2 See, e.g., Rhonda Copelon, 'Recognizing the Egregious in the Everyday: Domestic Violence as Torture' (1994) 25 *Colum Hum Rts L Rev* 291. A recent example, concerning restriction of access to abortion and involuntary sterilisation, is found in Ronli Sifris (2013), *Reproductive Freedom, Torture and International Human Rights: Challenging the Masculinisation of Torture* (Routledge 2013).

3 See overview given in Alice Edwards, 'The "Feminizing" of Torture under International Human Rights Law' (2006) 19 *Leiden Journal of International Law* 349.

4 Respectively *Pretty v. UK*, no. 2346/02, ECHR 2002-III; *Sufi and Elmi v. UK*, nos 8319/07 and 11449/07, 28 June 2011; *M.S.S. v. Belgium and Greece*, no. 30696/09, 21 January 2011.

5 Burgers and Danelius and Rodley and Pollard cite the drafting history of the UNCAT and note the drafters' perception that cruel, inhuman or degrading treatment or punishment was more difficult to define than torture; Herman J Burgers and Hans Danelius, *The United Nations Convention Against Torture: A Handbook on the Convention Against Torture and Other Cruel, Inhuman or Degrading Treatment or Punishment* (Martinus Nijhoff 1998) 70; Nigel Rodley and Matt Pollard, *The Treatment of Prisoners under International Law* (3rd edn, Oxford University Press 2009) 111.

contexts[6] and partly a reflection of external forces (notably Amnesty International's 1972 'Campaign for the Abolition of Torture'[7] which drew attention to the torture element of the wider right that had earlier been included in the Universal Declaration of Human Rights (UDHR) and the International Covenant on Civil and Political Rights (ICCPR)).[8] The UNCAT solidifies a distinction between torture and other harm in that it provides a detailed 'definition' of torture in its first Article but does not refer to the other forms of harm until Article 16 of the Convention, and does not provide an explicit picture of them.[9] These other forms of harm have also been less prominent elsewhere at the UN and other regional levels. These monitoring bodies do recognise distinctions between torture, cruel, inhuman and degrading treatment or punishment[10] but,

6 Rodley and Pollard 27–29.

7 See Kelly's discussion of the development of the prohibition of torture and in particular the impact of Amnesty International's 1970s anti-torture campaign; Tobias Kelly, *This Side of Silence: Human Rights, Torture, and the Recognition of Cruelty* (University of Pennsylvania Press 2011) 39; Rodley and Pollard 22, 25.

8 United Nations General Assembly, *Universal Declaration of Human Rights* (10 December 1948) 217 A (III), Article 5.

9 United Nations, *Convention Against Torture and Other Cruel, Inhuman or Degrading Treatment or Punishment* (adopted 10 December 1984, entered into force 26 June 1987) Article 16.

10 For example, some decisions of the UN Human Rights Committee, monitoring the International Covenant on Civil and Political Rights, refer to 'cruel, inhuman or degrading treatment' (e.g. *Mellet v. Ireland* (31 March 2016) Communication No. 2324/2013 CCPR/C/116/D/2324/2013, para. 7.6), a more specific 'inhuman and degrading treatment or punishment' (e.g. *T.V. and A.G. v. Uzbekistan* (11 March 2016) Communication No. 2044/2011 CCPR/C/116/D/2044/2011, para. 7.12), and also 'degrading treatment' standing alone (e.g. UN Human Rights Committee, *Young v. Jamaica* (4 November 1997) Communication No. 615/1995 CCPR/C/61/D/615/1995). See United Nations Human Rights Committee, *General Comment No. 20, Replaces General Comment 7 Concerning Prohibition of Torture and Cruel Treatment or Punishment (Art. 7)*, 10 March 1992, para. 4 on distinctions between the forms of harm. For examples of cases in which the Inter-American Court of Human Rights has upheld distinctions, and an overview of the approach of this body to the prohibition of torture, including cruel, inhuman or degrading treatment or punishment, see L Burgorgue-Larsen, AU de Torres and R Greenstein, *The Inter-American Court of Human Rights: Case Law and Commentary* (Oxford University Press 2011) Chapter 15. A systematic analysis of the approach under the African Charter of Human and People's Rights is more difficult to find, but there is evidence of the African Commission on Human and People's Rights upholding distinctions between the forms of harm; see African Commission on Human and Peoples' Rights, *Sudan Human Rights Organisation & Centre on Housing Rights and Evictions (COHRE) v. Sudan*, 45th Ordinary Session, Communication No. 279/03–296/05 (27 May 2009), para. 164. The UN Committee Against Torture and Other Cruel, Inhuman or Degrading Treatment or Punishment has *not* tended make distinctions between the forms of harm. It has tended to find only violations of Article 16 in general. This is seen, for example, in a survey of the Committee's judgments over the past three years (2014–2017): UN Committee Against Torture, *Kirsanov v. Russia* (14 May 2014) Communication No. 478/2011 CAT/C/52/D/478/2011; UN Committee Against Torture, *Kwami Mopongo and Ors v. Morocco* (7 November 2014)

in light of differing socio-political environments, they have had less opportunity to confront non-torture forms of harm.[11] These factors have contributed to a common perception of cruel, inhuman or degrading treatment or punishment as simply the 'other forms of ill-treatment'. Commentators use this language as an abbreviation but the effect, when used habitually, has been to mask the significance and independent scope of the other forms of treatment as integrated and influential parts of a whole. At the European level the picture differs – the jurisprudence of the European Convention on Human Rights[12] (ECHR; the Convention) manifests the centrality of the other forms of harm. The European Court of Human Rights (ECtHR; the Court) has been at the forefront of the interpretation and application of Article 3 of the Convention since the late 1970s.[13] It is in the European Convention protection system, rather than at the UN or other regional levels, that the interpretation of the other forms of ill-treatment has been pioneered. The ECtHR and its former sister body, the European Commission on Human Rights (ECommHR; the Commission), have established distinctions between inhuman and degrading treatment and punishment[14] and applied these forms of harm beyond the traditional deprivation-of-liberty settings – the above examples of the end-of-life, conflict, and socio-economic contexts are drawn from the Strasbourg jurisprudence. The ECtHR did not make its first finding of torture until 1996, almost 40 years after it came into existence[15] and decades after it had reached its first finding of a violation of Article 3 on the basis of the other forms of harm. The ECommHR had urged a finding of torture in 1978, in *Ireland v. UK*, but for the Court this case was instead the starting point for the development of the right not to be subjected to inhuman or degrading

Communication No. 321/2007 CAT/C/53/D/321/2007; UN Committee Against Torture, *Déogratias Niyonzima v. Burundi* (21 November 2014) Communication No. 514/2012 CAT/C/53/D/514/2012; UN Committee Against Torture, *Guerrero Larez v. Venezuela* (15 May 2015) Communication No. 456/2011 CAT/C/54/D/456/2011; UN Committee Against Torture, *F.K. v. Denmark* (23 November 2015) Communication No. 580/2014 CAT/C/56/D/580/2014; UN Committee Against Torture, *D.I.S. v. Denmark* (8 December 2015) Communication No. 671/2015 CAT/C/56/D/671/2015; UN Committee Against Torture, *Taoufik Elaïba v. Tunisia* (6 May 2016) Communication No. 551/2013 CAT/C/57/D/551/2013; UN Committee Against Torture, *B.R. v. Italy* (29 April 2016) Communication No. 598/2014 CAT/C/57/D/598/2014; UN Committee Against Torture, *Abdulrahman Kabura v. Burundi* (11 November 2016) Communication No. 549/2013 CAT/C/59/D/549/2013; UN Committee Against Torture, *Ennaâma Asfari v. Morocco* (15 November 2016) Communication No. 606/2014 CAT/C/59/D/606/2014.

11 Burgorgue-Larsen makes this point in relation to the Inter-American system: Burgorgue-Larsen, de Torres and Greenstein 370–371.

12 Council of Europe, *European Convention for the Protection of Human Rights and Fundamental Freedoms, as amended by Protocols Nos 11 and 14* (adopted 4 November 1950, entered into force 3 September 1953) ETS 5.

13 Beginning with the cases of *Ireland v. UK*, judgment of 18 January 1978, Series A, no. 25, and *Tyrer v. UK*, judgment of 25 April 1978, Series A, no. 26.

14 See David Weissbrodt and Cheryl Heilman, 'Defining Torture, Inhuman and Degrading Treatment' 29 *Law and Inequality* 343, 372.

15 *Aksoy v. Turkey*, no. 21987/93, *Reports* 1996-IV.

treatment or punishment. The ECtHR has come to be recognised as a leader of the international development of the right not to be subjected to torture, inhuman or degrading treatment or punishment.[16] The other forms of harm should not be seen as peripheral but as central to the on-going interpretive development of the right in international human rights law.

The aim of this book is to further an understanding of the reach, and limits, of states' protection of individuals from torture, cruel, inhuman or degrading treatment or punishment by drawing attention to the 'other forms of ill-treatment'. I do so by closely examining one particular form of harm – I explore, articulate, and evaluate past, present and possible interpretations of *degrading treatment.*

Why 'degrading treatment'?

The central question addressed in this book is, what is the interpretive scope of the right not to be subjected to degrading treatment as a distinct form of harm? That is, what does degrading treatment mean (the right's scope of meaning), and to which kinds of situations might the right apply (the right's scope of application)?[17] To describe degrading treatment (or the other harms) as distinct wrongs is not to suggest that it should be divorced from its place within the right not to be subjected to torture. It is to suggest that its place within this broader right means that its scope of interpretation merits greater attention – to generate a richer understanding of the whole, the doctrine that has developed on the constitutive elements of the right can and should be explored independently.

This book addresses the body of European Convention jurisprudence under Article 3, which states that 'no one shall be subjected to torture or to inhuman or degrading treatment or punishment'. Within this provision the Strasbourg organs have upheld distinctions between forms of harm. It was not inevitable that they would do so but were presumably motivated by the nature of the claims which it was asked to addressed, and it is not surprising that they have done so given the use of several different terms in the Convention's text. In normative terms we might ask whether it is desirable to treat the forms of harm as capable of standing alone as well as occurring in combination; in practical terms the distinctions have become ingrained in the jurisprudence. This book explores the rationale behind the jurisprudence pertaining to degrading treatment and aims to make sense of the range of interpretations of the right to date. From the perspective of considering the parameters of the right not to be subjected to torture or other prohibited harm, degrading treatment is a most interesting site of interpretation for five reasons: interpreters of the right generally perceive it to be at the bottom of a

16 Malcolm D. Evans and Rod Morgan, *Preventing Torture – A Study of the European Convention for the Prevention of Torture and Inhuman or Degrading Treatment or Punishment* (Clarendon Press 1998) 74.

17 I distinguish between scope of meaning and scope of application in order to emphasise the importance of focusing on the substantive meaning of the texts as a step distinct from asking whether the right has been violated. To express the coming together of both aspects, I will refer to the right's 'interpretive scope'.

hierarchy of harm within the prohibition of torture, thereby raising interesting questions about the line between what is prohibited and what is not prohibited by it; the nature of the established benchmarks of degradation; the perception of familiarity yet ambiguity invoked by the term 'degrading'; the linguistic association between degradation and the idea of dignity; and the pre-eminence of the idea of treatment over that of punishment.

Degrading treatment is generally seen to be at the lower end of a hierarchy of ill-treatment. As Evans and Morgan observe, the Strasbourg organs have endorsed the view that 'there is an hierarchical progression between three separate categories of ill-treatment and that the threshold between them is based on the severity of suffering'.[18] As early as 1969 the EComHR stated that all torture was necessarily inhuman and degrading, and all inhuman treatment was degrading.[19] In more recent cases the Court's view of degrading treatment as being at the bottom of a hierarchy of harm is subtly evident.[20] Other interpretive bodies and several commentators contest the idea that there should be a 'severity of suffering' scale within the prohibition of torture,[21] but they conceive of scales of different kinds.[22] Both in the international and European contexts, interpreters of the right perceive some form of progression within it, and harm that is degrading is seen as being at the bottom of the hierarchy.[23] Because it is perceived to be at the bottom of a hierarchy, degrading treatment may also be the focus of concerns about what should and should not be allowed within the ambit of the right. There have been longstanding concerns about the right's overexploitation[24]; as Judge Costa stated in one ECHR judgment: 'Article 3 should not be cheapened or trivialised through overuse.'[25] If, amongst the different forms of harm within the prohibition of torture and inhuman or degrading treatment or punishment, we perceive degradation to be closest to a line between prohibited harm and non-prohibited harm we will gain a richer understanding of the potential boundaries of the right as a whole by understanding the scope of the idea of degradation.

18 Evans and Morgan 77. See also John Cooper, *Cruelty – An Analysis of Article 3* (Sweet and Maxwell 2003) 7.

19 *The Greek case*, Commission Report, 5 November 1969, *Yearbook of the European Convention on Human Rights XII* (1969) 186, para. 2.

20 See, e.g., *Members of the Gldani Congregation of Jehovah's Witnesses and Others v. Georgia*, no. 71156/01, 3 May 2007, paras 104–105; *Frérot v. France*, no. 70204/01, 12 June 2007, para. 48.

21 For example, the UN Human Rights Committee refers to any distinction between forms of harm as dependent on a combination of nature, purpose and severity; *General Comment No. 20, Replaces General Comment 7 Concerning Prohibition of Torture and Cruel Treatment or Punishment (Art. 7)*, 10 March 1992, para. 4. See also Evans and Morgan 78–79, 97–98.

22 For example, degrees of purposive infliction of harm; see Rodley and Pollard 123.

23 See, e.g., Rodley and Pollard 124, and Clare McGlynn, 'Rape, Torture and the European Convention on Human Rights' (2009) 58 *Int'l & Comp LQ* 565, 570.

24 *Ireland v. UK*, judgment of 18 January 1978, Series A, no. 25, Separate Opinion of Judge Sir Gerald Fitzmaurice.

25 *McGlinchey and Others v. UK*, no. 50390/99, ECHR 2003-V, Concurring Opinion of Judge Costa, para. 2.

The ECtHR has configured the scope of the idea of degradation around a series of reference points; described by Jeremy Waldron as 'benchmarks'.[26] The ECtHR's benchmarks of degradation are feelings of fear, anguish or inferiority capable of humiliating or debasing a person, of breaking of a person's physical or moral resistance, of driving a person to act against will or conscience, or as having an adverse effect on personality.[27] These ideas themselves invite interpretation. They invite conceptual engagement to an extent that is not echoed in Strasbourg's narrower benchmarks of harm that is inhuman: that is premeditated, applied for hours at a stretch and causes intense physical and mental suffering.[28] There is an imbalance in conceptual depth between the two sets of benchmarks. It is surprising that those of inhuman treatment or punishment have not been further developed by the ECtHR.[29] This is perhaps because, unlike degrading treatment, the Court closely links torture to inhuman treatment, in that it has maintained an understanding of torture as 'aggravated' or 'deliberate' inhuman treatment.[30] (This reinforces the above point that degrading treatment is seen to be at the bottom of the hierarchy of harm). Whilst interpreters have questioned the relationship between the three forms of harm within the right, few have questioned the nature of the benchmarks of harm that is either inhuman or degrading, or the substance or conceptual cohesion of the relatively detailed benchmarks that compose degradation. As Waldron also notes:

> *There is one thing one misses in [inhuman and degrading treatment] case law and in the textbooks that summarize it. Neither judges nor scholars spend much time reflecting on the meaning of the predicates that are incorporated in the Article 3 standard – 'inhuman' and 'degrading' – and explaining how the Court is guided by their meanings in generating its principles, presumptions and benchmarks.*[31]

Exploring the conceptual thread that runs through the Court's benchmarks will inform debate about the current legal and/or normatively preferable view of the relationship between the forms of harm within the prohibition of torture as a whole.[32] This book stresses the value of enquiring into the scope of legal meaning and scope of application of the degradation benchmarks.

26 Jeremy Waldron, 'Inhuman and Degrading Treatment: The Words Themselves' (2010) 23 *Canadian Journal of Law and Jurisprudence* 269, 273.
27 See Chapter 2.
28 *Ireland v. UK*, para. 167.
29 Evans and Morgan 93.
30 *The Greek case* 186; *Ireland v. UK*, para. 167. See also Rodley and Pollard 86–87 and 110.
31 Waldron 273. The other notable exception is John Vorhaus, who drew attention to the concept of degradation in a duo of articles: John Vorhaus, 'On Degradation. Part One: Article 3 of the European Convention on Human Rights' (2002) 31 *Common Law World Review* 374–399, and John Vorhaus, 'On Degradation. Part Two: Degrading Treatment and Punishment' (2003) 32 *Common Law World Review* 65–92.
32 For examples of approaches to understanding the relationship between the forms of harm, see Rodley and Pollard 123 and Manfred Nowak and Elizabeth McArthur, 'The

The ordinary meaning of degradation is something we intuitively understand. It is a familiar term. It is used more commonly to describe an experience than the term 'inhuman', and more sincerely to describe an experience than the term 'torture'. In everyday language torture might be more familiar than the term 'inhuman' but it is often used as intentional embellishment.[33] The term 'degrading' is different: it is used to express a perception of harm actually witnessed or experienced. Yet, at the same time, we might find it difficult to pin down the meaning of degradation. In particular, we might ask, is one person's idea of suffering degradation different to another person's? If so, how does this play out within a right that is subject to no exceptions? Degradation is marked out from the two other forms of treatment prohibited alongside it in Article 3 because of such questions about the relationship between its legal and ordinary meanings.

The meaning of the term 'degrading' is a pertinent site of analysis within the prohibition of torture because, linguistically, it immediately invokes the idea of human dignity. Compared to torture and inhuman treatment, the term 'degrading' recalls dignity more directly. The concept of dignity has been the subject of unyielding interest across a number of fields of practice and theory. In the world of practice the currency of human dignity is strong amongst campaigning and advocacy organisations,[34] in diverse fields ranging from economic, social and cultural rights activism[35] to the 'death with dignity' debate.[36] Its relevance in international legal practice is seen in areas such as the development of minimum humanitarian standards[37] and international criminal law.[38] In literature there are cross-disciplinary anthologies that defend human dignity and explore its violation[39] and authors including Dworkin and Waldron in legal and political

Distinction between Torture and Cruel, Inhuman or Degrading Treatment' (2006) 16 *Torture* 147–151.

33 Kelly notes the use of the term 'torture' to 'signify displeasure or dislike', giving examples including spending time with one's in-laws; Kelly 9.

34 For example, Human Rights Watch, 'A Move to Restore Dignity to Syria's Victims', 15 September 2017; Dignity International.

35 See Paulo César Carbonari, 'Human Dignity as a Basic Concept of Ethics and Human Rights' in B Klein Goldewijk, AC Baspineiro and PC Carbonari (eds), *Dignity and Human Rights – The Implementation of Economic, Social and Cultural Rights* (Intersentia 2002) 39; Berma Klein Goldewijk, 'Economic, Social and Cultural Rights: Globalization and the Search for Alternatives and International Political Impacts' in B Klein Goldewijk, AC Baspineiro and PC Carbonari (eds), *ibid* 302; 'Michael Bochenek Interview, Part I' (15 May 2012) *Harvard Human Rights Journal* (on Amnesty International's *Demand Dignity* campaign).

36 See, e.g., third-party intervention by the Voluntary Euthanasia Society in *Pretty v. UK*, no. 2346/02, ECHR 2002-III, para. 25.

37 Klein Goldewijk 6.

38 See Béatrice Maurer, *Le Principe de Respect de la Dignité Humaine et la Convention Européene des Droits de l'Homme* (Jacques Bourrinet ed., La Documentation française 1999) 9, citing the first judgment of the International Criminal Tribunal for the Former-Yugoslavia, which makes reference to dignity; see *The Prosecutor v. Dražen Erdemović*, no. IT-96–22-T, 29 November 1996, para. 28.

39 For example, Marcus Düwell et al. (eds), *The Cambridge Handbook of Human Dignity: Interdisciplinary Perspectives* (Cambridge University Press 2014); Christopher

theory,[40] McCrudden in relation to judicial interpretation,[41] Rosen and Iglesias from a philosophical perspective[42] and Beyleveld and Brownsword in the bioethics context[43] have all contributed to the substantial body of scholarship on human dignity. Within the ever-increasing body of literature there has been recent interest in exploring the precise nature of the relationship between human dignity and human rights law.[44] Those discussing dignity from all perspectives invariably point to its prominent place within international human rights law in general, and the prohibition of torture in particular. The concept is one that has been described as a 'mystery'.[45] A common response to the idea of dignity is captured in Oscar Schachter's observation that 'I know it when I see it even if I cannot tell you what it is'.[46] Observing that the ideas of dignity and degradation have been described as 'two sides of the same coin'[47], but also that 'not every type of indignity' will amount to degrading treatment,[48] this book considers the influence of the 'mysterious' idea of dignity on the interpretive scope of the term 'degrading'.

If the idea of degradation might seem abstruse, the idea of treatment might seem uncomplicated. Talk of punishment has been almost entirely displaced in ECHR vocabulary by the term 'treatment'. Treatment is able to encompass punishment within it whilst punishment is a narrower idea, readily associated with detention settings. In order to consider the boundaries of the right, this book focuses on the broader idea of treatment. A meaning of treatment has not been

McCrudden (ed.), *Understanding Human Dignity* (Oxford University Press/British Academy 2013); Paulus Kaufman et al., *Humiliation, Degradation, Dehumanization: Human Dignity Violated* (Springer 2011); Robert P Kraynak and Glenn Tinder (eds), *In Defense of Human Dignity – Essays for Our Times* (University of Notre Dame Press 2003); David Kretzmer and Eckhart Klein (eds), *The Concept of Human Dignity in Human Rights Discourse* (Kluwer Law International 2003).

40 See Ronald Dworkin, *Is Democracy Possible Here? Principles for a New Political Debate* (Princeton University Press 2006); Jeremy Waldron, 'Dignity and Rank' (2007) 48 *European Journal of Sociology* 201.

41 Christopher McCrudden, 'Human Dignity and Judicial Interpretation of Human Rights' (2008) 19 *Eur J Int'l L* 655.

42 Michael Rosen, *Dignity: Its History and Meaning* (Harvard University Press 2012); Teresa Iglesias, 'Bedrock Truths and the Dignity of the Individual' (2011) 4 *Logos* 114–134.

43 David Beyleveld and Roger Brownsword, *Human Dignity in Bioethics and Biolaw* (Oxford University Press 2001).

44 Jeremy Waldron, 'Is Dignity the Foundation of Human Rights?' in Rowan Cruft, S Matthew Liao and Massimo Renzo (eds), *Philosophical Foundations of Human Rights* (Oxford University Press 2015); Conor Gearty, *Principles of Human Rights Adjudication* (Oxford University Press 2005) Chapter 5 in particular.

45 Glenn Tinder, 'Facets of Personal Dignity' in Robert P Kraynak and Glenn Tinder (eds), *In Defense of Human Dignity – Essays for Our Times* (University of Notre Dame Press 2003) 245.

46 Oscar Schachter, 'Human Dignity as a Normative Concept' (1983) 77 *American Journal of International Law* 848, 849.

47 Susan Millns, 'Death, Dignity and Discrimination: The Case of *Pretty v. United Kingdom*' (2002) 3 *German Law Journal* para. 5.

48 Ellie Palmer, *Judicial Review, Socio-economic Rights and the Human Rights Act* (Bloomsbury Publishing 2007) 69.

articulated by the ECtHR, which suggests that its interpretation is likely uncontroversial. The unassuming term provokes questions however, because the classic context of application of the prohibition of degrading treatment is *conditions* of detention. 'Treatment' as a set of conditions goes beyond the most common meaning of the word as an action or way of behaving towards an individual or group. This indicates that treatment does not have a one-dimensional legal meaning.

The premise of this book is that it is valuable to examine the interpretive scope of degrading treatment. Just as the other forms of ill-treatment are often in the shadow of torture, interpreters often amalgamate degrading treatment with cruel or inhuman treatment. This can to some extent explain why scholars have afforded little attention to the interpretation of the right not to be subjected to degrading treatment in particular. It is probable that the perceived ambiguity of the idea of degradation and the perceived simplicity of the idea of treatment can also to some extent explain why the interpretation of degrading treatment has rarely been closely analysed. It is nevertheless evident in writing on Article 3 and in general commentaries on the Convention that scholars widely acknowledge the doctrinal position of degrading treatment as a distinct kind of harm. Commentators detail the Court's benchmarks and the range of categories of application of the right.[49] This book goes further and interprets the Court's benchmarks of degradation, the meaning of treatment, the rationale that drives the interpretation of Article 3 and moves beyond the situations in which the right has already been argued to apply. Examining the terms 'degrading' and 'treatment' then, foregrounds important questions: Where is the line between harm that is degrading and harm that does not make it into the hierarchy of harm at its lowest point? What are the legal meanings of the terms 'degrading' and 'treatment'? To what extent can we understand the idea of dignity to shape the interpretation of degrading treatment? In short, how far does and should the legal category of degrading treatment stretch?

The central argument of this book is that the term 'degrading' should be understood to have a narrow conceptual core while the term 'treatment' should be understood to have a wide conceptual core. The meaning of both terms is circumscribed by the purpose driving the right within the ECHR system of interpretation and this purpose bounds the right's material scope of application in interaction with states' obligations of protection. A concern often expressed or recognised by interpreters of the prohibition of torture about dilution of the standard of suffering due to expansive interpretation of the idea of degradation is unwarranted.[50] Revealing a coherent rationale behind the right shows why its

49 There are many examples. Some recent works include Anthony Paul Lester, David Pannick and Javan Herberg, *Human Rights: Law and Practice* (3rd edn, LexisNexis 2009) 190–196; Bernadette Rainey, Elizabeth Wicks and Clare Ovey, *Jacobs, White, and Ovey: The European Convention on Human Rights* (Elizabeth Wicks and Clare Ovey eds, 7th edn, Oxford University Press 2017) 185–186; Alastair Mowbray, *Cases and Materials on the European Convention on Human Rights* (2nd edn, Oxford University Press 2007) 213–232.

50 See the well-known dissenting opinion of Judge Sir Gerald Fitzmaurice in *Ireland v. UK*, paras 25–28 and 36. See also, e.g., Lorna McGregor, 'Applying the Definition of

interpretive scope is important in and of itself and shows that it can lead to a new perspective for thinking about the interpretive scope of the broader right not to be subjected to torture.

The approach of the book

This book takes an interpretive approach. I label it explicitly as an interpretive exercise to draw attention to how I have determined the validity of sources of degrading treatment's meaning (sources in the sense of *who* and *what* contributes to constructing meaning). Describing this book's approach as interpretive draws attention to the valid contribution of non-authoritative interpretations, like the present scholarly analysis, to developing the scope of the right. Interpretation from this perspective implies a broader focus than the institutional contexts that are normally identified with legal interpretation. This broader focus is important because it aims to reinforce that non-authoritative interpretations like the present one can validly generate the content of human rights standards.[51] This broad perspective on interpretation also recognises that the meaning of legal standards derives from dialogues, over time, between interpreters outside and within official institutional contexts.[52] In the human rights field, it is through such dialogues that processes of interpretation have tested, and will continue to test, the boundaries of rights protection. This dialogic perspective on interpretation extends to the kinds of sources that are validly relied upon to assess the meaning of degrading treatment. Insights from literature in a range of fields are used to advocate particular legal meanings within interpretation because the ideas that are relevant to the conceptual essence of degrading treatment (like humiliation, will, and personality) of course have a life outside of the law. Insights, notably from social philosophy and social psychology literature, are channeled into the present interpretation of degrading treatment. This dialogue and permeability within interpretation have implications in a more general sense: for the present approach to current legal doctrine. The interpretation put forward is informed but not restricted by existing doctrine. It is informed by existing doctrine because authoritative readings of the right matter to those claiming a violation[53] of Article 3, and the book's principal aim is to reach conclusions that have potential for practical impact in the current human rights landscape. As such, it aims to put forward an interpretation that

Torture to the Acts of Non-State Actors: The Case of Trafficking in Human Beings' (2014) 36 *Hum Rts Q* 210, 214.

51 See concluding section in Elaine Webster and Deirdre Flanigan, 'Localising Human Rights Law: A Case-study of Civil Society Interpretation of Rights in Scotland' (2018) 22 *International Journal of Human Rights* 22.

52 For example, dialogue between the interpretative claims of legal advisors and interpretations of judicial decision-makers in response, or between the interpretive claims of rights-holders and the interpretive interventions of civil society groups.

53 See Webster and Flanigan, where this point is made in relation to why law matters within broader discourse around human rights.

remains within the current legal range of hearing.[54] In particular, it elaborates upon the Strasbourg interpretation in a way that is judged to be coherent with the favoured interpretive approach already existing under the Convention – an interpretation guided by the text's purpose, which integrates the idea of human dignity. At a more basic level, the present approach is necessarily informed by existing doctrine because, as an interpretive exercise, it takes into account preceding understandings when progressing those understandings, like all forms of 'creative interpretation'.[55] However, also in common with all forms of creative interpretation, the present approach is only partly constrained by existing understandings. All interpreters who put forward meanings of a legal standard – from judges to rights-holders to scholars – play an active role in creating law.[56] The scholarly interpretation in this book is inspired by the active, optimistic 'interpretive attitude' that Dworkin identifies as characteristic of constructive interpretation.[57] A constructive approach acknowledges that no interpretations are fixed, because different interpreters will always have a role in inventing meaning; as Donato writes, recognising this 'highlights law's nature as a fluid, human document open to change. Subjectivity in interpretation continually reminds us that understanding invites transformation.'[58] I approach the meaning of degrading treatment in a way that aims to make sense of its development to date and that can move our current understandings forward whilst presenting a basis for on-going interpretation in future. This book thereby provides an example of how human rights protection is shaped through processes of interpretation.

A comparative approach with national legal systems of States Parties to the ECHR or other states is not adopted. There is no significant evidence of the Court, in degrading treatment case-law, referring explicitly to the jurisprudence of other jurisdictions to inform its own understanding of the *meaning* of degrading

54 Wilson invokes this idea when describing the making of legal claims from a human rights perspective: 'A variety of social and material conflicts, from land titling to the language of instruction in schools, are now expressed in a way that law can hear them; that is, they seek to conform to legal convention and precedent.' Richard A Wilson, 'Tyrannosaurus Lex: The Anthropology of Human Rights and Transnational Law' in Mark Goodale and Sally Engle Merry (eds), *The Practice of Human Rights: Tracking Law Between the Global and the Local* (Cambridge University Press 2007) 351.

55 Ronald Dworkin, *Law's Empire* (Fontana Press 1986) 49–53.

56 James Donato, 'Dworkin and Subjectivity in Legal Interpretation' (1988) 40 *Stan L Rev* 1531.

57 Dworkin, *Law's Empire* 46–48, 52–53. See also Donato who provides an overview of parallels between Dworkin's understanding of constructive interpretation and the hermeneutic tradition, which highlights the dialogic dimension of interpretation and the dual role of interpreters in producing and reproducing meanings; Donato 1535–1537. Constructive interpretation in the Dworkinian sense also shares common ground with a purposive interpretive method (Dworkin, *Law's Empire* 51–52; Aharon Barak, *Purposive Interpretation* (Princeton University Press 2005) 296), which reflects a central part of this book's interpretive framework because, as will be argued, it is a central part of the authoritative approach to interpreting Article 3.

58 Donato 1540.

treatment.[59] When the Court refers to the law of the States Parties it does so in terms of the approach of the national state to a particular situation that bears upon the *application* of the right.[60] Carozza describes the Court's use of comparison as a 'justificatory method of comparative law'; that is, it is used to justify the Court's conclusion after it has exercised its discretion; it is not used expressly to arrive at the *meaning* of Convention provisions.[61] It can be presumed that national traditions indirectly influence the meanings of Convention provisions, given the range of national experience that is inherent in the composition of the Court through its judges.[62] The law of the ECHR is thereby treated as a self-standing body of law.

A comparative approach with other human rights monitoring bodies is not adopted. The work of the European Committee for the Prevention of Torture and Inhuman or Degrading Treatment or Punishment,[63] which also operates within the Council of Europe framework, is interesting but it draws upon the ECtHR's interpretation of Article 3, in particular as it relates to (inhuman and) degrading

59 Carozza notes that any comparative references in the Court's judgments tend not to be specific about the object or nature of the comparison; Paolo G Carozza, 'Uses and Misuses of Comparative Law in International Human Rights: Some Reflections on the Jurisprudence of the European Court of Human Rights' (1998) 73 *Notre Dame L Rev* 1217, 1224–1225. See also Peter E Quint, 'International Human Rights: The Convergence of Comparative and International Law' (2001) 36 *Tex Int'l LJ* 605, 607. A case that might appear to go against this trend is *Vinter v. UK*. In this case, concerning irreducible life sentences in the United Kingdom, the Court refers to the German Constitutional Court's use of the idea of dignity in a similar national case. This reference to dignity is ambiguous and might seem to be an example of the Strasbourg Court using the jurisprudence of this national jurisdiction to inform the meaning of the words within Article 3. Arguably, however, the Strasbourg Court does not use it in this way but instead to recognise that the question of review of life sentences has been seen not only as one of effectiveness but as one of dignity. It uses it to show trends in state practice, as it also does later in the judgment, referring to other national jurisdictions; see *Vinter v. UK*, nos 66069/09, 130/10, 3896/10, ECHR 2013 (extracts), paras 113, 117. Indeed, a criticism of the Court's reasoning in *Vinter* is that it does not actually examine at all what any of the terms within Article 3 actually mean, therefore it cannot be said to use comparative approaches in arriving at such meaning; see Partly Dissenting Opinion of Judge Villiger.

60 For example, in the Article 3 corporal punishment cases of *Tyrer v. UK* and *Campbell and Cosans v. UK*, the Court referred to developments in the penal policy of the Council of Europe states and observed the traditional and widely accepted nature of corporal punishment in the communities in question. See *Tyrer v. UK*, para. 31; *Campbell and Cosans v. UK*, judgment of 25 February 1982, Series A, no. 48, para. 29.

61 Carozza 1225, 1234; see Carozza generally for a helpful discussion of the use of comparative references by the Court.

62 Rudolf Bernhardt, 'The Convention and Domestic Law' in RSJ Macdonald, F Matscher and H Petzold (eds), *The European System for the Protection of Human Rights* (Martinus Nijhoff 1993) 35.

63 Established by the Council of Europe, *European Convention for the Prevention of Torture and Inhuman or Degrading Treatment or Punishment* (adopted 26 November 1987, entered into force 1 February 1989) ETS 126.

treatment and punishment,[64] and its reports are limited to places of detention. An ECHR focus is more appropriate for the present analysis. As already noted, in the Human Rights Committee's monitoring of the ICCPR, and in the Inter-American and African monitoring regimes, there has, to date, been less jurisprudence on the other forms of harm.[65] In cases in which these bodies have engaged with the other forms of harm there is some evidence of them drawing upon the ECtHR's approach. Examples include decisions concerning treatment of relatives of disappeared persons[66] and ill-treatment in detention.[67] Given the permeability of interpretations amongst international and regional approaches, the approach of the ECtHR is likely to continue to be influential. The present analysis aims for an interpretation of degrading treatment that builds on the ECHR approach and that is relevant to the broader international context.

The analysis begins from the jurisprudence on Article 3 that has developed under the supervision of the ECtHR and pre-1998, prior to the restructuring of the Convention system by Protocol no. 11, the ECommHR. Priority is given to judgments of the Court as the final and binding decisions. Some important insights can also be gained from the Commission's discussions in certain cases and some of these are drawn upon, including the rare cases that were not referred to the Court pursuant to the Commission's report. In terms of systematic analysis, the cases are limited to judgments on the merits handed down by the ECtHR since this body came into existence in 1959. The judgments analysed are those that relate to 'inhuman and degrading treatment' to ensure a comprehensive and accurate underpinning from which to draw an interpretation of degrading treatment. The number of judgments is now in excess of 1,500.[68]

64 See Evans and Morgan 241–245 for an overview and critique of the Committee's use of the terms 'inhuman' and 'degrading'. A recent example of the Committee invoking ideas used by the ECtHR is found in its *Report to the Government of the Netherlands on the visit to the Netherlands carried out by the European Committee for the Prevention of Torture and Inhuman or Degrading Treatment or Punishment from 2 to 13 May 2016*, CPT/Inf (2017) 1, para. 62, in which it refers to 'humiliation' and concludes by identifying degrading treatment.

65 See pp. 3–4 above.

66 See, e.g., *Bámaca-Velásquez v. Guatemala*, Merits, Inter-American Court of Human Rights Series C No 70 (25 November 2000), paras 162–163.

67 See, e.g., African Commission on Human and Peoples' Rights, *Gabriel Shumba v. Zimbabwe*, 51st Ordinary Session, Communication No. 288/04 (2 May 2012), paras 138–139 and 164.

68 The audit of judgments on which the book's analysis is based covers the period 1959 until 1 January 2017. Judgments have been searched and accessed via the Council of Europe's HUDOC database, holding all judgments of the Court. Printed case collections have been consulted for certain Commission reports and for admissibility decisions prior to 1986 that are not available via the HUDOC database. The HUDOC search (of Chamber and Grand Chamber judgments, limited by keywords 'degrading treatment' and 'inhuman treatment') returned 1659 results. Having excluded 154 returns (including claims that were struck out, inadmissible and not examined under Article 3), 1505 judgments have been systematically examined.

The structure of the book

In order to understand the prohibition of degrading treatment it must simultaneously be viewed as part of the right not to be subjected to torture and as a distinct form of harm. Chapter 2 includes an overview of the body of degrading treatment case-law. It details the degradation benchmarks and related principles. This chapter highlights general features of Article 3 jurisprudence that apply equally to the prohibition of degrading treatment and which have been and will remain key to the right's development and an evaluation of it. Firstly, it recognises the importance of the principle of evolutive interpretation. The idea that the interpretation of the ECHR should evolve to reflect current societal norms was in fact articulated in the first case in which degradation was recognised as a distinct form of harm – *Tyrer v. United Kingdom* in 1978. Secondly, this chapter sees the continuing evolution of the Convention against the backdrop of another major Strasbourg innovation – the development of positive state obligations of protection. Three decades ago, in relation to the evolving nature of obligations upon the state to encompass obligations of protection, Judge Evrigenis, formerly of the ECtHR, made a prescient observation when he noted the 'subtle, shifting synthesis between prohibited interference and compulsory intervention'.[69] The development of positive obligations has a substantial bearing upon the scope of application of the right not to be subjected to degrading treatment. There is not, however, consensus on the precise content of state obligations pertaining to Article 3 ECHR. Chapter 2 clarifies that degrading treatment can be analysed in its own right as a semi-distinct element of the wider prohibition and clarifies the applicable framework of obligations before moving on to consider the substantive meaning of the terms.

Detailing the meaning of the terms 'degrading' and 'treatment' is an exercise that involves preferring certain meanings and disregarding others. Chapter 3 lays out the framework for evaluating, selecting and proposing particular readings of the benchmarks of degradation and of the term 'treatment'. It describes three dimensions of interpretation that, taken together, are relevant to understanding the book's arguments about the boundaries of the right's meaning and its scope of practical application. These are an 'epistemological' dimension (which explains the basic approach that will be taken to deriving meaning from the case-law texts), a 'judicial' dimension (which describes the Strasbourg Court's approach to interpretation that will frame an understanding of degrading treatment) and a 'formative' dimension (which ties the book's approach to analysing the case-law to the current interpretations of the ECtHR). A key point in this chapter is that respect for human dignity is best understood as a fundamental value that embodies a core purpose of Article 3, and guides its interpretation. Dignity is described as an elemental status, which is diminished by, and demands freedom from, experiences

69 Dimitrios Evrigenis, 'Recent Case-Law of the European Court of Human Rights on Articles 8 and 10 of the European Convention on Human Rights' (1982) 3 *Human Rights Law Journal* 121, 136.

that undermine a minimal kind of regard or capacity. It is this limited meaning that should be understood to shape the interpretation of Article 3.

The terms 'degrading' and 'treatment' are considered in Chapters 4 and 5 respectively. In order to explore the boundaries of any human rights standard it is necessary to have a developed understanding of the kind of harm that might be captured by the text of the right. To separate analysis of the terms 'degrading' and 'treatment' is not the usual approach in human rights law scholarship but is used here to emphasise the desirability of exploring the meaning of both of the terms that compose the right.[70] Chapter 4 interprets the benchmarks of degradation that are routinely restated in ECHR case-law. It contributes a richer understanding than we currently have of what is relevant and significant in arriving at a finding of degradation via these benchmarks. In that sense, it aims to add substance to the space between the benchmarks and the case-law findings. From the perspective of the body of case-law and guided by the purpose seen to drive Article 3, this chapter argues that the idea of degradation in this context has a narrow core of conceptual concern. This is considered alongside the equally important interpretation of treatment, which Article 3 case-law and literature has tended to overlook.[71] Chapter 5 draws out the interpretation of treatment from the case-law. It argues that treatment has a broad legal meaning. Although the meaning of treatment has not been and need not be seen as controversial, the scope of this term's meaning implies that treatment will be a key anchor for future interpretations that push the boundaries of the right's application. In line with the framework defined in Chapter 3, both chapters interpret degrading treatment in a way that is deemed to be the best fit with the Court's interpretation to date. It is argued that degrading treatment should be understood as a social experience characterised by profound powerlessness and symbolic exclusion from the community of human beings, or by destruction of a minimal capacity to oppose the undermining of one's human status or to direct one's own actions.

Chapter 6 contextualises the newly developed interpretation of the right not to be subjected to degrading treatment through an example chosen to test its fringes of application. It considers an experience of socio-economic deprivation in which

70 See Brian Bix, *Law, Language, and Legal Determinacy* (Clarendon Press 1993) 19.

71 The case of *Pretty v. United Kingdom* in 2002 saw the ECtHR refer for the first time briefly but explicitly to the scope of the term 'treatment'. There are numerous references to inhuman and degrading treatment in ECHR literature, which do not consider the scope of meaning of treatment. For Clayton and Tomlinson, for example: 'Degrading treatment is treatment that humiliates or debases', highlighting the substantive character of treatment and not the meaning of treatment itself; Richard Clayton and Hugh Tomlinson, *The Law of Human Rights* (2nd edn, Oxford University Press 2009) 502 para. [8.90]. The same approach is also subtly reflected in Cassese's statement that: 'it is particularly difficult to pinpoint the exact scope and meaning of the bans enshrined in Article 3 regarding the notion of "inhuman" and "degrading" treatment or punishment'; Antonio Cassese, 'Prohibition of Torture, Inhuman or Degrading Treatment or Punishment' in RSJ Macdonald, F Matscher and H Petzold (eds), *The European System for the Protection of Human Rights* (Martinus Nijhoff 1993) 225. See also Cooper 22, and Rainey, Wicks and Ovey 185.

an individual's own active choices appear to play a decisive contributory role. It explores whether this situation could convincingly be argued to fall within the scope of the right not to be subjected to degrading treatment. Through this lens Chapter 6 highlights challenges for the interpretation of the right and reflects on its material scope of application. A key challenge is the idea of human dignity itself. It has both promise and peril as a factor in interpretation. While a particular dimension of the meaning of dignity is argued to be implicit in Article 3 case-law, this can only take us a limited distance when we come to imagine and justify the outer reaches of the prohibition of degrading treatment. The directions in which the prohibition might go must also navigate the limits of state responsibility – the point beyond which the Strasbourg Court will see it as unacceptable to hold states responsible for the suffering of degrading treatment. This chapter demonstrates that the outer limits of the right's interpretive scope revolve around these axes of dignity and responsibility; ideas that are both understood in socially embedded, context-dependent ways, and which simultaneously expand and restrain the right's scope. The discussion highlights, then, the inevitable confrontation between interpretive bodies' dedication to protecting fundamental human dignity and the limits of human rights law itself. There is, nevertheless, much that can be unpacked from Strasbourg jurisprudence and used to underpin a richer understanding of why certain practices or situations should or should not fall within the ambit of the right not to be subjected to degrading treatment.

Chapter 7 reflects on implications of the interpretation of degrading treatment for the interpretive boundaries of the broader right not to be subjected to torture. It briefly considers the meaning of torture and its relationship to degrading treatment, and how cruel and inhuman treatment might conceptually fit into this picture in terms of their specific meanings and their relationships with both torture and degrading treatment. An understanding of these relationships, as Evans and Morgan state, 'has a profound influence over the forms of treatment or punishment likely to be found to violate Article 3.'[72] This chapter demonstrates that the interpretation of each element should sit coherently within the conceptual umbrella of the right, and that a richer understanding of each element leads to a richer understanding of the interpretive scope of the whole.

The concluding chapter summarises how the book has arrived at an understanding of degrading treatment's interpretive scope, what this suggests about the past and future trajectories of the right not to be subjected to degrading treatment, and how the interpretation of degrading treatment can in turn be seen to impact on our understanding of the meanings and relationships within the broader right. Examining degrading treatment, therefore, is both an end in itself and a contribution to an understanding of the essence as well as the margins of the right not to be subjected to torture, cruel, inhuman or degrading treatment or punishment.

72 Evans and Morgan 73.

References

Barak, A, *Purposive Interpretation* (Princeton University Press, 2005)

Bernhardt, R, 'The Convention and Domestic Law' in Macdonald, RSJ, Matscher, F and Petzold, H (eds), *The European System for the Protection of Human Rights* (Martinus Nijhoff, 1993)

Beyleveld, D and Brownsword, R, *Human Dignity in Bioethics and Biolaw* (Oxford University Press, 2001)

Bix, B, *Law, Language, and Legal Determinacy* (Clarendon Press, 1993)

Burgers, HJ and Danelius, H, *The United Nations Convention against Torture: A Handbook on the Convention Against Torture and Other Cruel, Inhuman or Degrading Treatment or Punishment* (Martinus Nijhoff, 1998)

Burgorgue-Larsen, L, de Torres, AU and Greenstein, R, *The Inter-American Court of Human Rights: Case Law and Commentary* (Oxford University Press, 2011)

Carbonari, PC, 'Human Dignity as a Basic Concept of Ethics and Human Rights' in Klein Goldewijk, B, Baspineiro, AC and Carbonari, PC (eds), *Dignity and Human Rights – The Implementation of Economic, Social and Cultural Rights* (Intersentia, 2002)

Carozza, PG, 'Uses and Misuses of Comparative Law in International Human Rights: Some Reflections on the Jurisprudence of the European Court of Human Rights' (1998) 73(5) *Notre Dame L Rev* 1217

Cassese, A, 'Prohibition of Torture, Inhuman or Degrading Treatment or Punishment' in Macdonald, RSJ, Matscher, F and Petzold, H (eds), *The European System for the Protection of Human Rights* (Martinus Nijhoff, 1993)

Clayton, R and Tomlinson, H, *The Law of Human Rights* (2nd edn, Oxford University Press, 2009)

Cooper, J, *Cruelty – An Analysis of Article 3* (Sweet and Maxwell, 2003)

Copelon, R, 'Recognizing the Egregious in the Everyday: Domestic Violence as Torture' (1994) 25 *Colum Hum Rts L Rev* 291

Dayan, C, *The Story of Cruel and Unusual* (MIT Press, 2007)

Donato, J, 'Dworkin and Subjectivity in Legal Interpretation' (1988) 40 *Stan L Rev* 1517

Düwell, M et al. (eds), *The Cambridge Handbook of Human Dignity: Interdisciplinary Perspectives* (Cambridge University Press, 2014)

Dworkin, R, *Law's Empire* (Fontana Press, 1986)

Dworkin, R, *Is Democracy Possible Here? Principles for a New Political Debate* (Princeton University Press, 2006)

Edwards, A, 'The "Feminizing" of Torture under International Human Rights Law' (2006) 19 *Leiden Journal of International Law* 349

Evans, MD and Morgan, R, *Preventing Torture – A Study of the European Convention for the Prevention of Torture and Inhuman or Degrading Treatment or Punishment* (Clarendon Press, 1998)

Evrigenis, D, 'Recent Case-Law of the European Court of Human Rights on Articles 8 and 10 of the European Convention on Human Rights' (1982) 3 *Human Rights Law Journal* 121

Gearty, C, *Principles of Human Rights Adjudication* (Oxford University Press, 2005)

Iglesias, T, 'Bedrock Truths and the Dignity of the Individual' (2001) 4 *Logos* 114

Kaufman, P et al., *Humiliation, Degradation, Dehumanization: Human Dignity Violated* (Springer, 2011)

Kelly, T, *This Side of Silence: Human Rights, Torture, and The Recognition of Cruelty* (University of Pennsylvania Press, 2011)

Klein Goldewijk, B, 'Economic, Social and Cultural Rights: Globalization and the Search for Alternatives and International Political Impacts' in Klein Goldewijk, B, Baspineiro, AC and Carbonari, PC (eds), *Dignity and Human Rights – The Implementation of Economic, Social and Cultural Rights* (Intersentia, 2002)

Klug, F, 'A Bill of Rights: Do We Need One or Do We Already Have One?' (2007) Win *Public Law* 701

Kraynak, RP and Tinder, G (eds), *In Defense of Human Dignity – Essays for Our Times* (University of Notre Dame Press, 2003)

Kretzmer, D and Klein, E (eds), *The Concept of Human Dignity in Human Rights Discourse* (Kluwer Law International, 2003)

Lester, AP, Pannick, D and Herberg, J, *Human Rights: Law and Practice* (3rd edn, LexisNexis, 2009)

Maurer, B, *Le Principe de Respect de la Dignité Humaine et la Convention Européene des Droits de l'Homme* (Bourrinet, J ed., La Documentation Française, 1999)

McCrudden, C, 'Human Dignity and Judicial Interpretation of Human Rights' (2008) 19 *Eur J Int'l L* 655

McCrudden, C (ed.), *Understanding Human Dignity* (Oxford University Press/British Academy, 2013)

McGlynn, C, 'Rape, Torture and The European Convention on Human Rights' (2009) 58 *Int'l & Comp LQ* 565

McGregor, L, 'Applying the Definition of Torture to the Acts of Non-State Actors: The Case of Trafficking in Human Beings' (2014) 36 *Hum Rts Q* 210

Millns, S, 'Death, Dignity and Discrimination: The Case of *Pretty v. United Kingdom*' (2002) 3 *German Law Journal*

Mowbray, A, *Cases and Materials on the European Convention on Human Rights* (2nd edn, Oxford University Press, 2007)

Nowak, M and McArthur, E, 'The Distinction between Torture and Cruel, Inhuman or Degrading Treatment' (2006) 16 *Torture* 147

Palmer, E, *Judicial Review, Socio-economic Rights and the Human Rights Act* (Bloomsbury Publishing, 2007)

Quint, PE, 'International Human Rights: The Convergence of Comparative and International Law' (2001) 36 *Tex Int'l LJ* 605

Rainey, B, Wicks, E and Ovey, C, *Jacobs, White, and Ovey: The European Convention on Human Rights* (Wicks, E and Ovey, C eds, 7th edn, Oxford University Press, 2017)

Rodley, N and Pollard, M, *The Treatment of Prisoners under International Law* (3rd edn, Oxford University Press, 2009)

Rosen, M, *Dignity: Its History and Meaning* (Harvard University Press, 2012)

Schachter, O, 'Human Dignity as a Normative Concept' (1983) 77 *American Journal of International Law* 848

Sifris, R, *Reproductive Freedom, Torture and International Human Rights: Challenging the Masculinisation of Torture* (Routledge, 2013)

Tinder, G, 'Facets of Personal Dignity' in Kraynak, RP and Tinder, G (eds), *In Defense of Human Dignity – Essays for Our Times* (University of Notre Dame Press, 2003)

Vorhaus, J, 'On Degradation. Part One: Article 3 of the European Convention on Human Rights' (2002) 31 *Common Law World Review* 374

Vorhaus, J, 'On Degradation. Part Two: Degrading Treatment and Punishment' (2003) 32 *Common Law World Review* 65

Waldron, J, 'Dignity and Rank' (2007) 48 *European Journal of Sociology* 201

Waldron, J, 'Inhuman and Degrading Treatment: The Words Themselves' (2015) 23 *Canadian Journal of Law and Jurisprudence* 269

Waldron, J, 'Is Dignity the Foundation of Human Rights?' in Cruft, R, Liao, SM and Renzo, M (eds), *Philosophical Foundations of Human Rights* (Oxford University Press, 2015)

Webster, E and Flanigan, D, 'Localising Human Rights Law: A Case-study of Civil Society Interpretation of Rights in Scotland' (2018) 22 *International Journal of Human Rights* 22

Weissbrodt, D and Heilman, C, 'Defining Torture, Inhuman and Degrading Treatment' (2011) 29 *Law and Inequality* 343

Wilson, RA, 'Tyrannosaurus Lex: The Anthropology of Human Rights and Transnational Law' in Goodale, M and Merry, SE (eds), *The Practice of Human Rights: Tracking Law Between the Global and the Local* (Cambridge University Press, 2007)

2 Degrading treatment within Article 3

The right in Article 3 is constituted by forms of harm that are connected yet distinctive. They are connected because together they make up one holistic legal standard and presumably share some common conceptual ground, and they are distinctive because the text of the Convention uses several terms within this single right, which have been authoritatively interpreted by the Convention's monitoring bodies as expressing harms that are capable of occurring in combination and independently. This chapter singles out degrading treatment as a form of harm and gives an overview of the Court's case-law starting points that underpin the interpretation of degradation. This involves showing that degrading treatment is conceived by the Court as a form of harm that can stand alone and setting out the degradation benchmarks. This chapter also clarifies the broader Article 3 context that will have a bearing upon conclusions about the right's interpretive boundaries: the existence of degrading treatment is judged relative to the particular circumstances of an applicant; the idea of degrading treatment is interpreted flexibly and in line with prevailing societal norms; and the prohibition of degrading treatment is 'absolute'. The Article 3 context in which degrading treatment sits also guides the applicable range of obligations upon the state, obligations to refrain from causing harm as well as to protect against it. This chapter identifies the negative obligation not to inflict harm alongside a framework of three forms of protective, positive obligation: to conduct an effective investigation into allegations of degrading treatment; to take measures to protect individuals from suffering degrading treatment at the hands of state agents; and to take measures to protect individuals from suffering degrading treatment stemming from sources beyond the state. The extent of state obligations, as well as the adjudicatory practice of distinguishing between different forms of harm, could be subject to normative critique but that is not the task of this chapter. Rather, it sets the context for analysis of the boundaries of the right not to be subjected to degrading treatment on the basis of current legal practice. The central argument of this chapter is that, to understand the interpretive parameters of the right not to be subjected to degrading treatment, the right must be recognised as conveying a distinctive kind of harm and, at the same time, must be interpreted as an integral part of Article 3.

The category of degrading treatment

The Convention's use of several terms within Article 3 must be presumed to signal harms that are substantively different to some extent but its drafters held no discussion on distinctions between the forms of ill-treatment.[1] Distinctions have been made in the course of the Convention's interpretation. The ECtHR principally distinguishes between torture on the one hand and inhuman/degrading treatment on the other hand.[2] The Court also distinguishes between harm that is inhuman and harm that is degrading. This is evident in the separate sets of benchmarks that it has accorded to each form of harm[3] and in its case-law.[4] It is true that the Court, and applicants, often do not identify one precise form of prohibited treatment in Article 3 claims. Applicants have frequently alleged a violation of Article 3 without specifying the element of the prohibition that is argued to be transgressed,[5] or have alleged inhuman *and/or* degrading treatment.[6] It is common for the ECtHR not to specify whether it understands harm as inhuman and/or degrading; on rare occasions it has found treatment to be inhuman *or* degrading.[7] It is more usual for the Court to find treatment only 'contrary to', or 'in breach of', Article 3.[8] This practice often occurs in cases concerning unexplained injury whilst in state detention[9] and prospective harm in expulsion cases[10] – in both situations it may not be possible for the Court to specify one form of harm when it cannot establish the exact nature of what has happened or is likely to happen. On other occasions the Court does not specify the form(s) of harm when it would be possible for it to do so[11]; there is no settled pattern. Despite scores of findings of 'inhuman and degrading treatment' and of treatment 'contrary

1 Council of Europe, *Collected Edition of the 'Travaux Préparatoires' of the European Convention on Human Rights*, Vol. IV (Martinus Nijhoff 1977).
2 *Selmouni v. France*, para. 96. This confirmed the position set out in *Ireland v. UK* (para. 167) and follows earlier ECommHR decisions; see, e.g., *X. v. The Federal Republic of Germany*, no. 1628/62, 12 December 1963, Collection 12, 61–69.
3 *Ireland v. UK*, para. 167.
4 See, e.g., the following ECtHR cases: *Tyrer v. UK* ('degrading punishment'); *Yankov v. Bulgaria* ('degrading treatment'); *Bilgin v. Turkey*, no. 23819/94, 16 November 2000 ('inhuman treatment'); *Selmouni v. France* ('torture').
5 E.g. *Ahmed v. Austria*, judgment of 17 December 1996, *Reports* 1996-VI, para. 35; *Stanev v. Bulgaria*, no. 26760/06, judgment of 17 January 2012, para. 197.
6 E.g. *Tomasi v. France*, judgment of 27 August 1992, Series A, no. 241-A, para. 112; *Becciev v. Moldova*, no. 9190/03, 4 October 2005.
7 E.g. *Van der Ven v. the Netherlands*, no. 50901/99, ECHR 2003-II, para. 63.
8 *E. and Others v. UK*, no. 33218/96, 26 November 2002; *Pantea v. Romania*, no. 33343/96, ECHR 2003-VI; *R.L. and M.-J.D. v. France*, no. 44568/98, 19 May 2004; *McGlinchey and Others v. UK*, no. 50390/99, ECHR 2003-V.
9 E.g. *Mehmet Emin Yüksel v. Turkey*, no. 40154/98, 20 July 2004; *Karayiğit v. Turkey*, no. 63181/00, 20 September 2005.
10 E.g. *Salah Sheekh v. The Netherlands*, no. 1948/04, 11 January 2007, paras 136 and 148; *Jabari v. Turkey*, no. 40035/98, ECHR 2000-VIII, para. 42.
11 Contrast, e.g., *Taş v. Turkey*, no. 24396/94, 14 November 2000 (in breach of Article 3), with *Bazorkina v. Russia*, no. 69481/01, 27 July 2006 (inhuman treatment) both concerning harm suffered by an applicant in a forced disappearance case.

to Article 3', it is also common for the Court to be more precise in the way it characterises suffering. In numerous cases the Court classifies harm specifically as one form as opposed to another,[12] as was also the practice of its former sister body, the ECommHR.[13] It is clear that each form of Article 3 harm is capable of standing alone.

A range of claims, both successful and unsuccessful, show a perception and acceptance, on the part of the Court and of applicants, that harm can be argued and/or assessed explicitly and uniquely as degrading. The Court has considered on the merits: corporal punishment[14]; discrimination on grounds of sex, race or birth[15]; living conditions caused by pollution from a waste treatment plant[16]; interrogation[17]; application of an official policy of exclusion of homosexuals from the armed forces[18]; repeated imprisonment for refusal to carry out military service[19]; (prison and immigration) detention conditions[20] (including conditions not adapted to physical disability[21] and solitary confinement[22]); the shaving of a prisoner's hair[23]; strip searches[24]; severe suffering caused by a terminal illness[25]; physical ill-treatment by state agents[26] (including the witnessing of the ill-treatment of close family

12 See, e.g., *Tyrer v. UK* ('degrading punishment'); *Yankov v. Bulgaria* ('degrading treatment'); *Bilgin v. Turkey*, no. 23819/94, 16 November 2000 ('inhuman treatment'); *Selmouni v. France* ('torture').

13 See, e.g., *X. v. The Federal Republic of Germany*, no. 3040/67, 7 April 1967, Collection 22, 133–138 ('inhuman treatment'); *East African Asians v. UK*, no. 4403/70, et al., Commission Report of 14 December 1973, Decisions and Reports 78, at 55, paras 180 and 182 ('degrading treatment').

14 *Campbell and Cosans v. UK; Tyrer v. UK.*

15 *Abdulaziz, Cabales and Balkandali v. UK*, judgment of 28 May 1985, Series A, no. 94.

16 *López Ostra v. Spain*, judgment of 9 December 1994, Series A, no. 303-C.

17 *Raninen v. Finland.*

18 *Smith and Grady v. UK*, no. 33985/96; 33986/96, ECHR 1999-VI.

19 *Ülke v. Turkey*, no. 39437/98, 24 January 2006.

20 Cases include *Dougoz v. Greece*, no. 40907/98, ECHR 2001-II; *Peers v. Greece*, no. 28524/95, ECHR 2001-III; *Price v. UK*, no. 33394/96, ECHR 2001-VII; *Valasinas v. Lithuania*, no. 44558/98, ECHR 2001-VIII; *Mayzit v. Russia*, no. 63378/00, 20 January 2005; *Nevmerzhitsky v. Ukraine*, no. 54825/00, 5 April 2005; *Romanov v. Russia*, no. 63993/00, 20 October 2005; *Nicolae Augustin Rădulescu v. Romania*, no. 17295/10, 11 February 2014; *Aleksandr Vladimirovich Smirnov v. Ukraine*, no. 69250/11, 13 March 2014; *F.H. v. Greece*, no. 78456/11, 31 July 2014; *Apostu v. Romania*, no. 22765/12, 3 February 2015; *Drăgan v. Romania*, no. 65158/09, 2 February 2016.

21 *Price v. UK*, no. 33394/96, ECHR 2001-VII; *Vincent v. France*, no. 6253/03, 24 October 2006; *Weiser v. Austria*, no. 2293/03, 22 February 2007; *Engel v. Hungary*, no. 46857/06, 20 May 2010; *Helhal v. France*, no. 10401/12, 19 February 2015.

22 *Nikitenko v. Ukraine*, no. 62609/00, 16 July 2009.

23 *Yankov v. Bulgaria.*

24 E.g. *Wainwright v. UK*, no. 12350/04, ECHR 2006-X; *Frérot v. France, no. 70204/01, 12 June 2007; Jaeger v. Estonia*, no. 1574/13, 31 July 2014.

25 *Pretty v. UK.*

26 *Barbu Anghelescu v. Romania*, no. 46430/99, 5 October 2004; *Saba v. Italy*, no. 36629/10, 1 July 2014; *Kitanovski v. The Former Yugoslav Republic of Macedonia*,

members)[27] and by private persons[28]; failure to provide adequate medical care in detention[29]; failure to provide a detainee with adequate food[30]; anguish caused to a father by the mutilation of his son's body[31]; suffering caused by a deficient state investigation into a disappearance[32]; subjection to extremely poor living conditions (combined with racial discrimination and authorities' mishandling of complaints)[33]; suffering of an elderly applicant required to undertake military service not adapted to his physical ability[34]; the holding of detainees in a metal cage during a court hearing[35]; obliging a detainee to wear a hood in court and in meetings with lawyers and family[36]; depriving an applicant of glasses in detention[37]; situations of indefinite socio-economic deprivation suffered by asylum seekers[38]; conduct of medical examinations in detention[39] (including a gynaecological examination of a young woman)[40]; forced subjection to psychiatric treatment in hospital[41]; living conditions in social care homes[42]; prolonged uncertainty for an applicant whose deceased husband's organs had been removed without consent[43]; forced undressing during a military line-up[44]; handcuffing during a police transfer to hospital[45]; conduct of a police raid and arrest[46]; and failure to provide supervision for a child whose parents were arrested.[47] Some of these claims were successfully argued whilst others were not, but all show that applicants and the Court perceive degradation as a distinct kind of harm that can be the independent object of Article 3 claims.

no. 15191/12, 22 January 2015; *Bouyid v. Belgium [GC]*, no. 23380/09, ECHR 2015.

27 *Iljina and Sarulienė v. Lithuania*, no. 32293/05, 15 March 2011.

28 *Members of the Gldani Congregation of Jehovah's Witnesses and Others v. Georgia.*

29 E.g. *Farbtuhs v. Latvia*, no. 4672/02, 2 December 2004; *Nevmerzhitsky v. Ukraine; Sarban v. Moldova*, no. 3456/05, 4 October 2005; *Marian Chiriță v. Romania*, no. 9443/10, 21 October 2014.

30 *Moisejevs v. Latvia*, no. 64846/01, 15 June 2006.

31 *Akkum and Others v. Turkey*, no. 21894/93, 24 March 2005.

32 *Gongadze v. Ukraine*, no. 34056/02, 8 November 2005.

33 *Moldovan and Others v. Romania*, no. 41138/98; 64320/01, 12 July 2005.

34 *Taştan v. Turkey*, no. 63748/00, 4 March 2008.

35 *Ramishvili and Kokhreidze v. Georgia*, no. 1704/06, 27 January 2009; *Čalovskis v. Latvia*, no. 22205/13, 24 July 2014; *Pugžlys v. Poland*, no. 446/10, 14 June 2016.

36 *Petyo Petkov v. Bulgaria*, no. 32130/03, 7 January 2010.

37 *Slyusarev v. Russia*, no. 60333/00, 20 April 2010.

38 *M.S.S. v. Belgium and Greece*, no. 30696/09, *Reports* 2011; *F.H. v. Greece*, no. 78456/11, 31 July 2014; *V.M. and Others v. Belgium*, no. 60125/11, 7 July 2015.

39 *Duval v. France*, no. 19868/08, 26 May 2011.

40 *Yazgül Yılmaz v. Turkey*, no. 36369/06, 1 February 2011.

41 *Gorobet v. Moldova*, no. 30951/10, 11 October 2011.

42 *Stanev v. Bulgaria*, no. 36760/06, *Reports* 2012; *Stefan Stankov v. Bulgaria*, no. 25820/07, 17 March 2015.

43 *Elberte v. Latvia*, no. 61243/08, ECHR 2015.

44 *Lyalyakin v. Russia*, no. 31305/09, 12 March 2015.

45 *Ilievska v. The Former Yugoslav Republic of Macedonia*, no. 20136/11, 7 May 2015.

46 *Slavov and Others v. Bulgaria*, no. 58500/10, 10 November 2015; *Govedarski v. Bulgaria*, no. 34957/12, 6 February 2016.

47 *Ioan Pop et Autres v. Romania*, no. 52924/09, 6 December 2016.

This overview of degrading treatment claims also gives an impression of the diversity of the situations that applicants and the Strasbourg Court have associated with degrading treatment. Conditions of detention are common but the range stretches much wider than this: from discrimination[48] to living conditions in a social care home.[49] This spectrum of degrading treatment claims attests to the interpretative creativity[50] of both applicants and the Court.

The degradation benchmarks

The benchmarks are the Court's guide to the interpretation of degrading treatment. They in fact encapsulate degradation and not treatment, the meaning of which has not been substantively fleshed out by the Court. They are used by the Court to assess whether the situation being complained of should fall within the Article 3 meaning of degradation and are constituted by a range of concepts that invoke emotional states. Commonly recognised features of degrading treatment case-law are restated here as the starting point for subsequent chapters, and a number of nuances of interpretation are noted, details that might often be overlooked but are relevant to an understanding of the right's potential parameters.

In the landmark case of *Ireland v. UK* in the late 1970s, the Court stated that the 'five techniques' of interrogation under discussion were degrading 'since they were such as to arouse in their victims feelings of fear, anguish and inferiority capable of humiliating and debasing them and possibly breaking their physical or moral resistance'.[51] This formulation remains the Court's most frequently cited description of degrading treatment. The co-existence of all the elements is not required: whereas the Court in *Ireland* used the phrase 'fear, anguish *and* inferiority', in the case of *Pretty v. UK*, the Court looked for 'fear, anguish *or* inferiority'.[52] Similarly, the Court has referred to harm as 'humiliating *and* debasing' and to 'humiliation *or* debasement'.[53]

The Court has associated two principles with the interpretation of the benchmark concept of humiliation. First, it stipulates that a person may be humiliated despite the lack of an intention to bring about humiliation. The ECtHR explicitly accepts that the inflictor of harm need not intend to humiliate or cause suffering to an applicant and stresses that a finding of degrading treatment is possible nevertheless.[54]

48 *Abdulaziz, Cabales and Balkandali v. UK.*
49 *Stanev v. Bulgaria.*
50 This term in used by Mowbray. See Alistair Mowbray, 'The Creativity of the European Court of Human Rights' (2005) 5 *Human Rights Law Review* 57.
51 *Ireland v. UK*, para. 167 (emphasis added).
52 *Pretty v. UK*, para. 52 (emphasis added).
53 *Ireland v. UK*, para. 167 (emphasis added); *Campbell and Cosans v. UK*, para. 28 (emphasis added).
54 See, e.g., *T. v. UK*, no. 24724/94, 16 December 1999, para. 69; *Price v. UK*, para. 30; *Mayzit v. Russia*, para. 42; *Shishkov v. Russia*, no. 26746/05, 20 February 2014, para. 93.

Although the presence or lack of intention is not decisive, intention remains significant and the Court assesses whether the object of the treatment was indeed to humiliate and/or debase, and if such intention is apparent this is a central factor in an eventual finding of a violation;[55] if the treatment is carried out in public the Court may see this as relevant in assessing whether the harm was intentional.[56] Secondly, the Court considers whether or not treatment has occurred in public as part of its determination of the nature of the harm. In the 1978 case of *Tyrer* a 15-year-old boy was sentenced to three strokes of the birch by a juvenile court on the Isle of Man, administered by a policeman in the presence of the boy's father and a doctor, and this was found to be degrading within the meaning of Article 3. The Court referred to the relevance of a public dimension:

> *Publicity may be a relevant factor in assessing whether a punishment is 'degrading' within the meaning of Article 3 ... but the Court does not consider that absence of publicity will necessarily prevent a given punishment from falling into that category: it may well suffice that the victim is humiliated in his own eyes, even if not in the eyes of others.*[57]

The Court regularly reiterates that it may be sufficient for a person to be humiliated in her or his own eyes.[58]

The Court most often relies on the *Ireland v. UK* formulation of degradation but the European Commission's Report on *The Greek case* in 1969 in fact provided the original formulation of degrading treatment: treatment that drives the victim to act against his 'will or conscience'.[59] In its judgments the Court has relied upon this formulation infrequently, but does continue to do so.[60]

The Court's interpretation of degrading treatment also asks whether the treatment has had an adverse effect on the victim's personality. *Albert and Le Compte v. Belgium* was the first time in which the Court referred to this particular benchmark. The Court held that a disciplinary measure against one of the applicants did not intend to debase his personality and did not 'adversely affect his personality in a manner incompatible with Article 3 ...'.[61] This has been repeated in subsequent cases.[62] The Court made a similar statement shortly afterwards in *Abdulaziz, Cabales and Balkandali*, in which it questioned whether the treatment

55 *Raninen v. Finland*, para. 55.

56 *Raninen v. Finland*, para. 55; *Berktay v. Turkey*, no. 22493/93, 1 March 2001, para. 175.

57 *Tyrer v. UK*, para. 32.

58 *Smith and Grady v. UK*, para. 120.

59 *The Greek Case*, Commission Report, Chapter IV, section A (2), at 186.

60 *Keenan v. UK*, no. 27229/95, ECHR 2001-III, para. 110.

61 *Albert and Le Compte v. Belgium*, judgment of 10 February 1983, Series A, no. 58, para. 22.

62 See, e.g., *Raninen v. Finland; Ahmet Özkan and Others v. Turkey*, no. 21689/93, 6 April 2004.

complained of showed contempt or lack of respect for the applicants' personalities.[63]

These benchmarks are a series of reference points that encapsulate the characteristics accorded by the Court to degradation. Case-law tells us only what the benchmarks are and includes additional points in relation to the idea of humiliation in particular. It does not tell us what the benchmarks themselves mean or why they co-exist in the way that they do.

Relative assessment of a minimum level of severity

In the Court's assessment of whether alleged harm falls within the scope of the degradation benchmarks it takes into account all the circumstances of the case before it. Such circumstances include the duration of the treatment, its effects on an individual, and whether the individual's sex, age or state of health adds a special dimension.[64] The Court takes account of such variables individually and cumulatively (made explicit by the Court in cases concerning conditions of detention).[65] A relative assessment implies a tailored conclusion for each case.

The Court undertakes a relative assessment in order to consider whether harm falls within the interpretive scope of Article 3. Harm must be something other than 'difficult' or 'undoubtedly unpleasant or even irksome'.[66] The ECtHR has stated that a practice was 'discreditable and reprehensible',[67] and that a situation may have been 'distressing and humiliating',[68] whilst neither fell within the scope of Article 3. The line between harm that is prohibited by the terms of Article 3

63 *Abdulaziz, Cabales and Balkandali v. UK*, para. 91. One other description has arisen relating to personality: the idea of 'rank, position, reputation or character'. This is not a reference point that has become an established element of degrading treatment. Before reference to adverse effect on personality had occurred, the Commission in its report on the *East African Asians* case considered the definition of degrading treatment *offered by the applicants*: that treatment could be degrading if it lowered the victim in 'rank, position, reputation or character' (the definition that is in fact found in the Oxford Dictionary under 'degraded'). The Commission was of the opinion that this general definition could be a useful starting point but stressed that the purpose of Article 3 was to 'prevent interferences with the dignity of man of a particularly serious nature', and suggested that the definition offered must be narrowed to take account of this (*East African Asians v. UK*, no. 4403/70, et al., Commission Report of 14 December 1973, Decisions and Reports 78, at 55, para. 189). The Commission again mentioned lowering of rank alongside feelings of fear, anguish, etc, as well as the question of whether contempt or lack of respect had been shown, in its Report in the case of *Raninen v. Finland* (no. 20972/92, Commission Report of 24 October 1996, paras 50–52). In the judgment in *Raninen*, however, the Court adopted adverse effect on the applicant's personality (para. 55).

64 *Ireland v. UK*, para. 162. See also, e.g., *Tyrer v. UK*, para. 30; *Labzov v. Russia*, no. 62208/00, 16 June 2005, para. 41.

65 *Kalashnikov v. Russia*, para. 95; see also *Van der Ven v. the Netherlands*, para. 40.

66 *López Ostra v. Spain*, para. 60; *Guzzardi v. Italy*, judgment of 6 November 1980, Series A, no. 39, para. 107, respectively.

67 *Ireland v. UK*, para. 181.

68 *Smith and Grady v. UK*, para. 121.

and harm that is not prohibited by it is expressed by the Court as a threshold of severity.[69] The relative assessment of the minimum level of severity applies across Article 3 as a whole but it takes on particular importance in respect of degrading treatment – if this is seen to be the entry point to Article 3 at the bottom of the right's hierarchy of harm. The protection of Article 3 is activated when the minimum level of severity threshold is crossed. The threshold has been described as a 'boundary'.[70] It is also usefully thought of as a filter; in the case of degradation, a filter between forms of treatment that are degrading and forms of treatment that do not make it into the sphere of degradation as this is understood by the Court.

The inherent scope for evolution

The assessment of the Court is not only relative to individual circumstances but also to societal context. In *Campbell and Cosans v. UK* the ECtHR stated that: 'simply because the measure [corporal punishment] has been in use for a long time or even meets with general approval ...' does not necessarily exclude it from being degrading.[71] Treatment that was in the past excluded from the scope of application of Article 3 could be considered as portraying the minimum degree of severity in future.[72] The Court stresses that the right can evolve to encompass new situations:

> *Given the fundamental importance of Article 3 ... in the Convention system, the Court must reserve to itself sufficient flexibility to address the application of that Article ... in other contexts which might arise.*[73]

One of the hallmarks of the Strasbourg Court is its interpretation of the Convention as a flexible and adaptable system of rights protection. It is widely recognised that the Convention, including Article 3, has been linked to an expanding range of contexts,[74] and that the Court has achieved this by relying upon the notions of 'practical and effective' protection and of the Convention as a 'living instrument'.

69 When this condition is met the Court may simply state that treatment 'reached the threshold' (*Z. and Others v. UK*, para. 74) or was of 'sufficient severity' (*Yankov v. Bulgaria*, para. 120).

70 John Cooper, *Cruelty – An Analysis of Article 3* (Sweet & Maxwell 2003), 27.

71 *Campbell and Cosans v. UK*, para. 29.

72 *Farbtuhs v. Latvia*, para. 53. See also *Selmouni v. France*, para. 101

73 *D. v. UK*, judgment of 2 May 1997, *Reports* 1997-III, para. 49. See also *Pretty v. UK*, para. 50.

74 See, e.g., Mowbray 58; David J Harris, Michael O'Boyle and Colin Warbrick, *Law of the European Convention on Human Rights* (Butterworths 1995) 88; JJ Cremona, *Selected Papers 1946–1989* (Publishers Enterprises Group (PEG) Ltd. 1990) 246; Alberta Fabbricotti, 'The Concept of Inhuman or Degrading Treatment in International Law and its Application in Asylum Cases' (1998) 10 *International Journal of Refugee Law* 637, 638.

The Court has maintained that the ECHR 'is intended to guarantee not rights that are theoretical or illusory but rights that are practical and effective', since first stating this principle in the 1979 case of *Airey v. Ireland.*[75] The Court for the first time made explicit the idea of evolutive interpretation in *Tyrer v. UK*, where it described the Convention as a living instrument that must be interpreted in light of present day conditions.[76] This position had recently been expressed by the then-President of the Commission in a report entitled 'Do the rights set forth in the ECHR in 1950 have the same significance in 1975?', in which he concluded that the Convention had to adapt in order to keep pace with social change.[77] When asked whether a particular situation crosses the threshold to fall within the scope of meaning of the terms in Article 3, the Court's response is not a static one.

An absolute right

If the Strasbourg Court does find harm to come within the interpretive scope of Article 3, and if responsibility can be attributed to a Respondent State, the Court accepts no justifications for the harm suffered. Article 3 is 'absolute' in the sense that it is unqualified. This contrasts with the majority of rights found alongside the prohibition in international instruments, to which legitimate limitations are permitted. The difference is most visible when Article 3 ECHR is compared with Articles 8–11 ECHR – limitations of the right in the interests of national security and/or public safety, for the protection of public order, health, or morals, and so on, are not permissible in respect of the prohibition of torture, inhuman or degrading treatment or punishment. This is unlike even the right to life, susceptible to limitation in some circumstances.[78] The Strasbourg organs have repeatedly reaffirmed Article 3's absolute nature.[79]

The absolute nature of the right applies, not only to torture, but equally to the other forms of harm. The ECtHR forcefully made this point in its first expulsion case, *Soering v. UK*. The harm that the applicant risked suffering – the death row phenomenon in the United States – was not identified as torture, but as inhuman and degrading treatment or punishment. The Court reiterated that a person must not be extradited to face a real risk of torture, and that this protection extended to

75 *Airey v. Ireland*, judgement of 9 October 1979, Series A, no. 32.

76 *Tyrer v. UK*, para. 31. See also *Selmonui v. France*, para. 101; *T. v. UK*, para. 70.

77 Søren C Prebensen, 'Evolutive interpretation of the European Convention on Human Rights' in P Mahoney et al. (eds), *Protection des droits de l'homme: la perspective européenne* [*Protecting Human Rights: The European Perspective – Studies in Memory of Rolv Ryssdal*] (Heymanns 2000) 1123.

78 As a result of a sentence imposed by law, or as a result of a proportionate use of force in defence of a person from unlawful violence, to effect a lawful arrest or prevent escape of a detainee, or in lawful action to quell a riot or insurrection (Article 2 ECHR).

79 See, e.g., *Ireland v. UK*, para. 163; *Raninen v. Finland*, para. 55; *Pretty v. UK*, para. 49; *Yankov v. Bulgaria*, para. 103.

a real risk of the other forms of harm.[80] This reinforces the equal prohibition of the non-torture harms. As Addo and Grief observe: 'all forms of ill-treatment which fall within the scope of Article 3 are prohibited with equal force no matter which end of the spectrum they fall'.[81]

The absolute label accords to the right significant weight and places significant demands on States Parties to the ECHR. Addo and Grief write that the 'absolute' label endows Article 3 with certain 'conceptual characteristics'. Building on Alan Gewirth's theoretical conceptualisation of absolute rights,[82] these authors note that there is an expectation that the right will be subject to the most rigorous protection possible; that if there is any doubt about the scope of the right the benefit of that doubt must be given to the alleged victim; that 'potential violators ... should enjoy only limited discretion in respect of such a right'; and that redress must be ensured if a violation is established.[83] The existence of such characteristics is supported in the Court's case-law. Notably, the ECtHR has held that the right must be protected 'irrespective of the victim's conduct',[84] and has upheld its application in extremely challenging situations, from cases of expulsion of convicted and suspected terrorists[85] to cases in which economic constraints have been offered as a defence against a finding of a violation.[86] Due to the absolute nature of the right the Court has not afforded to states a margin of appreciation. The margin is a 'latitude of discretion'[87] allowed to States Parties and is applied in various situations.[88] The consequences of its application are significant: within the permitted area of discretion the Court will not intervene to question the state's judgment; the margin limits the scope of the Court's review. There is evidence of a Respondent State claiming a margin of appreciation before the ECtHR in determining the extent of protective state obligations under Article 3, and literature on

80 *Soering v. UK*, judgment of 7 August 1989, Series A, no. 161, para. 88.
81 Micheal K Addo and Nicholas Grief, 'Does Article 3 of the European Convention on Human Rights Enshrine Absolute Rights?' (1998) 9 *European Journal of International Law* 510, 512.
82 See Alan Gewirth, *Human Rights. Essays on Justification and Applications* (University of Chicago Press 1982) Chapter 9. Gewirth's approach to absolute rights is part of his rational account of moral rights and human dignity, founded on the basis of the agency of human persons. Three senses of absolutism are identified by Gewirth (Principle, Rule and Individual Absolutism), which are succinctly explained by Addo and Grief and mapped onto Article 3 ECHR; see Addo and Grief 514–515.
83 Addo and Grief 516.
84 See, e.g., *Ireland v. UK*, para. 163.
85 E.g. *Saadi v. Italy*, no. 37201/06, 28 February 2008; *Chahal v. UK*, no. 22414/93, *Reports* 1996-V.
86 *Kalashnikov v. Russia*, no. 47095/99, ECHR 2002-VI.
87 Howard Charles Yourow, *The Margin of Appreciation Doctrine in the Dynamics of European Human Rights Jurisprudence* (Martinus Nijhoff Publishers 1996) 13. In the landmark *Handyside* judgment the Court explained its understanding of, and motivations for, the attribution of a margin of appreciation; *Handyside v. United* Kingdom, no. 5493/72, judgment of 7 December 1976, Series A, no. 24, para. 48.
88 Yourow 12.

the issue is also ambiguous,[89] but the case-law on which the analysis in this book is based shows no evidence that the Court accepts its application. If a margin of appreciation is referred to by the Court, it is in cases that concern other Convention provisions alongside Article 3. For example, in the case of *Marckx* the margin of appreciation is relied upon as part of the Article 8 claim in conjunction with Article 14 but not in relation to Article 3.[90] The margin of appreciation was referred to in the 2002 case of *Pretty v. UK*, not by the Court but by the UK government, who argued that a margin of appreciation existed for it to judge the scope of positive obligations.[91] (Conversely, Mrs Pretty argued that there was no scope for a margin of appreciation in relation to Article 3).[92] The Court stopped short of engaging with this question, estimating that no positive obligation existed and therefore the issue of its scope did not need to be determined.[93] The Court's body of inhuman and degrading treatment case-law lends no support to the application of a margin of appreciation.[94] Its absence is a consequence of the absolute nature of Article 3. A further consequence is that Article 3 is removed from the ambit of

89 For example, Yourow 188; Pieter Van Dijk, '"Positive Obligations" Implied in the European Convention on Human Rights: Are the States Still the "Masters" of the Convention?' in Monique Castermans-Holleman, Fried van Hoof and Jacqueline Smith (eds), *The Role of the Nation State in the 21st Century; Human Rights, International Organisations and Foreign Policy: Essays in Honour of Peter Baehr* (Kluwer Law International 1998) 22–23.

90 *Marckx v. Belgium*, judgment of 13 June 1979, Series A, no. 31, paras 31 and 53–54.

91 *Pretty v. UK*, para. 48; see also *R (Pretty) v. Director of Public Prosecutions* [2001] 3 WLR 1598, para. 15.

92 *Pretty v. UK*, para. 46.

93 *Pretty v. UK*, para. 56.

94 Calleweart, writing in 1998, agreed that the Court had not allowed a margin of appreciation in the application of Article 3 but does not refer specifically to determination of the scope of positive obligations. Rather, he distinguishes between two stages in the process of applying Article 3 in order to demonstrate clearly that a margin of appreciation is not applicable in either – these are the establishment of the facts, and the legal classification of the facts. The reasons he gives for the non-applicability of a margin include the following: its flexibility is incompatible with the absolute nature of Article 3. Under Article 3 the same circumstances must allow the same conclusion to be reached, i.e. the effect of the circumstances may be different based on the circumstances of the case but not based on conceptions held within the state. A margin would be incompatible since it would have the consequence of accepting differences in the *Convention's effects* in light of local circumstances. Also, given the nature of adjudication on Article 3, which requires a process of legal classification in order to determine whether or not the right has been violated, the Court must retain control over this process – the authoritative interpretation and definition of the Convention and its requirements, having effects on all of the Contracting States, is reserved to the Court by Article 45 of the Convention (now Article 32). As well as being incompatible with the territorially limited competence of domestic authorities, allowing individual states to limit the 'interpretive freedom' of the Court would not be in line with the purpose of the margin of appreciation. He also emphasises the need for common standards in the application of Article 3, which he sees as the most prominent right symbolising universality. See Johan Calleweart, 'Is there a Margin of Appreciation in the Application of Articles 2, 3 and 4 of the Convention?' (1998) 19 *Human Rights Law Journal* 6.

temporary abrogation in time of war or public emergency. It is one of few rights that are non-derogable.[95] Once the Court finds Article 3 to be engaged, and if it finds that responsibility is attributable to a State Party, the exigencies of Article 3, as Mavronicola writes, are 'non-displaceable'.[96] The absolute nature of Article 3 subjects States Parties to special restrictions and places upon them special demands.

The obligations of states under Article 3

The protection afforded by Article 3 is activated if the Court attributes to a Respondent State responsibility for a violation of the Convention. Responsibility is attributed when an act or omission triggers a breach of an obligation. An understanding of obligations, of the things that the state cannot do, and must do, is a necessary prelude to an assessment of whether a violation of the right has or has not occurred. In other words, whether a state can properly be seen as responsible for harm suffered by an individual applicant depends on an understanding of the state's human rights obligations.

Article 1 ECHR anchors a dual obligation upon states not to inflict harm and to intervene in order to protect – States Parties shall 'secure' the Convention rights to everyone within their jurisdictions. Since the early days of the Convention[97] this dual obligation has been expressed in the form of negative and positive obligations. The former demand that states do not interfere with the enjoyment of rights; the latter address 'the question of the state as a guarantor rather than a violator of human rights.'[98] The boundary between positive and negative obligations is not always easily defined.[99] A positive/negative dichotomy can seem artificial in light of the multidimensional nature of rights and rights protection, and some have questioned the usefulness of the distinction.[100] It is the case that the label attached

95 Article 3 ECHR is explicitly removed from the scope of Article 15, which details derogation.

96 See Natasa Mavronicola, 'What is an "Absolute Right"? Deciphering Absoluteness in the Context of Article 3 of the European Convention on Human Rights' (2012) 12 *Human Rights Law Review* 723. This analysis of the meaning of 'absoluteness' as a quality of Article 3 ECHR also foregrounds the significance of definitional questions in light of Article 3's absolute nature.

97 See *Belgian Linguistics Case*, judgment of 23 July 1968, Series A, no. 6; see section 1, A and B.

98 Cordula Dröge, *Positive Verpflichtungen der Staaten in der Europäischen Menschenrechtskonvention* [*Positive Obligations of States under the European Convention of Human Rights*] (Springer 2003) 380.

99 Anthony Paul Lester, David Pannick and Javan Herberg, *Human rights: Law and Practice* (3rd edn, LexisNexis 2009) at 196, para. 4.3.15; Keir Starmer, 'Positive Obligations under the Convention' in Jeffrey Jowell and Jonathan Cooper (eds), *Understanding Human Rights Principles* (Hart Publishing 2001) 158.

100 In a number of cases on the right to respect for private and family life, home and correspondence, the ECtHR has stated that the distinction between negative and positive obligations has been irrelevant; the legitimate limitation test has been seen as broadly similar regardless of whether negative or positive obligations are in question. See, e.g., *López Ostra v. Spain*, para. 51.

to the nature of the state's obligation is not always pivotal. This is so in situations when a state both acts and fails to act, but in which its responsibility is evident and not disputed. Where the attribution of responsibility is unproblematic, and will not be a barrier to a finding of a violation of a Convention right, it makes little difference whether the obligation is labelled as positive or negative. This one instance does not detract from the value of a scheme of obligations for understanding what human rights law expects of the state. In the following discussion the negative/positive distinction forms the primary framework.

An overview of the negative obligation is followed by more extensive consideration of positive obligations pertaining to Article 3. Negative obligations are the prototypical obligations, in line with the classic notion of human rights as protection of the individual against intrusion by the state. Such obligations impose upon the state a duty not to intrude into an individual's life; to leave individuals free to lead the lives they choose without undue restriction or incursion. Positive obligations were traditionally seen as being reserved for economic, social and cultural rights but this is no longer the case; it is firmly established that civil and political rights also require states to take positive measures. The catalyst behind this was recognition that rights would not be effectively secured if states were never obliged to undertake 'affirmative tasks'.[101] Starmer highlights the historical context in which the Convention came into existence that further justifies the adoption by the Convention organs of positive obligations: in comparing the approach to positive obligations of the US Supreme Court and the ECtHR, he notes that the purpose of the ECHR is not primarily the protection of individual freedom from the excesses of the state but rather the protection of human dignity. This, he writes, stems from the particular experience of World War II, in which atrocities were committed against minorities and dissidents with the widespread collaboration of ordinary citizens.[102] Positive obligations are now ingrained in the fabric of the Convention and have transformed the landscape of European human rights law. They are the practical manifestation of a change in the perceived role of the state. As Dimitrios Evrigenis has observed: 'Modern human rights legislation increasingly relies on the concept of a "State conferring benefits" ...'.[103] The 'shifting synthesis', as this change has been described by Evrigenis, has not yet abated.[104] The continuing development of positive obligations is critical to an assessment of the potential scope of application of the right not to be subjected to degrading treatment within Article 3. Accounts of positive obligations, under Article 3 in particular and the ECHR in general, vary substantially from one author to another. There is agreement that positive obligations require the state to

101 Alastair Mowbray, *Development of Positive Obligations under the European Convention on Human Rights by the European Court of Human Rights* (Hart Publishing 2004) 2.
102 Starmer 144–145.
103 Dimitrios Evrigenis, 'Recent Case-Law of the European Court of Human Rights on Articles 8 and 10 of the European Convention on Human Rights' (1982) 3 *Human Rights Law Journal* 121, 136.
104 Evrigenis 136.

take action,[105] but in answering the question in what circumstances and to what extent, although there is significant overlap, there is not a uniform approach.[106] The Strasbourg Court itself has not expounded general principles on the content and scope of positive obligations.[107] In the absence of a settled approach to categorising these obligations, and in order to make plain the forms of obligation that will shape the scope of application of the right not to be subjected to degrading treatment, this section identifies a framework of state obligations on the basis of the inhuman and degrading treatment jurisprudence that informs the rest of the book.[108]

The ECtHR has specified that Article 3 imposes primarily a negative obligation[109] but positive obligations have now become an integral part of this right's application. A paradigmatic negative obligation is associated with the traditional image of torture, inhuman or degrading treatment or punishment, of abuse inflicted by state officials behind closed doors. Going beyond the 'classic' examples of ill-treatment, cases that rely on negative obligations include *Selçuk and Asker v. Turkey*, in which the destruction of homes and the ensuing treatment of the applicants demonstrated a breach of a negative obligation, and *Yankov v. Bulgaria*, in which the forcible shaving of the applicant's head constituted degrading treatment and breached the state's negative obligation.[110] The counterpart to the

105 See, e.g., Mowbray, *Development of Positive Obligations under the European Convention on Human Rights by the European Court of Human Rights* 2, referring to the opinion of Judge Martens in the case of *Gül v. Switzerland*, no. 23218/94, *Reports* 1996-I; Frédéric Sudre, 'Les "Obligations Positives" dans la Jurisprudence Européene des Droits de l'Homme' in P Mahoney et al. (eds), *Protection des Droits de l'Homme: La Perspective Européene [Protecting Human Rights: The European Perspective – Studies in Memory of Rolv Ryssdal]* (Heymanns 2000) 1359 referring to *López Ostra v. Spain*.

106 For example, Starmer extracts general principles through an analysis of the Court's case-law resulting in five positive obligations (Starmer 147–158); Mowbray arrives at three broad groupings (Mowbray, *Development of Positive Obligations under the European Convention on Human Rights by the European Court of Human Rights* 225–227); Dröge uses two broad categories (Dröge 381–383); and Sudre also highlights two forms but focuses on the way in which obligations can be breached rather than what they demand (Sudre 1365–1368).

107 See *Plattform Ärzte für das Leben v. Austria*, judgment of 21 June 1988, Series A, no. 139, para. 31. See Starmer and Dröge, who both find this lack of general theory characteristic of the ECtHR, and also unfortunate; Starmer 139 and Dröge 379.

108 The present discussion does not draw upon torture jurisprudence but it is presumed that the framework of obligations put forward here could apply to Article 3 as a whole. This presumption finds support in the work of Palmer and Mowbray; two authors who have discussed positive obligations as they apply to Article 3 specifically rather than the Convention in a more general sense. Despite some differences in the way the categories are constructed, the obligations identified are essentially the same. See Stephanie Palmer, 'A Wrong Turning: Article 3 ECHR and Proprtionality' (2006) 65 *Cambridge Law Journal* 438, 440–441; Mowbray, *Development of Positive Obligations under the European Convention on Human Rights by the European Court of Human Rights*, Chapter 3.

109 *Pretty v. UK*, para. 50.

110 *Selçuk and Asker v. Turkey*, judgment of 24 April 1998, *Reports* 1998-II; *Yankov v. Bulgaria*.

negative obligation in Article 3 is the implied (rather than express) positive obligation.[111] The scope of implied obligations attract greater controversy as obligations that were not anticipated by states who were early signatories to the Convention. In this vein some have suggested that a consequence of implied obligations is subjection to a test of proportionality (discussed below).[112] The fact that implied obligations have become ingrained in the Convention is nevertheless undisputed.[113] In *Costello-Roberts v. UK*, an Article 3 case concerning corporal punishment in an independent school, the positive obligation was expressed as follows:

> *The Court has consistently held that the responsibility of a State is engaged if a violation of one of the rights and freedoms defined in the Convention is the result of non-observance by that State of its obligation under Article 1 ... to secure those rights and freedoms in its domestic law to everyone within its jurisdiction.*[114]

This general positive obligation is manifested in the case-law as, firstly, an obligation to conduct an effective investigation into allegations of degrading treatment; secondly, as an obligation to take measures to protect individuals from suffering degrading treatment at the hands of the state; and thirdly, as an obligation to take measures to protect individuals from suffering degrading treatment that stems from 'actors' beyond the State Party (for example, another state). In inhuman and degrading treatment jurisprudence the negative obligation sits alongside these three specific forms of positive obligation.

The first is to conduct an effective investigation, although several of the relevant cases do not explicitly state the nature of this obligation. An example is found in *Kuznetsov v. Ukraine*:

> *The Court recalls that where an individual raises an arguable claim that he has been subjected to ill-treatment by the police or other agents of the State unlawfully and in breach of Article 3 of the Convention, that provision, read in conjunction with the State's general duty under Article 1 of the Convention to 'secure to everyone within their jurisdiction the rights and freedoms defined in ... [the] Convention', requires by implication that there should be an effective official investigation.*[115]

111 Certain requirements to take action are included expressly in the text of the Convention (e.g. Art. 5 (2–4)), whereas others have been read into the text by the Strasbourg organs. For discussion, see Van Dijk.

112 See the UK House of Lords judgment in *R (Munjaz) v. Mersey care NHS Trust* [2005] 3 WLR 793, para. 78.

113 Harris, O'Boyle and Warbrick 19–20; Starmer 159.

114 *Costello-Roberts v. UK*, judgment of 25 March 1993, Series A, no. 247-C, para. 26.

115 *Kuznetsov v. Ukraine*, para. 105. See also *Ahmet Ozkhan and Others v. Turkey*, para. 358; *Toteva v.* Bulgaria, no. 42027/98, 19 May 2004, para. 62.

This invocation of Article 1 suggests that the procedural guarantee[116] of conducting an effective investigation is a positive obligation. In the later case of *Afanasyev v. Ukraine* this is made explicit: 'The Court recalls that Article 3 of the Convention creates a positive obligation to investigate effectively allegations of ill-treatment ...'.[117]

The second form of positive obligation is to take measures to protect individuals from suffering prohibited treatment at the hands of the state. This is the essence of states' protective obligation towards persons deprived of liberty. In *Mouisel v. France* the Court stated that Article 3 imposed 'an obligation on the State to protect the physical well-being of persons deprived of their liberty, for example by providing them with the requisite medical assistance'.[118] This case concerned the continued detention in prison of an individual suffering from a progressive illness and the conditions in which he was transferred to hospital for treatment. By failing to take adequate positive measures to ensure that the applicant did not suffer prohibited treatment the state had breached its obligation.[119] In *Farbtuhs v. Latvia*, in which an 84 year old disabled applicant was suffering from several chronic illnesses, the Court explicitly confirms that the protection of the physical well-being of detainees is viewed as a positive rather than negative obligation: Article 3 is said to impose a positive obligation to ensure that prisoners are detained in conditions compatible with their human dignity, and the health and well-being of detainees must be adequately safeguarded, notably through the provision of adequate medical care.[120] The Court's reasoning in *Pretty v. UK* also supports the existence of an Article 3 positive obligation to provide appropriate medical care.[121] This obligation to safeguard the health and wellbeing of persons deprived of liberty can be expressed in more general terms as an obligation to take positive measures to protect individuals from suffering degrading treatment *at the hands of the state.*

This form of obligation, in the body of inhuman and degrading treatment and punishment case-law, is most often at play in situations of detention but the geography of the harm should not be crucial. The critical aspect is the engagement of state responsibility. Responsibility is engaged when state authorities are at the root of the harm, and this is the case where persons are physically under state control but could also be the case where a person is not under such physical control. When treatment finds it source in the state itself the responsibility of that state for a violation of the right is clearly engaged. As such, this obligation might be perceived as being almost indistinguishable from a negative obligation. The line between the forms of obligation here is fluid but the jurisprudence indicates that it is an obligation to take positive action to prevent the suffering of prohibited harm. It is helpful to describe the second form of positive obligation in these more

116 *Naumenko v. Ukraine*, no. 42023/98, 10 February 2004, para. 129.
117 *Afanasyev v. Ukraine*, no. 38722/02, 5 April 2005, para. 69.
118 *Mouisel v. France*, no. 67263/01, ECHR 2002-IX, para. 40.
119 *Mouisel v. France*, para. 48.
120 *Farbtuhs v. Latvia*, para. 51. See also *Nevmerzhitsky v. Ukraine*, para. 81.
121 *Pretty v. UK*, para. 55.

general terms because it allows for a more streamlined framework of Article 3 obligations by drawing attention to the question of who or what is at the source of the harm. The obligation to take measures to protect the health and well-being of persons deprived of liberty then is alternatively expressed as an obligation to take positive measures to protect individuals from suffering prohibited treatment at the hands of the state.

The third form of positive obligation is a progressive extension from the obligation to protect individuals from prohibited harm at the hands of the state. It is an obligation to take positive measures to protect individuals from suffering degrading treatment that stems from a source beyond the state and has been pivotal to the development of Article 3. It is evident in *Z. and Others v. UK*, in which the harm did not stem from the state but was inflicted by a private individual:

> *The obligation on High Contracting Parties under Article 1 of the Convention to secure to everyone within their jurisdiction the rights and freedoms defined in the Convention, taken in conjunction with Article 3, requires States to take measures designed to ensure that individuals within their jurisdiction are not subjected to torture or inhuman or degrading treatment, including such ill-treatment administered by private individuals.*[122]

This approach is repeated by the Court in *E. and Others v. UK*[123] and confirmed in subsequent cases.[124] In expulsion cases the existence of a positive obligation is made less explicit by the Court but the form of obligation is the same. In *Soering*, agreeing with the applicant and confirming the Commission's approach, the Court held that Article 3:

> *Not only prohibits the Contracting States from causing inhuman or degrading treatment or punishment to occur within their jurisdiction but also embodies an associated obligation not to put a person in a position where he will or may suffer such treatment or punishment at the hands of other States.*[125]

The Court concluded that extradition could give rise to an issue under the Convention if it established that there existed a real risk that the applicant would be subjected to prohibited treatment in the requesting state.[126] The obligation of the state in this and other expulsion cases[127] is to protect against potential harm

122 *Z. and Others v. UK*, paras 70 and 73.
123 *E. and Others* v. UK, para. 88.
124 *Pretty v. UK*, paras 50–51.
125 *Soering v. UK*, para. 82.
126 *Soering v. UK*, para. 91.
127 E.g. *Nsona v. the Netherlands*, judgment of 28 November 1996, *Reports* 1996-V, para. 91. See also, e.g., *Ahmed v. Austria*, para. 39, and *H.L.R. v. France*, judgment of 29 April 1997, *Reports* 1997-III, para. 34; *Khodzhayev v. Russia*, no. 52466/08, 12 May 2010, para. 90. Non-*refoulement* claims brought by applicants who are receiving

stemming from 'actors', or 'sources', beyond the Respondent State.[128] 'Sources' refers to who or what can inflict or bring about the prohibited treatment without implying that there is an active, identifiable inflictor of harm. The ECtHR has gradually, and significantly, expanded the range of sources of Article 3 harm from which the protection of States Parties might be sought.

There is clear evidence of three non-state sources in the case-law – another state, private persons, and no one identifiable actor or institution – and less clear evidence of one further source – naturally occurring illness. The original non-state actor that a Respondent State was asked to positively protect against was another state. The many examples of expulsion and extradition cases demonstrate this. In *Soering v. UK* the death row phenomenon stemmed directly from a state institution, but not an institution of the State Party to the Convention; in this case the United States government. In *Chahal v. UK* the risk of prohibited Article 3 ill-treatment would have stemmed from Indian security forces. Had the individuals been returned, the treatment would have been inflicted by the state in the receiving country. Prohibited treatment by a private person can be seen in *E. and Others v. UK* concerning the abuse – which amounted to inhuman and degrading treatment – of children by their step-father. An example of treatment by a group of private persons is found in the case of *Pantea v. Romania*, in which the applicant was subjected to physical violence by fellow prison inmates, found by the Court to amount to inhuman or degrading treatment.[129] Another example is found in *H.L. R. v. France*, in which the applicant feared inhuman or degrading treatment at the hands of drug dealers in Colombia.[130] There is increasingly well-established evidence in the case-law of another, very different source of harm. The Court recognises harm brought about by no one identifiable actor or institution, a source

life-sustaining medical care form an exceptional category; for discussion see Elaine Webster, 'Medical-Related Expulsion and Interpretation of Article 3 of the European Convention on Human Rights' (2013) 6 *Inter-American and European Human Rights Journal* 36.

128 It is possible that an overlap could occur between the first and second forms of positive obligation. The case of *Pantea v. Romania* provides an example of this. The prison authorities in this case, in which the applicant was beaten by other inmates during his detention, were held to have failed in their positive obligation to protect the physical integrity of the applicant through insufficient surveillance and protection from harm. The Court stated that the injuries caused by the fellow detainees whilst under control of the prison authorities were: '[e]lements of fact that ... are in themselves severe enough for the offences complained of to constitute inhuman or degrading treatment ...' and found that this treatment was 'contrary to' Article 3. The Court then went on to establish 'whether the authorities in the respondent state [could] be held responsible for this.' The Court noted that the state had an obligation to take the practical preventative measures necessary to protect the physical integrity and health of persons who have been deprived of their liberty. This seems to suggest a confluence of the obligation to take measures to protect individuals from prohibited treatment stemming from both the state and private persons; *Pantea v. Romania*, paras 185–196.

129 *Pantea v. Romania*. See also *Premininy v. Russia*, no. 44973/04, 10 February 2011.

130 *H.L.R. v. France*, paras 39–40.

of harm that seems gradually to have become established by the Court. It was originally implied by the Court in the first medical-related expulsion case that it examined, the well-known case of *D. v. UK* in 1997. The Court stated in this case that an applicant's claim could be scrutinised even when the proscribed harm in the country to which the applicant was to be expelled stemmed from no one actor or institution in particular. The root of the conditions complained of was found in factors which could not 'engage either directly or indirectly the responsibility of the public authorities of that country.'[131] That is to say, the receiving state could not be held responsible for inflicting prohibited treatment. The conditions of adversity that would await the applicant were nobody's fault as such; no one actor or institution could be said to have caused them. A more recent example is found in *N. v. Sweden.*[132] Besides this indeterminate source, there is now some evidence that the Court is moving towards extending the non-state-sources positive obligation to naturally occurring illness. If the Court accepts that illness can bring about the kind of treatment prohibited by Article 3 it implies that a state could be held responsible for failing to mitigate the harm. In a 2007 judgment against Lithuania the Court indicated that the positive obligation entailed a need to protect against inhuman or degrading treatment 'whatever its source' and gave the example of naturally occurring illness.[133] The Court's reference to Article 3 was brief and no violation was found in this case. This can be seen also in the 2012 case of *Hristozov and Others v. Bulgaria*:

> *Suffering flowing from a naturally-occurring illness may be covered by Article 3 where it is or risks being exacerbated by treatment stemming from measures for which the authorities can be held responsible ... However, the threshold in such situations is high, because the alleged harm emanates not from acts or emissions of the authorities but from the illness itself.*[134]

The Court's approach here, the idea that the suffering emanates from the illness and that the authorities' 'refusals' do not cross the severity threshold,[135] seems incoherent. This incoherence is a symptom of the irregularity found in the niche category of medical-related expulsion cases under Article 3.[136] My view is also that an expansion of the positive obligation in this direction, to require the state to protect against Article 3 prohibited treatment from *any source*, is not only illogical but conceptually a wrong turning; a point that will be become clear in the interpretation of the degradation benchmarks in Chapter 4. As it stands, however, the current Strasbourg position in any case indicates an increase in the range of non-

131 *D. v. UK*, para. 49.
132 *N. v. Sweden*, no. 23505/09, para. 62. The development of this source of Article 3 harm is discussed in Webster (2013).
133 *L. v. Lithuania*, no. 27527/03, para. 46.
134 *Hristozov and Others v. Bulgaria*, no. 47039/11; 358/12, ECHR 2012 (extracts), para. 111.
135 *Hristozov and Others v. Bulgaria*, para. 113.
136 Webster 48–49.

state sources of harm that can be encompassed within the third form of positive obligation. In summary, the Court has moved over time from invoking a positive obligation where harm stems from a third state, to having its source in non-state actors, to harm that stems from no one identifiable actor or institution in particular.

In order for the Court to hold a state responsible under Article 3 for suffering that stems, or would stem, from any non-state source, that state must have had specific knowledge of, or judged reasonably, should have had knowledge of, the impugned acts. Assessment of this criterion is commonly referred to as the '*Osman* test'. The applicants in the *Osman* case stipulated, in allegations under Article 2, that a 'careful scrutiny of events' demonstrated that the police did not take adequate measures to protect the second applicant and his family from the acts of a private person which lead to the injury of this applicant and the killing of his father. The government argued that the response of the authorities, in light of the information they held, was reasonable.[137] The Court's assessment found that the applicant had to show 'that the authorities did not do all that could be reasonably expected of them', and this is 'a question which can only be answered in the light of all the circumstances of any particular case.'[138] The Court conducted such an evaluation, including assessment of the levels of knowledge available, of how the input of professionals impacted upon the decisions of authorities, of the series of events and of what could reasonably have been deduced from them, and it considered whether the lack of action of the authorities at particular points could be considered unreasonable.[139] In considering all such circumstances of a case, the Court is in a position to determine whether the state could have been *expected to do more* to prevent a violation. And the same approach is used in Article 3 cases: the Court refers to the taking of reasonably available measures[140] and to the need to avoid an impossible burden upon the state when taking practical preventive action to protect individuals.[141] An applicant must show that the authorities did not do all that could reasonably be expected of them to protect against a certain and immediate risk of ill-treatment of which they had or ought to have had knowledge.[142]

This test of reasonable expectation is distinct from a proportionality test. The doctrine of proportionality 'implies the need to strike a proper balance between various competing interests'.[143] There are several 'versions' of proportionality[144]

137 *Osman v. UK*, no. 23452/94, ECHR 1998-VIII, paras 103 and 109.
138 *Osman v. UK*, para. 116.
139 *Osman v. UK*, paras 115–122.
140 *E. and Others v. UK*, para. 92. See also *Z. and Others v. UK*, para. 73.
141 *Pantea v. Romania*, para. 190.
142 *Pantea v. Romania*, para. 190.
143 Pieter Van Dijk et al. (eds), *Theory and Practice of the European Convention on Human Rights* (4th edn, Intersentia 2006) 80.
144 Richard Clayton and Hugh Tomlinson, *The Law of Human Rights* (2nd edn, Oxford University Press 2009) 397, para. 6.258.; Lord Hope citing *Osman v. UK* in *R. (Munjaz) v. Mersey Care NHS Trust*, para. 78; the UK government in *Pretty v. UK*, para. 47.

that have different implications in different contexts. Proportionality is 'most evident'[145] in relation to the rights found in Articles 8–11 ECHR that can be legitimately restricted. Some have expressed the view that a form of proportionality test is used by the Strasbourg Court when defining the limits of positive obligations.[146] As Palmer rightly argues, proportionality should not be seen as relevant to the absolute right in Article 3; not in relation to the interpretation of Article 3 (i.e. in determining whether a certain practice amounts to one or more of the forms of harm within Article 3), or in relation to the scope of the Article 3 positive obligation[147] (i.e. in determining the extent of the state's obligation to take action). Limitations on the scope of the obligation to protect against non-state harm instead pertain to reasonable expectation.[148] The test of reasonable expectation takes into account practical constraints on the state's capacity of action rather than any assessment of a 'proper balance'. It is a limit, or a line drawn, at the point at which what is being asked of the state exceeds what is reasonable. It is not reasonable to expect the state to do something impossible or something that would place a disproportionate burden upon it. The Strasbourg Court has unhelpfully used the word 'disproportionate',[149] inviting confusion with the doctrine of proportionality but it has also used 'intolerable' or 'excessive'.[150] It would be unachievable for the state to prevent all attacks on physical and/or mental integrity by non-state sources and it is therefore unreasonable to expect the state to do so. As Dworkin has stated in an example pertaining to absolute legal rights, the only reason for not protecting such rights is impossibility.[151] The reasonable expectation test leaves the 'non-displaceable'[152] nature of the right intact, contrary to what would be suggested by the use of the term 'proportionality'.

The test of reasonable expectation comes into play when the Court accepts that prohibited treatment has stemmed, or will stem, from a source outside of the state, and when an applicant argues that state responsibility is nevertheless engaged. If prohibited treatment stems from state agents/institutions it would be illogical to see the scope of the positive obligation as limited by constraints of knowledge.[153] Only where harm finds its source beyond the state can the scope of

145 Harris, O'Boyle and Warbrick 11.

146 Clayton and Tomlinson 368, para. 6.178. See also Stephen Grosz, Jack Beatson and Peter Duffy, *Human Rights: The 1998 Act and the European Convention* (Sweet & Maxwell 2000) 172, para. C0–16.

147 Palmer 446. It seems that Palmer sees the first example as a dangerous use of a proportionality test that would gain currency if proportionality were to be mistakenly applied in the second sense of determining the scope of an obligation.

148 Palmer 448.

149 *Osman v. UK*, para. 116.

150 *Pantea v. Romania*, para. 189.

151 Ronald Dworkin, 'Hard Cases' (1975) 88 *Harv L Rev* 1057, 1069: '... a political theory which holds a right to freedom of speech as absolute will recognize no reason for not securing the liberty it requires for every individual; no reason, that is, short of impossibility.'

152 Mavronicola.

153 Palmer 450.

the positive obligation be limited by what can reasonably be expected of the state in the circumstances.

To summarise the positive obligations that accompany the negative obligation under Article 3: there is an obligation to conduct an effective investigation into allegations of prohibited treatment; an obligation to take measures to protect individuals from suffering prohibited treatment at the hands of the state; and an obligation to take measures to protect individuals from suffering prohibited treatment stemming from sources other than the State Party. A framework of obligations is necessary to underpin analysis of the scope of application of the right not to be subjected to degrading treatment.

Degrading treatment: interpretation in context

If there is no obligation that has been breached by a state, Article 3 – including degrading treatment – cannot be brought into play. Equally, if there is no actual, or real risk of, treatment that falls within the scope of meaning of Article 3 harm, the right cannot be brought into play. The breach of a state obligation within the vertical ECHR protection system thereby goes hand-in-hand with the interpretation of the Convention's terms. In the current analysis assessment of the interpretive scope of the right not to be subjected to degrading treatment relies upon the framework of obligations detailed above to inform it. This framework will support arguments about the potential reach of the right. It might be objected, for example, that an obligation is excessively wide and unacceptable because a state will be found to have violated the Convention when it has not inflicted the treatment, had nothing to do with the prohibited treatment, or could not have prevented it. Such objections are most likely to arise in connection with an obligation to protect against non-state sources of harm. The framework of obligations indicates that the concern should not be with the demands of the obligation itself but with whether, in a particular situation, state responsibility should be engaged. State responsibility is implicitly shown by the framework of obligations to be one element that cannot be foreseen in an assessment of the right's interpretive parameters (the exception is expulsion cases in which state responsibility is by default foreseeable; questions should instead revolve around whether the Court is likely to accept that the *risk* to the individual is *real* and whether the prospective treatment would fall within the interpretation of Article 3 harm). Whether state responsibility is likely to be engaged is a question that will often be inextricable from the practical constraints and factual circumstances of an individual applicant and, as such, cannot be predicted in the abstract.

The filtering point between harm that Article 3 will not condemn and harm that is absolutely prohibited is not fixed and is of great consequence. The relative assessment means that the severity threshold will shift depending on the particular circumstances of each applicant and the forms of harm within Article 3 will encompass new situations when the Court deems this appropriate. The Court will shift the threshold in line with changing social and political contexts and neither a margin of appreciation nor a proportionality balancing exercise are afforded to a

Respondent State. If responsibility is attributed to the state, harm is absolutely prohibited once it falls within the scope of meaning of Article 3.

In respect of the meaning of the terms 'degrading' and 'treatment', there is a gap between restating the benchmarks of degradation and understanding how the Strasbourg Court chooses to label certain sets of factual circumstances. There is also a gap between the degradation benchmarks and the idea of treatment. Treatment's meaning is usually assumed to be straightforward or uninteresting, or probably both, but it informs the interpretive scope of the prohibition in the same way as the meaning of degradation. The benchmarks construct degradation as a distinct form of harm within Article 3. They are themselves constituted by concepts that can only be given minimal content in Strasbourg judgments. The concept of humiliation, for example, is limited in case-law to a state induced by fear, anguish or feelings of inferiority, whereas it is evident in social philosophical literature that it encompasses a complex interplay of facts and emotions. In order to better understand when and why humiliation or debasement, and so on, have occurred, we can learn something by exploring the space between the benchmarks and the case-law findings. The following chapter underpins this exploration of the benchmark concepts, and of the term 'treatment', later in the book. It lays out the rubric that I use for selecting and evaluating these interpretations, which includes considering how their interpretation is driven by Article 3's *purpose*.

References

Addo, MK and Grief, N, 'Does Article 3 of the European Convention on Human Rights Enshrine Absolute Rights?' (1998) 9 *European Journal of International Law* 510

Calleweart, J, 'Is there a Margin of Appreciation in the Application of Articles 2, 3 and 4 of the Convention?' (1998) 19 *Human Rights Law Journal* 6

Clayton, R and Tomlinson, H, *The Law of Human Rights* (2nd edn, Oxford University Press, 2009)

Cooper, J, *Cruelty – An Analysis of Article 3* (Sweet & Maxwell, 2003)

Council of Europe, *Collected Edition of the 'Travaux Préparatoires' of the European Convention on Human Rights*, Vol. IV (Martinus Nijhoff, 1977)

Cremona, JJ, *Selected Papers 1946–1989* (Publishers Enterprises Group (PEG) Ltd., 1990)

Dröge, C, *Positive Verpflichtungen der Staaten in der Europäischen Menschenrechtskonvention* [*Positive Obligations of States under the European Convention of Human Rights*] (Springer, 2003)

Dworkin, R, 'Hard Cases' (1975) 88 *Harv L Rev* 1057

Evrigenis, D, 'Recent Case-Law of the European Court of Human Rights on Articles 8 and 10 of the European Convention on Human Rights' (1982) 3 *Human Rights Law Journal* 121

Fabbricotti, A, 'The Concept of Inhuman or Degrading Treatment in International Law and its Application in Asylum Cases' (1998) 10 *International Journal of Refugee Law* 637

Gewirth, A, *Human Rights. Essays on Justification and Applications* (University of Chicago Press, 1982)

Grosz, S, Beatson, J and Duffy, P, *Human Rights: The 1998 Act and the European Convention* (Sweet & Maxwell, 2000)

Harris, DJ, O'Boyle, M and Warbrick, C, *Law of the European Convention on Human Rights* (Butterworths, 1995)

Lester, AP, Pannick, D and Herberg, J, *Human Rights: Law and Practice* (3rd edn, LexisNexis, 2009)

Mavronicola, N, 'What is an "Absolute Right"? Deciphering Absoluteness in the Context of Article 3 of the European Convention on Human Rights' (2012) 12 *Human Rights Law Review* 723

Mowbray, A, *Development of Positive Obligations under the European Convention on Human Rights by the European Court of Human Rights* (Hart Publishing, 2004)

Mowbray, A, 'The Creativity of the European Court of Human Rights' (2005) 5 *Human Rights Law Review* 57

Palmer, S, 'A Wrong Turning: Article 3 ECHR and Proportionality' (2006) 65 *Cambridge Law Journal* 438

Prebensen, SC, 'Evolutive Interpretation of the European Convention on Human Rights' in Mahoney, P et al. (eds), *Protection des Droits de l'homme: La Perspective Européenne* [*Protecting Human Rights: The European Perspective – Studies in Memory of Rolv Ryssdal*] (Heymanns, 2000)

Starmer, K, 'Positive Obligations under the Convention' in Jowell, J and Cooper, J (eds), *Understanding Human Rights Principles* (Hart Publishing, 2001)

Sudre, F, 'Les "Obligations Positives" dans la Jurisprudence Européene des Droits de l'Homme' in Mahoney, P et al. (eds), *Protection des Droits de l'Homme: La Perspective Européene* [*Protecting Human Rights: The European Perspective – Studies in Memory of Rolv Ryssdal*] (Heymanns, 2000)

Van Dijk, P, '"Positive Obligations" Implied in the European Convention on Human Rights: Are the States Still the "Masters" of the Convention?' in Castermans-Holleman, M, van Hoof, F and Smith, J (eds), *The Role of the Nation State in the 21st Century: Human Rights, International Organisations and Foreign Policy: Essays in Honour of Peter Baehr* (Kluwer Law International, 1998)

Van Dijk, P et al. (eds), *Theory and Practice of the European Convention on Human Rights* (4th edn, Intersentia, 2006)

Webster, E, 'Medical-Related Expulsion and Interpretation of Article 3 of the European Convention on Human Rights' (2013) 6 *Inter-American and European Human Rights Journal* 36

Yourow, HC, *The Margin of Appreciation Doctrine in the Dynamics of European Human Rights Jurisprudence* (Martinus Nijhoff Publishers, 1996)

3 Framing the conceptual boundaries of degrading treatment

How should the meaning of degrading treatment be approached? The starting point in addressing the meaning of degrading treatment must reflect the desired end point: to articulate this meaning in a way that facilitates an understanding of the prohibition of torture *today*; that is, in a way that is not abstract and can contribute to the protection of human dignity in the current human rights landscape. The most effective way of achieving this end is by acknowledging the existing approach of the right's authoritative interpreters and the context within which they operate. I acknowledge these factors by placing considerations of current judicial practice and context at the heart of the present methodological approach. This approach does not fall on either side of a simplified descriptive/normative dichotomy; it is somewhere in between.[1] It is essentially *interpretative*; the meaning of degrading treatment will be articulated through a process of interpretation.

As stated in Chapter 1, interpretation in the field of human rights discourse, practice and scholarship tends to be associated with the institutions who have legal authority to say what particular rights should mean, but interpretation is a broader interaction with human rights texts. Multiple stakeholders – including rights-advocates, legal practitioners, and scholars – make specific claims about what particular rights should encompass. They espouse 'extra-judicial' interpretations, which have different characteristics from judicial interpretations but are nevertheless processes of interpretation.[2] Extra-judicial human rights interpretations differ in that they might be radical or conservative, in part depending on the interpreter's motivations; they might be motivated by particular theoretical convictions (for example, as in feminist scholarship on the scope of the prohibition of torture), or by an urgent practical imperative (for example, as in the arguments of grassroots political activists). Interpreters' different motivations will influence their

1 See discussion in Anne Ruth Mackor, 'Explanatory Non-Normative Legal Doctrine. Taking the Distinction between Theoretical and Practical Reason Seriously' in Mark Van Hoecke (ed.), *Methodologies of Legal Research: Which Kind of Method for What Kind of Discipline?* (Bloomsbury Publishing 2011).

2 See Elaine Webster and Deirdre Flanigan, 'Localising Human Rights Law: A Case-study of Civil Society Interpretation of Rights in Scotland' (2018) 22 *International Journal of Human Rights* 22.

interpretative conclusions. Extra-judicial interpretations also differ in that they can potentially be of a depth that could not be expected from judicial or human rights monitoring bodies.[3] Again as stated in Chapter 1, the category of extra-judicial interpretation encompasses the present academic exercise, which seeks to articulate an in-depth meaning of degrading treatment that will resonate within the current practical landscape.

In this chapter I make the key elements of this interpretive process explicit in order to make clear the framework that I use in subsequent chapters to evaluate and select which doors should be opened and which doors should be closed when exploring and articulating degrading treatment's legal meaning. This framework is particularly important where there are fundamental question marks about meaning, as in respect of degrading treatment,[4] and where an idea like human dignity, which comes with significant baggage,[5] is perceived to play a role. This chapter proposes, in detail, a relevant methodology of interpretation.

I present the key elements of this methodology of interpretation through the lens of three questions: How do I understand the foundations of legal interpretation? How do I understand the drivers behind the legally authoritative interpretation of the right not to be subjected to degrading treatment? How will the present interpretive exercise incorporate these responses into an articulation of the right's interpretive scope? These three questions can be seen as inter-related dimensions of the interpretative process: 'epistemological', 'judicial' and 'formative' dimensions. The first, 'epistemological' dimension, clarifies in the most basic sense how meaning is derived from the relevant texts. I make some brief points in this regard. These points comprise an understanding of the concept of interpretation itself, of the valid objects of interpretation, and of the relationship between semantic meaning and legal meaning. The second, 'judicial' dimension, articulates the ECtHR's approach to choosing particular legal meanings from amongst a range of possible semantic meanings; namely, the Court's favoured 'purposive' method of interpretation. It is in relation to this judicial method of interpretation that the idea of human dignity assumes a central place. The idea of dignity is a substantial subject of discussion in itself and could merit its own dedicated chapter, but I have chosen instead to integrate it within the interpretive methodology to emphasise that, in terms of its impact on *degrading treatment's meaning*, the idea is best understood through this interpretive route. I argue that the idea of dignity is best understood as a fundamental value that expresses a core element of the purpose of Article 3 ECHR. The third, 'formative', dimension of interpretation describes this book's approach to probing the conceptual boundaries of degrading treatment in a way that respects the mechanics of legal meaning as well as the dignity-centred purposive approach taken by the authoritative interpreters of Article 3. This includes arguing for a particular meaning of the dignity idea in this context – dignity as an

3 See Chapter 1, pp. 11–12.
4 See Chapter 1, pp. 8–10.
5 Laying out the approach in detail in this way simultaneously invites replication and critique by other extra-judicial interpreters of this or other rights.

elemental status, which is diminished by, and demands freedom from, experiences that undermine a minimal kind of regard or capacity. It explains why the interpretation of degrading treatment comes from looking backwards as well as forwards, and is neither totally unconstrained, nor totally constrained. Taken together, these three dimensions of interpretation are at the heart of the book's analysis and will *frame* degrading treatment's meaning.

The epistemological dimension – foundations of legal meaning

Interpretation aims to render meaning intelligible[6]; it is 'an understanding or explanation of *the meaning* of an object.'[7] Interpretation is not a response to lack of clarity. Contemporary understandings of interpretation generally regard *all understanding* as interpretation. As Barak states: 'Every text requires interpretation. To understand is to interpret.'[8] Texts subject to interpretation may be written or oral. The present exercise acknowledges the text of Article 3 while focusing primarily on Article 3 case-law decisions.[9] Barak describes *legal* interpretation as the exercise of pinpointing the legal meaning of the text from amongst the range of possible semantic meanings.[10] This implies limits to *possible* interpretations constituted by the limits of semantic meaning, where semantic meaning refers to all the possible meanings that may be attached to the language of the text by those who speak the language. The language of a text comprises the text itself and its immediate context; it includes 'what we can infer from the text, its structure, organization, and the relationship among its different provisions.'[11] The exercise of pinpointing legal meaning also implies that this meaning, although it should be

6 Joseph Raz, 'Why Interpret?' (1996) 9 *Ratio Juris* 355.
7 Andrei Marmor, *Interpretation and Legal Theory* (2nd edn, Hart 2005) 9. For further discussion of the meaning of 'meaning' see, e.g., Marmor Chapter 2.
8 Aharon Barak, *Purposive Interpretation* (Princeton University Press 2005) 38. See also Barak 4: 'The plainness of a text does not obviate the need for interpretation, because such plainness is itself a result of interpretation. Even a text whose meaning is undisputed requires interpretation, for the absence of dispute is a product of interpretation.' The alternative possibility is to view interpretation as necessary only when a text is unclear. Dascal and Wróblewski describe the association of interpretation with a lack of clarity as the 'classical conception of legal interpretation'; one which has been criticised in contemporary approaches. For discussion of the critique of the 'classical' view, see Marcelo Dascal and Jerzy Wróblewski, 'Transparency and Doubt: Understanding and Interpretation in Pragmatics and in Law' (1988) 7 *Law and Philosophy* 203, 209–212 (cf. Michael S. Moore, 'Interpreting Interpretation' in A Marmor (ed.), *Law and Interpretation: Essays in Legal Philosophy* (Clarendon Press 1995)).
9 Barak 3, 11. In the international law context, reference has been made to interpretation of treaties *and* interpretation of international judicial decisions; see Maarten Bos, *A Methodology of International Law* (Elsevier Science Publishers 1984) Chapters vi and vii. Raz views the decisions of legal authorities as the *primary* objects of interpretation where the aim is to establish the content of the law that such authorities develop (Raz 362).
10 Barak 6 and see generally 3–30.
11 Barak 22.

found within the limits of semantic meaning, will not necessarily accord with the way the language is employed in everyday use. 'Legal language' has been described as a 'sub-type of natural language'.[12] The legal and the everyday uses of terms may accord with each other, or they may diverge. Interpretation involves deciding which of the semantic meanings constitute the proper legal meaning; 'Interpretive activity extracts or extricates the legal ... norm from its semantic vessel.'[13]

This overview is brief but it conveys a key point: the legal meanings derived from the relevant objects of interpretation may, but do not necessarily, coincide with the most common usage of the language. This will aid understanding and acceptance of meanings of degrading treatment put forward in the book that may otherwise be criticised for appearing to be uncommon or unusual. The interpretation of degrading treatment that will be derived from the 'language' of the Convention text and the associated case-law can be 'expansive' or 'constrictive', 'natural' or 'innovative'[14] whilst remaining within the bounds of legitimate interpretation.

The judicial dimension – justifying legal meanings

In subsequent chapters I will integrate this foundational understanding of *how* the legal meaning of degrading treatment can be derived with an understanding of *why* certain legal meanings are preferred over others. In this section I am interested in why the authoritative interpreters of Article 3 choose certain meanings over others.

The 'why' question forms part of what Barak calls 'systems of interpretation in law'.[15] Different systems posit different preferred approaches to arriving at interpretive outcomes. The Strasbourg Court's system of interpretation is the methodological approach it uses to guide its choice of particular legal meanings from amongst a range of possible semantic meanings. This system is its guide for navigating towards an interpretive conclusion; it establishes criteria for finding the legal meaning of the relevant texts.[16] This section establishes that the ECtHR favours a purposive method of interpretation. It then develops the following points: respect for human dignity is a fundamental value within the Convention system, which expresses one of the Convention's multiple purposes; respect for human dignity is a fundamental value that guides interpretation at different levels of abstraction; the text and jurisprudence of Article 3 show that the value of respect for human dignity guides interpretation of Article 3 in an immediate way. This section concludes that respect for human dignity drives the legal meaning of degrading treatment within Strasbourg's purposive method.

12 Jerzy Wróblewski, 'Legal Language and Legal Interpretation' (1985) 4 *Law and Philosophy* 239, 240.
13 Barak 12.
14 Barak 18.
15 Barak 9, 30
16 Barak xiii.

Interpretation with recourse to 'object and purpose'

Awareness of 'object and purpose' is central to the interpretation of the Convention provisions. The ECtHR interprets the Convention, as an international treaty, in line with Article 31 of the Vienna Convention on the Law of Treaties[17]: a 'treaty shall be interpreted in good faith in accordance with the ordinary meaning to be given to the terms of the treaty in their context and in light of its object and purpose'.[18] 'Ordinary' meaning is not commonly used meaning but a basic linguistic perspective. Linderfalk describes ordinary meaning as one that accords with the conventions of the language; with the system of rules underlying the language (including rules about how 'phrases and sentences are put together', 'how linguistic expressions are used in certain kinds of situations', and he gives the example of Article 5(2) ECHR: we know that 'arrested' describes a past event, that the reference to 'he' or 'his' refers to everyone, etc.).[19] The 'ordinary' meaning is understood within the context of the surrounding text and preambles.[20] The meaning of the terms in their treaty context is interpreted in light of object and purpose. As Bos argues, object and purpose are best viewed as a unitary expression 'reflecting two closely interrelated aspects of a single idea.'[21] Linderfalk describes these terms as 'a single lexical unit'.[22] The Strasbourg Court has elevated the importance of purpose in the text's interpretation.

The Court distinguishes the Convention as a special species of international treaty, one whose 'normative nature',[23] 'as a treaty for the collective enforcement of human rights and fundamental freedoms',[24] leads it to privilege recourse to purpose (over other considerations, such as deference to state sovereignty[25]). The

17 *Golder v. UK*, no. 4451/70, judgment of 21 February 1975, Series A, no. 18, paras 28–29. Although the Vienna Convention was not in force in 1950 when the ECHR was adopted and is not retroactive, the Court nevertheless recognised the rules therein as accepted principles of international law.

18 United Nations, *Vienna Convention on the Law of Treaties* (adopted 23 May 1969, entered into force 27 January 1980) 1155 UNTS 331.

19 Ulf Linderfalk, *On the Interpretation of Treaties: The Modern International Law as Expressed in the 1969 Vienna Convention on the Law of Treaties* (Springer 2007) 62. For further discussion, including on the everyday and technical varieties of language as included within 'ordinary meaning', see also 63–73.

20 Vienna Convention 1969, Article 31; *Soering v. UK*, judgment of 7 July 1989, Series A, no. 161, para. 103; *Abdulaziz, Cabales and Balkandali v. UK*, judgment of 28 May 1985, Series A, no. 94, para. 60.

21 Bos 153–154.

22 Linderfalk 204–210.

23 François Ost, 'The Original Canons of Interpretation of the European Court of Human Rights' in M Delmas-Marty (ed.), *The European Convention for the Protection of Human Rights – International Protection versus National Restrictions* (Martinus Nijhoff 1992) 311; see also Béatrice Maurer, *Le Principe de Respect de la Dignité Humaine et la Convention Européene des Droits de l'Homme* (Jacques Bourrinet ed., La Documentation Française 1999) 219.

24 *Soering v. UK*, para. 87; *Golder v. UK*.

25 Francis G. Jacobs, *The European Convention on Human Rights* (Clarendon Press 1975) 17; see also John G Merrills, *The Development of International Law by the*

'purposive'[26] or 'teleological'[27] method is widely recognised as central to the interpretation of human rights treaties.[28] The purposive system permeates the Court's interpretation of the Convention guarantees, and is reflected in individual cases as well as in key doctrines. Doctrines pertaining to the need to ensure 'practical and effective' protection, and to interpret the Convention as a 'living instrument' constitute integral parts of a system of interpretation that seeks to realise the Convention's purpose.[29] For example:

> *The object and purpose of the Convention as an instrument for the protection of individual human beings require that its provisions be interpreted and applied so as to make its safeguards practical and effective.*[30]

The Convention does not have one single purpose, but multiple purposes operating at various levels of specificity. As Barak has argued, there is a presumption that any text will have multiple purposes,[31] some local to particular provisions and some that may constitute part of the purpose of the surrounding text and even of many other texts. In this sense, purpose operates at different levels of abstraction.[32] The different strands of purpose act as a substantive guiding force for interpretation of the text; they are the 'substance that gives meaning to the form'.[33]

Dignity's expression in purpose and meaning

One substantive strand of the Convention's purpose is the protection of human dignity and human freedom. The Court made this point in *S.W. v. UK*, concerning marital rape:

> *The abandonment of the unacceptable idea of a husband being immune against prosecution for rape of his wife was in conformity not only with a civilised concept of marriage but also, and above all, with the fundamental objectives of the*

European Court of Human Rights (Manchester University Press 1993) 70. For a detailed argument about the Court's interpretive approach, see George Letsas, *A Theory of Interpretation of the Euorpean Convention on Human Rights* (Oxford University Press 2007).

26 E.g. Barak.

27 Anthony Aust, *Handbook of International Law* (Cambridge University Press 2005); Ost.

28 Alexander Orakhelashvili, 'Restrictive Interpretation of Human Rights Treaties in Recent Jurisprudence of the European Court of Human Rights' (2003) 14 *Eur J Int'l L* 529, 535.

29 Ost 294–302.

30 *Soering v. UK*, 87; *Svinarenko and Slyadnev v. Russia*, no. 32541/08 and 43441/08, 17 July 2014.

31 Barak 113.

32 Barak 113–115.

33 Barak 93.

> *Convention, the very essence of which is respect for human dignity and human freedom.*[34]

Protection of human dignity and freedom is the 'essence' of what the Convention as a whole aims to achieve. The Court states that it aims to reflect this in its interpretation of the Convention provisions. It has made repeated reference to human dignity as part of the Convention's purpose in more recent cases,[35] including in the context of findings of degrading treatment by the Grand Chamber. In *Svinarenko and Slyadnev v. Russia*, the Court stated:

> *Respect for human dignity forms part of the very essence of the Convention ... The object and purpose of the Convention as an instrument for the protection of individual human beings require that its provisions be interpreted and applied so as to make its safeguards practical and effective. Any interpretation of the rights and freedoms guaranteed has to be consistent with the general spirit of the Convention, an instrument designed to maintain and promote the ideals and values of a democratic society.*[36]

Here, the Court integrates purpose at various levels: the purpose of Article 3 is understood to be part of broader connected purposes of promoting the fundamental values of democratic societies and of providing practical and effective protection by protecting individuals' human dignity.

The dignity idea is a common denominator across the references to substantive purpose[37] and is the preeminent strand of purpose in the Article 3 context, where it operates at a lower level of abstraction. In the early days of the Convention system, the Commission and Court referred explicitly to the purpose of Article 3. The Commission stated, in its 1973 Report in the *East African Asians Case*, that the purpose of this right was to 'prevent interferences with the dignity of man'.[38] The Court, in its 1978 *Tyrer* judgment, stated:

> *His punishment ... constituted an assault on precisely that which it is one of the main purposes of Article 3 ... to protect, namely a person's dignity and physical integrity.*[39]

These are the Strasbourg bodies' most direct references to the purpose of Article 3.

34 *S.W. v. UK*, no. 20166/92, Judgment of 22 November 1995, Series A, no. 335-B, para. 44.
35 *Pretty v. UK*, no. 2346/02, ECHR 2002-III, para. 65.
36 *Svinarenko and Slyadnev v. Russia*, paras 118 and 138.
37 The Strasbourg bodies have sometimes referred to dignity alongside freedom (relating to the Convention as a whole) and physical integrity (relating to Article 3) and sometimes they have not.
38 *East African Asians Case*, no. 4403/70, et al., Commission Report of 14 December 1973, Decisions and Reports 78, para. 189.
39 *Tyrer v. UK*, judgment of 25 April 1978, Series A, no. 26.

In addition to the early references to dignity-protection as an element of the right's object and purpose, the language of dignity has become ingrained in the Court's everyday vernacular. It is ubiquitous across the body of Article 3 case-law. In the words of the Court: 'treatment ... may be incompatible with the standards imposed by Article 3 in the protection of fundamental human dignity ...',[40] and persons must be detained (and in one case required to perform military service) 'in conditions which are compatible with respect for his human dignity'.[41] The Court has described particular forms of treatment as having failed to be 'respectful' of dignity,[42] as having 'undermined' dignity,[43] 'diminished' dignity,[44] 'stripped' an individual of dignity,[45] as having been an 'affront' to dignity,[46] as having 'impaired' dignity,[47] and as having caused an individual to feel 'hurt in his dignity'.[48] The Court has made the dignity idea prominent in this body of case-law through these recurrent references. It has directed Article 3 towards dignity-respect and the situations that it has found to fall foul of the provision embody, in its judgment, dignity-disrespect. *All of the case-law references* indicate the influence of the dignity idea on the Court's understanding of what the right means. The forms of treatment, including degrading treatment, are expressions of disrespect for an individual's human dignity. There is a perceived binary relationship; a polarity that conforms to common intuitions that what is prohibited by Article 3 is antithetical to respect for dignity.[49] The Court suggests in its jurisprudence that the language of the text carries the idea of dignity within it, and that the idea of dignity definitively shapes how the text is interpreted.

40 For example, *Keenan v. UK*, no. 27229/95, ECHR 2001-III, para. 113.

41 On detention, see, e.g., *McGlinchey and Others v. UK*, no. 50390/99, ECHR 2003-V, para. 46; *Karalevičius v. Lithuania*, no. 53254/99, 7 April 2005, para. 34; *Valasinas v. Lithuania*, no. 44558/98, ECHR 2001-VIII, para. 102; *Vidish v. Russia*, no. 53120/08, 15 March 2016, para. 26. On military service, see *Lyalyakin v. Russia*, no. 31305/09, 12 March 2015, para. 70; *Akkoyunlu v. Turkey*, no. 7505/06, 13 October 2015, para. 33.

42 *Sochichiu v. Moldova*, no 28698/09, 15 May 2012, para. 40; *V.M. and Others v. Belgium*, no. 60125/11, 7 July 2015, para. 162.

43 *Mouisel v. France*, no. 67263/01, ECHR 2002-IX, para. 48; *Mayzit v. Russia*, no. 63378/00, 20 January 2005, para. 42.

44 For example, *Peers v. Greece*, no. 28524/95, ECHR 2001-III, para. 75; *Kalashnikov v. Russia*, no. 47095/99, ECHR 2002-VI, para. 101; *Salikhov v. Russia*, no 23880/05, 3 May 2012, para. 92; *M.S. v. UK*, no. 24527/08, 3 May 2012, para. 44; *Nogin v. Russia*, no 58530/08, 15 January 2015, para. 97; *Abdi Mahamud v. Malta*, no. 56796/13, 3 May 2016, para. 89.

45 *Piechowicz v. Poland*, no. 20071/07, 7 April 2012, para. 141.

46 *M.S. v. UK*, no. 24527/08, 3 May 2012, para. 45.

47 *Khlaifia and Others v. Italy*, no. 16483/12, ECHR 2016 (extracts), para. 162.

48 *Mouisel v. France*, no. 67263/01, ECHR 2002-IX, para. 48; *Yankov v. Bulgaria*, no. 39084/97, 11 December 2003, para. 113.

49 D Feldman, 'Human Dignity as a Legal Value – Part I' (1999) Win *Public Law*, 682, 690; Joshen Abr. Frowein, 'Human Dignity in International Law' in David Kretzmer and Eckart Klein (eds), *The Concept of Human Dignity in Human Rights Discourse* (Kluwer Law International 2002) 124.

The dignity idea is relevant in understanding the scope of all of the elements of Article 3 but the ideas of dignity and degrading treatment have long appeared in the case-law to be particularly closely related. The following examples evidence a specific link between dignity and degrading treatment:

> *Where treatment humiliates or debases an individual, showing a lack of respect for, or diminishing, his or her human dignity, or arouses feelings of fear, anguish or inferiority capable of breaking an individual's moral and physical resistance, it may be characterised as degrading.*[50]
>
> *[The treatment] in the Court's view, showed a lack of respect for the applicant's human dignity ... the Court is of the view that in the present case such behaviour which humiliated and debased the applicant, amounted to degrading treatment contrary to Article 3.*[51]
>
> *[The treatment] showed a clear lack of respect for the applicant, and diminished in effect his human dignity. It must have left him with feelings of anguish and inferiority capable of humiliating and debasing him. The Court concludes, therefore, that the [behaviour complained of] amounted to degrading treatment.*[52]
>
> *The Court finds that the conditions which the applicant was required to endure were an affront to human dignity and reached the threshold of degrading treatment for the purposes of Article 3.*[53]

These statements indicate a perception that the ideas of dignity and degrading treatment have a particularly close connection. One author has described dignity and degrading treatment as 'two sides of the same coin'.[54] This relationship was for the first time *explicitly* recognised in the 2015 case of *Bouyid v. Belgium* by the Grand Chamber: '... there is a particularly strong link between the concepts of "degrading" treatment or punishment within the meaning of Article 3 of the Convention and respect for "dignity"'.[55] This perceived 'close link'[56] presumably stems from a partly linguistic and partly intuitive connection between the language of degrading treatment and the language of dignity. Degrading treatment is in this sense an optimal site for examining the dignity idea's influence on interpretation of Article 3.

The dignity idea is therefore reflected in the language of the right and dignity-protection is positioned as its core goal – a combination which indicates that, underpinning Article 3, respect for dignity takes the form of a fundamental value. This is implied in the Court's repeated affirmations that Article 3 protects the

50 *Pretty v. UK*, no. 2346/02, ECHR 2002-III, para. 52.
51 *Iwańczuk v. Poland*, no. 25196/94, 15 November 2001, para. 59.
52 *Valasinas v. Lithuania*, no. 44558/98, ECHR 2001-VIII, para. 117.
53 *M.S. v. UK*, no. 24527/08, 3 May 2012, para. 45.
54 Susan Millns, 'Death, Dignity and Discrimination: The Case of *Pretty v. United Kingdom*' (2002) 3 *German Law Journal* para. 5.
55 *Bouyid v. Belgium* [GC], no. 23380/09, ECHR 2015, para. 90.
56 *Bouyid v. Belgium*, para. 90.

'fundamental values of democratic society'.[57] Simply put, respect for human dignity is a basic tenet of the ECHR value system. Fundamental values are 'goods'[58] that underlie and constitute the background of a legal context. Values are 'principles, policies and other sorts of standards' that can be distinguished from legal rules.[59] They provide reasons that argue in a particular *direction* in the context of a decision, rather than pointing towards one particular outcome.[60] Dworkin observes that principles and rules may overlap, notably in the sense that rules may contain language that entails references to principles:

> *Words like 'reasonable', 'negligent', 'unjust', and 'significant' often perform just this function. Each of these terms makes the application of the rule which contains it depend to some extent upon principles or policies lying beyond the rule.*[61]

The terms within Article 3 could be added to this list and respect for human dignity has been recognised to constitute a fundamental value.[62] Viewing dignity in the form of a fundamental value validates the idea that the underlying concept of dignity is reflected in the language of Article 3 and of degrading treatment. Barak notes that: 'fundamental values are embodied in the words ... that require interpretation as well as the objective purpose guiding the interpretation'.[63] Barak and others have observed that fundamental values can form part of the purpose of a text.[64] Once we understand dignity as a fundamental value, we can make a clear link between *purpose* and *dignity* in interpretation. Frowein, referring to the international law context and explicitly invoking the dignity idea, describes human dignity in the form of a fundamental value or principle acting as a guide to interpretation.[65] Through this route, respect for human dignity can be seen to drive the legal meaning of Article 3, and degrading treatment, within Strasbourg's purposive method.

The formative dimension – developing the parameters of legal meaning

How will the conclusions about the dignity-driven purpose of the right in Article 3, and about the foundations of legal meaning, be incorporated into the overall

57 For example, *Selmouni v. France* [GC], no. 25803/94, ECHR 1999-V, para. 95; *Soering v. UK*, para. 88.
58 Nikolaos K Tsagourias, *Jurisprudence of International Law: The Humanitarian Dimension* (Manchester University Press 2000) 91.
59 Ronald Dworkin, *Taking Rights Seriously* (Duckworth 1977) 22.
60 Dworkin 26.
61 Dworkin 27–28.
62 Maurer 86–141 and 190–92; Tsagourias 91; Barak 381; Aharon Barak, *Human Dignity: The Constitutional Value and the Constitutional Right* (Cambridge University Press 2015) 89.
63 Barak, *Purposive Interpretation* 381.
64 Barak, *Purposive Interpretation* 154, 381; Maurer 192, 197.
65 Frowein 114–115.

interpretation of degrading treatment? The specific implications of the dignity-centred purpose that envelops Article 3 are methodologically challenging and I shall return to these implications below. Initially, I want to make the basic point that developing the legal meaning of degrading treatment in a way that acknowledges the limits and possibilities that derive from the 'epistemological' and 'judicial' dimensions requires an approach that incorporates and builds upon them.[66] This step in the present interpretive methodology is the third dimension, which I have described as 'formative'. The process of developing the interpretation of degrading treatment is one that will look backwards as well as forwards, and will be neither totally unconstrained, nor totally constrained. The resulting interpretive claims are formed in a way that mirrors the constructive approach that threads throughout this book: they are anchored in existing legal doctrine but move beyond it where necessary and maintain the aim of arriving at practicable claims.

This process is envisaged as contributing to a 'chain novel' of interpretation, to borrow Dworkin's metaphor. This metaphor is one for all 'creative' interpretations, including interpretation of legal standards.[67] A key aspect of this metaphor is the idea that each author who writes a chapter in the novel sees her or his role as 'adding a chapter to the novel rather than beginning a new one'.[68] Each contributor:

> *Must take up some view about the novel in progress, some working theory about its characters, plot, genre, theme, and point, in order to decide what counts as continuing it and not as beginning anew.*[69]

In all interpretation there is an inherent tension between looking backwards, to what already exists, and looking forwards, to create new chapters of meaning; between 'conservation' and 'innovation'.[70]

The balance between 'conservation' and 'innovation' in the interpretation of degrading treatment that is put forward in subsequent chapters is, I argue, the

66 I see this approach as similar to Barak's approach to interpretation of the idea of human dignity from a constitutional perspective: 'Indeed, the intellectual process of understanding the meaning of the constitutional value and the constitutional right to human dignity is a process of constitutional interpretation.' Here Barak makes this point to stress that his constitutional frame of interest demands a constitutional and not philosophical approach to understanding the idea of human dignity; the constitutional approach 'rests upon the long theological and philosophical history of human dignity' but it is at the same time distinct from it; Barak, *Human Dignity: The Constitutional Value and the Constitutional Right* 4. It is thereby an approach that incorporates external sources but does not mirror them.

67 Ronald Dworkin, *Law's Empire* (Fontana Press 1986) 158–60.

68 Ronald Dworkin, *A Matter of Principle* (Clarendon Press 1985) 158.

69 Dworkin, *Law's Empire* 230.

70 Raz 361, 363. Dickson notes that there is wide agreement amongst legal theorists that interpretation contains both a backward- and a forward-looking perspective; Julie Dickson, 'Interpretation and Coherence in Legal Reasoning' Stanford Encyclopedia of Philosophy, para. 2.2, available at: <http://plato.stanford.edu/entries/legal-reas-interpret/> (accessed 29 September 2017).

'best' balance.[71] That is, again borrowing from Dworkin and his 'analytical devices' of 'fit' and 'substance', it is the best interpretation in the sense that it aims to align, or fit, with existing interpretations,[72] while its substance is judged to be the most appropriate content that could be given to the jurisprudential texts.[73] Focusing on fit and substance is not an abstract idea; as Guest describes it, 'you make the best of what you have before you.'[74] This is what I aim to do, and the questions of fit and substance are tools for judging the appropriateness and persuasiveness of particular interpretative possibilities.[75]

There is one major gap that must be filled before we can begin to articulate the meaning of degrading treatment in this formative sense – we need to know the meaning of the dignity idea that should feed into the meaning of degrading treatment. The meanings of the forms of harm within Article 3, including degrading treatment, are driven by the right's purpose of respecting dignity as a fundamental value. Therefore, to develop the meaning of degrading treatment it is necessary to be able to articulate the meaning of dignity. The Court has not explicitly stated in its case-law how it understands this idea's meaning. In 2015, three dissenting judges in *Bouyid v. Belgium* questioned the majority of the Grand Chamber's observations on the place of dignity in international human rights law, which they rightly noted sheds no further light on the dignity idea's meaning.[76] This can be addressed as part of the present interpretive process.

Circumscribing the meaning of dignity in this context poses a number of challenges. I have written about these challenges in other work, which has focused specifically on the question of how human rights scholars and practitioners should go about articulating a meaning of the dignity idea that is relevant to, and useful for, interpretation of the prohibition of torture, cruel, inhuman or degrading treatment or punishment.[77] In summary, the challenges in circumscribing the dignity idea's meaning are threefold: First, identifying the meaning of dignity means looking beyond the texts of human rights law (both the text of the treaties themselves and related case-law). Secondly, outside of the legal texts the landscape of the dignity idea is a vast and complex one of theoretical conceptualisations that are sometimes overlapping and in some ways competing. We know that the idea of dignity is intimately linked to the question of what it means to be a human being, that it expresses something about the worth of human beings, and that its invocation signals a demand for certain forms of respectful treatment, but beyond this

71 Dworkin, *Law's Empire* 63.

72 The interpretation must be plausible, although it is not required to 'fit every bit of the text'; Dworkin, *Law's Empire* 230.

73 See Dworkin, *Law's Empire* 231, 233.

74 Stephen Guest, *Ronald Dworkin* (Edinburgh University Press 1997) 8.

75 Dworkin, *Law's Empire* 230–231.

76 *Bouyid v. Belgium* [GC], no. 23380/09, ECHR 2015, Joint Partly Dissenting Opinion of Judges De Gaetano, Lemmens and Mahoney.

77 Elaine Webster, 'Interpretation of the Prohibition of Torture: Making Sense of "Dignity" Talk' (2016) 17 *Human Rights Review* 371. In this section I summarise and expand on the points made in this article.

the idea commonly defies attempts at order and clarity. Thirdly, there is perhaps a common assumption about the meaning of dignity that is relevant specifically to the right not to be subjected to torture, cruel, inhuman or degrading treatment: that dignity must mean something very basic, which is insufficient to guide interpretation.[78] I have argued that these challenges can be overcome through a 'constructive' approach to human rights interpretation, which aligns with the present study's general approach.

I my previous work I described a constructive perspective on human rights interpretation as one which sees legal texts (including oral texts like the Strasbourg jurisprudence) as integrated within the broader social domain.[79] This perspective understands that the Court must derive an understanding of the dignity idea from the 'outside'. This reflects Dworkin's approach to legal interpretation. Referring specifically to the example of dignity, Dworkin describes his imaginary judge Hercules as engaging with its substance by considering this idea's 'life' within the community in which he operates, necessarily fusing this with his own perceptions as a member of that community.[80] A constructive approach sees legal interpretation as a dynamic process that simultaneously integrates social values when applying the law in particular cases. Conceptual understandings or accounts of particular values are an integral (even if implicit) part of the practical context of applying human rights law to individual complaints because the legal texts themselves provide only a skeletal account and need to be supplemented. At the same time, conceptual understandings or accounts of particular values cannot be untethered from the practical context; put differently, these accounts can feed into decisions in the legal setting but the legal setting itself determines the extent to which they are relevant.[81] Interpretation from a constructive perspective has a pragmatic core – it aims to find a space within, and to build upon, existing understandings in order to maximise its conclusions. In asking how to go about articulating a meaning of the dignity idea that is relevant to, and useful for, interpretation of the prohibition of torture, cruel, inhuman or degrading treatment or punishment, I argued that the substance of the dignity idea should be identified using authoritative judicial decisions as the reference point, although these decisions must be interpreted in light of conceptual accounts of dignity as a social value.[82]

78 Webster 374–376.

79 Webster 376–377.

80 Dworkin, *Taking Rights Seriously* 127 and 123–130 and for further discussion Ronald Dworkin, 'The Secular Papacy' in R Badinter and S Breyer (eds), *Judges in Contemporary Democracy: An International Conversation* (NYU Press 2003) 67–111 and Ronald Dworkin, *Justice in Robes* (The Belknap Press 2006) 251–254.

81 This is also similar to Barak's approach; Barak, *Human Dignity: The Constitutional Value and the Constitutional Right* 4.

82 This contrasts with approaches that begin from accounts of the dignity idea's meaning and then show how a particular meaning is detectable in legal decisions; see D Shultziner and I Rabinovici, 'Human Dignity, Self-Worth, and Humiliation: A Comparative Legal-Psychological Approach' (2012) 18 *Psychology, Public Policy and Law* 105.

Taking Article 3 ECHR as a case-study, I argued that the result of this constructive approach to understanding dignity was that the relevant meaning of the dignity idea was limited to certain aspects of dignity's character, its different dimensions, and its different demands. Conceptual accounts of the dignity idea provide parameters for articulating the idea's Article 3 meaning. I argued that dignity, in the context of Article 3, should be understood as an elemental status, which is diminished by, and demands freedom from, experiences that undermine a minimal kind of regard or capacity (hereafter such experiences are abbreviated as 'injury to elemental status'). This meaning derived from a comprehensive analysis of Article 3 case-law,[83] which tells a story about what harm to dignity means in the eyes of its authoritative interpreters. In order to use this story of dignity-harm in a way that was useful to inform interpretive questions, I argued that it was necessary to remain rooted in this story *and* supplement it (not change it, but integrate it) by looking to broader accounts of the dignity idea's meaning. The unruly nature of dignity scholarship was overcome by taking a birds-eye view of the dignity idea's 'webs of meaning',[84] by acknowledging its multi-faceted nature, and being clear on what the idea's Article 3 meaning should *not* include as much as what it should include. On this basis, I argued that dignity's Article 3 meaning is not immediately concerned with dimensions of dignity that relate to whatever it is about human beings that motivates the recognition of human dignity in the first place, or to conceptions of community or species-level dignity. The relevant meaning *can* say something about whether dignity is, for example, a sort of quality, or capacity, or position; whether dignity is something that is an integral part of human beings or something variable and unequal amongst human beings; and whether dignity demands that human beings must not be treated in certain ways, or must be enabled to flourish in certain ways.[85] Through this approach, mediating between authoritative interpretation of Article 3 and conceptual accounts of dignity, I argued that dignity disrespect in the Article 3 context should be understood as injury to elemental status. This leads to an understanding of the dignity idea's meaning that fits its ECHR legal context. It works because it is built, and builds, upon the case-law narrative – of experiences of certain living environments; of physical and/or psychological force, intrusion, pressure, or restraint; of relationships that engender insecurity, helplessness, and indifference[86] – in a way that has sufficient depth to guide interpretive decisions but says no more than is necessary

83 The meaning of dignity was derived from a comprehensive analysis of Article 3 judgments in which the Court had found a violation. The analysis focused on judgments which found a violation of Article 3 because, in light of the binary relationship between dignity-respect and prohibited harm, this ensured the strongest foundation for drawing conclusions about how the Court understands the substance of the dignity idea. See Webster 378–382.

84 YM Barilan, *Human Dignity, Human Rights, and Responsibility: The New Language of Global Bioethics and Biolaw* (MIT Press 2012) 89.

85 Webster 382–385.

86 Webster 378–382.

for this purpose. As such, this approach is an interpretively useful way of expressing the dignity idea's meaning.

The meaning of dignity disrespect as injury to elemental status should feed into decisions about the *legal meaning* of the forms of harm within Article 3, including degrading treatment. This meaning of the dignity idea should be seen to act as more than a vague interpretive guide. It should give 'substance to the form,'[87] since respect for dignity takes the form of a fundamental value captured in the text as well as the purpose of Article 3. It should contribute to an interpretive *frame*. As such, the meaning of degrading treatment within Article 3 should be limited by this meaning of dignity. This provides one yardstick for understanding and judging existing Strasbourg interpretations and for evaluating the coherence of new directions in interpretation. If respect for dignity in this context does not extend to things like, for example, personal preferences, freedom of choice, or the availability of opportunities to live a maximally fulfilling life, this limits the scope of interpretation of degrading treatment. It excludes the extension of degrading treatment to a range of wrongs that might reflect concern with human dignity in a different, more maximal sense. Whilst certain doors may close, however, others open. Dignity as undermined by injury to elemental status is the meaning of dignity that I will use in framing the conceptual boundaries of degrading treatment.

The processes of articulating the relevant meaning of the dignity idea and of putting this meaning into practice in interpretive decisions both reflect new chapters in degrading treatment's interpretation. By explicitly addressing the nature of this 'formative' dimension of the overall interpretive methodology, I aim to emphasise the balance between 'conservation' and 'innovation' in the interpretation. The interpretation that I will put forward is the result of judgments about what the 'best' interpretation is, not the result of an argument for what the most normatively desirable interpretation would be.[88] Thereafter comes room for critique; the 'best' interpretation provides a basis for a critique of the directions in the case-law. In the context of this book, the advantage of a 'best' interpretation over an argument for the most normatively desirable understanding is that it is better aligned with the aim of maximising the practicability of the outcomes of the analysis. Explications of, as well as innovations in, degrading treatment's meaning are firmly tied to, but not limited by, existing jurisprudence. The meaning of degrading treatment within the prohibition of torture is thereby explored in a way which both describes the text's interpretation to date and, in light of this, evaluates preferable options in arriving at a 'best' interpretation.[89]

Chapter summary

This chapter has laid out the book's interpretative methodology. It has aimed to ensure that the meaning of degrading treatment will develop from a place of

87 Barak, *Purposive Interpretation* 93.
88 Guest 22.
89 See Dworkin, *A Matter of Principle* 146–148.

clarity. The central aspects of the reasoning within this process have been laid out as transparently as space will allow. The focus and transparency of this discussion are intended to maximise the persuasiveness of the meaning of degrading treatment that will emerge, in a way that makes the findings useable and impactful in the current human rights landscape. This is why such close attention is paid to the contribution of the text's authoritative interpreters from within a perspective of extra-judicial interpretation. It is obvious that engagement with the meaning of degrading treatment is an interpretative process when thinking about *judicial* interaction with the text of the Convention, but it might be less obvious when thinking about scholarly analysis of the jurisprudence. The approach that has been taken here provides a solid basis for understanding and critiquing the text's interpretive limits; or at the very least, it facilitates other interpreters' engagement with the steps in the present interpretive process.

The interpretive process comprises three dimensions: the first asks about the foundations of meaning; the second asks what directs the Court's authoritative interpretation of the Convention text; and the third asks how the parameters of legal meaning of the case-law text should be developed. Depending on the reader's perspective, some of the points might seem evident. Such points are, however, central to the process of interpreting the substance of a right that is commonly perceived to be 'difficult' to pin down. It is helpful to clarify things like the relationship between semantic meaning and legal meaning, the possibility from a legal perspective to 'interpret' the authoritative jurisprudence as a primary text, and that the need to interpret should not be taken to reinforce perceptions of a lack of clarity because interpretation is always required to deduce meaning from any text. Making these basic points should underpin the persuasiveness of the interpretation that will be put forward by, for example, leaving no doubt that a legal meaning of degrading treatment might not align with any commonly used or presumed meaning; the term 'degrading treatment' might legitimately have a 'special' legal meaning. These points constitute some of the limits within which the meaning of degrading treatment will be interpreted in the fullest way possible. Barak writes that the 'interpreter's job is to extract from the text all that it contains'[90] – that is the aim of this analysis. It aims to conserve the case-law developments whilst being innovative within the boundaries of an interpretive exercise, in order to make the best sense of the existing jurisprudence.

A central limitation of this process – but also an opportunity – derives from the presence of the idea of dignity, both as an intuitive element and as an explicit feature of the Strasbourg Court's Article 3 jurisprudence. The dignity idea continues to attract criticism for being 'ambiguous'[91], primarily in contexts beyond, but also to a limited extent within, the Strasbourg system.[92] As such, advocating

90 Barak, *Purposive Interpretation* 57.

91 David Ludan, 'Human Rights Pragmatism and Human Dignity' in Rowan Cruft, Matthew Liao and Massimo Renzo (eds), *Philosophical Foundations of Human Rights* (Oxford University Press 2015) 274.

92 *Bouyid v. Belgium*, Joint Partly Dissenting Opinion of Judges De Gaetano, Lemmens and Mahoney.

reliance upon the dignity idea in interpretation might seem counter-productive. But the dignity connection is unavoidable in an interpretive analysis like this one; an analysis that conserves existing authoritative interpretations in which the dignity idea has been positioned as a key purpose driving interpretation (of the Convention, of Article 3, and of degrading treatment). I suggest that this unavoidable dignity connection can and should be seen as a *positive* feature of the jurisprudence. It makes sense that this idea should be relevant in the process of the right's interpretation because there is an inescapable intuition that it *does* influence our perceptions of the kinds of harm that *should be* classed as torture, cruel, inhuman or degrading. To move from a connection that is intuitive to one that is practicable requires that a number of challenges be overcome. These challenges (a lack of explicit indication of dignity's meaning in human rights law, a sprawling body of entangled multi-perspective literature on the dignity idea's meaning, and presumptions about an uncomplicated meaning of dignity in the prohibition-of-torture context) are surmountable. Addressing these challenges is a kind of methodological detour, which I have addressed in other work. With a relevant meaning of the dignity idea in place, subsequent chapters will demonstrate that the inclusion of the dignity idea in this way is a valuable tool. The idea of dignity can act as a concrete guiding force in the exercise of justifying degrading treatment's legal meaning.

Drawing inspiration from Kelsen, Barak notes that interpretation gives meaning to a particular 'picture' whose 'frame' is constituted by the language of the text being interpreted.[93] In a similar sense, the 'epistemological', 'judicial', and 'formative' dimensions of the interpretative process together constrain which situations may or may not enter into the 'picture', actively framing the conceptual boundaries of degrading treatment.

References

Aust, A, *Handbook of International Law* (Cambridge University Press, 2005)

Barak, A, *Purposive Interpretation* (Princeton University Press, 2005)

Barak, A, *Human Dignity: The Constitutional Value and the Constitutional Right* (Cambridge University Press, 2015)

Barilan, YM, *Human Dignity, Human Rights, and Responsibility: The New Language of Global Bioethics and Biolaw* (MIT Press, 2012)

Bos, M, *A Methodology of International Law* (Elsevier Science Publishers, 1984)

Dascal, M and Wróblewski, J, 'Transparency and Doubt: Understanding and Interpretation in Pragmatics and in Law' (1988) 7 *Law and Philosophy* 203

Dickson, J, 'Interpretation and Coherence in Legal Reasoning' *Stanford Encyclopedia of Philosophy*, available at: <http://plato.stanford.edu/entries/legal-reas-interpret/> (accessed 29 September 2017)

Dworkin, R, *Taking Rights Seriously* (Duckworth, 1977)

Dworkin, R, *A Matter of Principle* (Clarendon Press, 1985)

Dworkin, R, *Law's Empire* (Fontana Press, 1986)

93 Barak, *Purposive Interpretation* 20.

Dworkin, R, 'The Secular Papacy' in Badinter, R and Breyer, S (eds), *Judges in Contemporary Democracy: An International Conversation* (NYU Press, 2003)

Dworkin, R, *Justice in Robes* (The Belknap Press, 2006)

Feldman, D, 'Human Dignity as a Legal Value – Part I' (1999) Win *Public Law* 682

Frowein, JA, 'Human Dignity in International Law' in Kretzmer, D and Klein, E (eds), *The Concept of Human Dignity in Human Rights Discourse* (Kluwer Law International, 2002)

Guest, S, *Ronald Dworkin* (Edinburgh University Press, 1997)

Jacobs, FG, *The European Convention on Human Rights* (Clarendon Press, 1975)

Letsas, G, *A Theory of Interpretation of the European Convention on Human Rights* (Oxford University Press, 2007)

Linderfalk, U, *On the Interpretation of Treaties: The Modern International Law as Expressed in the 1969 Vienna Convention on the Law of Treaties* (Springer, 2007)

Ludan, D, 'Human Rights Pragmatism and Human Dignity' in Cruft, R, Liao, M and Renzo, M (eds), *Philosophical Foundations of Human Rights* (Oxford University Press, 2015)

Mackor, AR, 'Explanatory Non-Normative Legal Doctrine. Taking the Distinction between Theoretical and Practical Reason Seriously' in Van Hoecke, M (ed.), *Methodologies of Legal Research: Which Kind of Method for What Kind of Discipline?* (Bloomsbury Publishing, 2011)

Marmor, A, *Interpretation and Legal Theory* (2nd edn, Hart, 2005)

Maurer, B, *Le Principe de Respect de la Dignité Humaine et la Convention Européene des Droits de l'Homme* (Bourrinet, J ed., La Documentation Française, 1999)

Merrills, JG, *The Development of International Law by the European Court of Human Rights* (Manchester University Press, 1993)

Millns, S, 'Death, Dignity and Discrimination: The Case of *Pretty v. United Kingdom*' (2002) 3 *German Law Journal*

Moore, MS, 'Interpreting Interpretation' in Marmor, A (ed.), *Law and Interpretation: Essays in Legal Philosophy* (Clarendon Press, 1995)

Orakhelashvili, A, 'Restrictive Interpretation of Human Rights Treaties in Recent Jurisprudence of the European Court of Human Rights' (2003) 14 *Eur J Int'l L* 529

Ost, F, 'The Original Canons of Interpretation of the European Court of Human Rights' in Delmas-Marty, M (ed.), *The European Convention for the Protection of Human Rights – International Protection versus National Restrictions* (Martinus Nijhoff, 1992)

Raz, J, 'Why Interpret?' (1996) 9 *Ratio Juris* 349

Shultziner, D and Rabinovici, I, 'Human Dignity, Self-Worth, and Humiliation: A Comparative Legal-Psychological Approach' (2012) 18 *Psychology, Public Policy and Law* 105

Tsagourias, NK, *Jurisprudence of International Law: The Humanitarian Dimension* (Manchester University Press, 2000)

Webster, E, 'Interpretation of the Prohibition of Torture: Making Sense of "Dignity" Talk' (2016) 17 *Human Rights Review* 371

Webster, E and Flanigan, D, 'Localising Human Rights Law: A Case-study of Civil Society Interpretation of Rights in Scotland' (2018) 22 *International Journal of Human Rights* 22

Wróblewski, J, 'Legal Language and Legal Interpretation' (1985) 4 *Law and Philosophy* 239

4 Understanding the benchmarks of degradation

This chapter progresses the book's analysis from a focus on the frame to a focus on the substance of the degrading treatment picture. Within that picture, the ECtHR has viewed the term 'degrading' as a sort of outline, which it has filled in with an additional layer of detail. This layer is constructed around a series of reference points, or benchmarks: feelings of fear, anguish and inferiority capable of causing humiliation or debasement; the breaking of physical or moral resistance; being driven to act against one's will or conscience; and suffering contempt or lack of respect for one's personality. The meanings of the terms that constitute the benchmarks are not obvious. This is not an implied criticism of Strasbourg practice. In the judicial forum an understanding of the concepts relied upon only requires to extend so far.[1] In day-to-day judgments questioning is contained at the level of the particular (i.e. were the facts correct and was the reaction reasonable?).[2] A more substantive understanding of the concepts is valuable when enquiry moves away from particular facts and is undertaken at a greater level of generality; at this point an 'account' of the concepts becomes helpful.[3] So the Court has not given an account of the conceptual substance of these benchmarks, and legal human rights literature has not analysed the case-law in an attempt to fill that gap.[4] The meanings of the benchmarks may be perceived as inevitably indeterminate, perhaps reinforced by perceptions of the idea of degradation as itself indeterminate, but this is not a sufficient reason to preclude their examination. This chapter unpacks the conceptual substance of the benchmarks in a way that can usefully inform our understanding of degrading treatment's scope of meaning. It does so in line with the previous chapter's threefold framework of interpretation, incorporating the foundations of legal meaning, a purposive reading of the text (where a key purpose is to protect – only – an elemental status, which is diminished by, and demands freedom from, experiences that undermine a minimal kind of regard or capacity), and an interpretation that progresses, rather than re-invents, the existing authoritative interpretations. I do not

1 Nussbaum considers the emotions of anger and fear in the context of the criminal law and the questioning of juries; see Martha C Nussbaum, *Hiding from Humanity: Disgust, Shame and the Law* (Princeton University Press 2004) Chapter 1.
2 Nussbaum 67–68.
3 Nussbaum gives the example of the Aristotelian account of anger; Nussbaum 68.
4 See Chapter 1, p. 7.

refer to the framework at every stage in the ensuing discussion but it provides the parameters for the meanings of degradation's conceptual constituents.

Against the backdrop of this framework, I use insights from literature, primarily in social philosophy and social psychology, to interpret the benchmarks of degradation.[5] This approach recognises, in short, that the benchmark concepts are entangled with social concepts; ideas about human emotions and social interaction. This chapter justifies an interpretation of 'humiliation/debasement' as erosion of one's self-respect as a result of profound powerlessness to live up to standards befitting of a human person and exclusion from the human community; 'the breaking of physical or moral resistance' as the destruction of a person's ability to oppose such exclusion; 'being driven to act against one's will or conscience' as tied to a particular dimension of the concept of autonomy; and 'personality' as a reference to human status. The analysis shows that the kind of harm that should be captured by the term 'degrading' is constituted by an extremely limited conceptual core.

Feelings of fear, anguish and inferiority

The 'feelings of fear, anguish and inferiority' aspect of the jurisprudence, which might seem to be a mere preface to the core benchmarks of degradation, can be seen to indicate an important distinction. The presence of feelings of fear, anguish and/or[6] inferiority draws our attention to the internal emotional aspects of degradation at the same time as it draws our attention to an external standard for judging whether these emotions should signal the existence of treatment that is degrading. We can understand the choice of terms as significant – fear, anguish, inferiority, as opposed to, say, worry or embarrassment. We can also understand the use of the term 'capable' (feelings of fear, anguish and/or inferiority *capable* of bringing about humiliation or debasement) as significant – this can be interpreted as a signal that some feelings of fear, anguish and/or inferiority will be sufficient to cause humiliation, and so on, while some such feelings will not.[7] Even this aspect of the jurisprudence can be understood to reveal a threshold between experiences that should be labelled as degrading and experiences that are undesirable in some other sense. This tension carries through to all of the benchmarks.

Humiliation and debasement

In the Article 3 jurisprudence, humiliation and debasement tend to come as a package.[8] At the same time, the jurisprudence elaborates a number of principles related to

5 Some of the points in this chapter build upon Elaine Webster, 'Degradation: A Human Rights Law Perspective' in Paulus Kaufmann et al. (eds), *Humiliation, Degradation, Dehumanization: Human Dignity Violated* (Springer 2011).

6 *Ireland v. UK*, judgment of 18 January 1978, Series A, no. 25, para, 167; *Pretty v. UK*, no. 2346/02, ECHR 2002-III, para. 52.

7 E.g. *Guzzardi v. Italy*, judgment of 6 November 1980, Series A, no. 39, para. 107.

8 E.g. *Ireland v. UK*, judgment of 18 January 1978, Series A, no. 25, para. 167; *Campbell and Cosans v. UK*, judgment of 25 February 1982, Series A, no. 48, para. 28.

humiliation specifically (the possibility of humiliation in one's own eyes only, etc), which gives the impression that in determining whether degrading treatment has occurred (or will occur) humiliation is the more dominant idea of the two. A sense of a greater focus on humiliation perhaps derives simply from its being referred to first, and nothing more. I understand the idea of debasement as an important reinforcement for, and in a sense qualification to, the idea of humiliation.

Both ideas share a common etymological core which fits their legal meaning in this context – the idea of lowering. Amongst the range of semantic meanings of the term 'debasement', a sense of lowering is a recurrent theme. Debase derives from the proposition 'de', meaning from, down from, off, etc, and 'base', meaning the lowest point, the most important element, or a fundamental starting point. To debase is defined in the *Oxford English Dictionary* as to lower in position, rank or dignity; to lower in estimation, to decry; to lower in quality, value or character, to make base, to degrade. The meaning of debasement has also been described simply as degradation.[9] Within the range of semantic meanings the idea of lowering recurs, whether it is rank/dignity, estimation, or value/character that is being lowered. To humiliate is defined in the *Oxford English Dictionary* as to make low or humble, or to lower or depress dignity or self-respect. The sense of lowering remains central. The etymology of the word 'humiliate' lies in the Latin *humus*, meaning 'earth'. Lindner highlights the centrality of 'lowering' with reference to the idea of 'orientational metaphors': 'Spatially, [humiliation] entails a downward orientation, literally a "de-gradation"'; she continues: 'To humiliate is … to strike *down*, put *down* or take *down*.'[10]

From within this range of semantic meanings there is at least one thing that debasement adds which humiliation does not semantically capture. This is the 'de' proposition, which provides a strong tie to the idea of degradation. Lindner's linking of humiliation and 'de-gradation' ties these ideas together, but 'debase' provokes a more immediate link to 'degrade'. Arguably, debasement should be seen as an equally important idea as humiliation despite a sense that it takes second place within the jurisprudence. I understand it is an idea whose presence hints at, and reinforces, humiliation's relevant meaning.

These observations as to semantic meaning only provide initial parameters for the interpretation of humiliation and debasement. The idea of humiliation is the subject of not extensive but nevertheless significant attention in literature, which likely reflects to some extent its common usage outside of the human rights context. The same cannot be said of the idea of debasement. The most fruitful way to proceed then, is to bear in mind the critical reinforcement of the 'downward orientation' provided by the idea of debasement, and to focus on articulating a relevant meaning of humiliation.

9 *The Compact Edition of the Oxford English Dictionary* (Clarendon Press); *The Chambers English Dictionary* (Chambers).

10 Evelin Gerda Lindner, 'Humiliation and the Human Condition: Mapping a Minefield' (2001) 2 *Human Rights Review* 46, 51.

Humiliation

The Strasbourg Court's inclusion of the term 'humiliation' in the degrading treatment benchmarks has perhaps been a poisoned chalice. From one perspective it makes the idea of degradation accessible, and from another perspective it risks derailing interpretations. Both possibilities stem from the term 'humiliation's familiarity in common language use. Its inclusion is positive in that, because of its familiarity, it is potentially a resource for empowering rights-holders and advocates to engage with the language of degrading treatment[11]; its inclusion is problematic in that it potentially contributes, again because of its familiarity as a common experience, to perceptions of degrading treatment as wide and sprawling. Articulating the legal meaning of humiliation is imperative in order to understand degrading treatment's boundaries.

Humiliation is an everyday occurrence. In William Ian Miller's study of the concept he talks about our fear of feeling humiliation whilst recognising that, within daily social interaction, it is normal. Miller describes how humiliation is physically experienced in the 'deepest center' of the body[12]; how it invokes painful memories.[13] At the same time, he writes, '[h]umiliation inheres in every nook and cranny of the normal'.[14] We easily recognise 'commonplace'[15] humiliation. Miller cites an enduring example found in Robert Burns' poem *To A Louse.*[16] The humiliation resides in the combination of elevated social status within a mixed social setting and the obliviousness of the 'fine' lady in the poem to the crawling louse upon her.[17] Anthony Quinton gives a more contemporary example: a woman who accepts congratulations by her dinner guests on a meal only for her husband to later reveal that she had bought the food ready-made.[18] In Miller's words, humiliation is the 'unmasking of pretension' and the feeling one has when pretensions are discovered.[19]

This breed of humiliation does not form part of degradation's conceptual make-up. In one sense it seems obvious that degradation in the context of human rights violations will not be triggered by situations that are 'trivial'.[20] In another sense it is not obvious, and the familiarity of commonplace humiliation probably hovers below concerns about the fluidity of degrading treatment's meaning. Both senses

11 Elaine Webster and Deirdre Flanigan, 'Localising Human Rights Law: A Case-study of Civil Society Interpretation of Rights in Scotland' 2018 (2) *International Journal of Human Rights* 22.
12 William Ian Miller, *Humiliation – and Other Essays on Honor, Social Discomfort and Violence* (Cornell University Press 1993) 160–161.
13 Miller 152.
14 Miller 10.
15 Miller 165.
16 Miller 136–137.
17 Carol McGuirk (ed.), *Robert Burns: Selected Poems* (Penguin 1993) 85–86.
18 Anthony Quinton, 'Humiliation' (1997) 64 *Social Research* 77, 80.
19 Miller 144.
20 Maury Silver et al., 'Humiliation: Feeling, Social Control and Construction of Identity' (1986) 16 *Journal for the Theory of Social Behaviour* 269.

can co-exist. There is some conceptual continuity between how we understand commonplace humiliation and degrading treatment's humiliation. Miller talks about the 'perversion' of commonplace humiliation.[21] This perverse form, he describes as 'humiliation with a big *H*'.[22] He, and others, describe sites of 'humiliation with a big *H*' as the torture chamber and the concentration camp.[23] This is a perversion because, instead of humiliation that brings someone down from a pretended social status, this 'grave'[24] kind of humiliation brings someone down from a justified social status – the status of a member of the human community.[25] This understanding sees both kinds of humiliation as linked. The idea of the perversion of a common social interaction is convincing, although this idea of lowering of human status should not be limited to the paradigmatic contexts of the torture chamber and the concentration camp. The meaning of dignity that anchors the framework for interpreting degrading treatment tells us that a core purpose of Article 3 as a whole is to protect against experiences that undermine a basic, minimal kind of regard or capacity, whether this manifests as torture or as degrading treatment. As degrading treatment is normally perceived to be at the lower end of a hierarchy of severity of harm, there might be an accompanying perception that a grave kind of humiliation (characterised by 'sadism and brutal cruelty', as Miller writes[26]) is not, or should not, be encompassed within the meaning of degradation. In fact, we should understand the connections here as beginning to reveal that the essence of humiliation actually lies in the lowering of human status. These connections also begin to reveal that there is a common conceptual thread running from degrading treatment to torture within the right. Humiliation within Article 3 jurisprudence should be understood as a class of treatment/experience that undermines a minimal regard towards a person, or minimal capacity of a person to act. Simply put, it is a serious kind of humiliation. This continuity in understandings of different forms of humiliation makes it all the more important to be clear about these distinctions, and about the legal meaning of humiliation.

Humiliation is thus seen to be relevant in one particular sense. This distinction highlights the distance between the idea of humiliation in this context and ideas that might be seen as similar, such as embarrassment or shame.[27] Embarrassment can be seen to sit alongside Miller's conception of 'normal' humiliation. Miller sees these ideas as related[28] but embarrassment is not as dark a concept as even

21 Miller 165–167.
22 Miller 165.
23 Miller 165; Silver et al. 269.
24 Silver et al. 269.
25 Miller 165–167.
26 Miller 165.
27 Nussbaum explicitly discusses the relationship between shame, embarrassment and humiliation; see Nussbaum 203–206.
28 Miller notes that it is possible that particularly intense feelings of embarrassment could increase on an 'intensity scale' to become feelings of humiliation; see Miller 152.

this 'normal' humiliation. The emotional context of embarrassment is different: one of friendship and good humour, whether induced by teasing or praise.[29] Nussbaum also observes the possibility of embarrassment invoked by public praise, understanding it to concern undesirable social awkwardness which need not involve any sense of 'defect'.[30] Embarrassment is obviously very distant from the kind of humiliation that is relevant in the interpretation of degrading treatment. The idea of shame is less distant. This comes across in the literature, which does not maintain a consistent distinction between humiliation and shame.[31] Instead, the literature often collapses the distinction, based on differing uses of the terms 'shame' and 'humiliation' (and the related ideas of self-respect and self-esteem).[32] The idea of shame encompasses a sense of a failure to conform to certain socially claimed or socially recognised ideals. 'Living up to ideals' suggests commonality with the idea of humiliation (in both of Miller's senses). Shame can be relevant in arguing for, or recognising, humiliation in the degrading treatment context, but the two ideas of humiliation and shame should be seen as conceptually distinct. Nussbaum's analysis of 'primitive shame' maintains a distinction between shame and humiliation, although she touches upon this only briefly: while the core of shame is a failure to live up to ideals, shame is a different, and broader notion to humiliation; notably, it is often touted as having a constructive role, unlike humiliation.[33] It is important in the degrading treatment context to be clear that 'humiliation with a big *H*' is fundamentally damaging, with no possibility of a constructive role. On this basis alone it is helpful to recognise a distinction between humiliation and shame. Note that Nussbaum suggests that particular forms of severe shaming *can* involve humiliation.[34] Diegh's understanding of shame and its sources points towards a convincing explanation for this: shame results from an injury to one's worth that derives from membership of a social group.[35] Conversely, we can understand humiliating-shame as injury to one's sense of worth on the basis of belonging, not to a social group, but to the community of human beings. Severe shaming on the basis of membership of a social group can escalate into humiliation if a whole social group is not perceived to belong to the community of human beings. This understanding echoes Margalit's:

29 Miller 157; see also 152–153.
30 Nussbaum 204–206.
31 Compare Donald C Klein, 'The Humiliation Dynamic: An Overview' (1991) 12 *The Journal of Primary Prevention* 93, 105, with Aaron Ben-Ze'ev, *The Subtlety of Emotions* (MIT Press 2000) 512–513.
32 See section on 'Self-respect' below.
33 Nussbaum focuses on shame in a fundamental manifestation – 'primitive shame' – which occurs in the face of human vulnerability, need and impotence (Nussbaum 189–93 in particular). Note that, despite recognition of shame's constructive possibility, Nussbaum argues squarely against a constructive role for shame in the law of liberal societies (see generally Chapter 5).
34 Nussbaum 203–204.
35 John Deigh, 'Shame and Self-Esteem – A Critique' in Robin S Dillon (ed.), *Dignity, Character and Self-Respect* (Routledge 1995) 149–151.

'[s]haming a person for legitimate identity traits is an act of humiliation.'[36] Humiliation might be described then as shaming on the basis of a failure to live up to basic ideals of what is appropriate for human beings to be like, thus recognising a relationship between shame and humiliation but nevertheless maintaining a distinction between these terms. This approach aligns with an understanding of humiliation as an experience that undermines a *minimal* kind of regard, or *minimal* capacity to act in certain ways, which is fundamental to understanding and explaining the boundaries of degrading treatment.

Humiliation as a social fact

Literature contributes another key distinction – between humiliation as a feeling and humiliation as a fact. I unpack recurrent principles that the Court has established in relation, primarily, to the idea of humiliation with reference to this distinction. These concern the relevance, or otherwise, of intention to cause humiliation and a public dimension of humiliation. A feeling/state distinction explains why, as a benchmark of degrading treatment, humiliation is not subjective to either the source or the recipient. The scope of meaning of humiliation becomes clearer when humiliation is understood to be a socially observable fact.

Literature on humiliation includes a distinction between *feeling* humiliated and *being* humiliated. It uses language like the 'emotion'[37] or 'emotional experience'[38] of humiliation, and the 'state',[39] 'social situation',[40] and 'social fact'[41] of humiliation. This distinction anchors the possibility of us *feeling* humiliated without *being* humiliated, and *being* humiliated without *feeling* humiliated.[42] Margalit's work on humiliation in the public sphere links both aspects when he talks about having *sound reasons for feeling* humiliated.[43] This integrates the emotional and the observable. I see this idea of having sound reasons for feeling humiliated in the Strasbourg Court's case-law when it asserts that applicants 'must have' felt humiliated and debased,[44] or that certain experiences are 'in principle' capable of giving rise to treatment prohibited by Article 3.[45] To judge whether someone has sound

36 Margalit continues: 'Shaming a person for achievement aspects of his identity ... may be an insult, but it does not constitute humiliation'; Avishai Margalit, *The Decent Society* (Harvard University Press 1996) 133 and see generally 132–135.

37 Silver et al. 273.

38 Jeremy Waldron, 'On Humiliation' (1995) 93 *Mich L Rev* 1787, 1794, footnote 14.

39 Miller 146.

40 Waldron 1794, footnote 14.

41 Silver et al. 273.

42 Miller 151, 166. See also Waldron 1800 and Silver et al. 273.

43 Margalit 9.

44 *Mayzit v. Russia*, no. 63378/00, 20 January 2005, para. 42; see also *Farbtuhs v. Latvia*, no. 4672/02, 2 December 2004, para. 61.

45 E.g. the forced shaving of an applicant's hair (*Yankov v. Bulgaria*, no. 39084/97, 11 December 2003, para. 114) and use of physical violence towards people in detention (*Ribitsch v. Austria*, judgment of 4 December 1995, Series A, no. 336, para. 38; *Tekın v. Turkey*, judgment of 9 June 1998, *Reports* 1998-IV, para. 53).

reasons for feeling humiliated is always an engagement with social norms; the question can only be answered with recourse to 'common morality'.[46] Asking whether someone has sound reasons for feeling humiliated is akin to a reasonable person standard, in the sense of asking whether a reasonable person would agree that someone had been humiliated, rather than in the subtly different sense of asking whether a reasonable person would have felt humiliated.

Subjective perspectives on the part of an alleged victim cannot be determinative of whether humiliation (and so potentially degrading treatment) has occurred; an approach underpinned by the emotion/social fact distinction. A central aspect of the Article 3 jurisprudence is the stipulation that it is sufficient that someone is humiliated in her or his own eyes, even if not in the eyes of others:

> *The public nature of the punishment or treatment may be a relevant factor. At the same time, it should be recalled, the absence of publicity will not necessarily prevent a given treatment from falling into that category: it may well suffice that the victim is humiliated in his or her own eyes, even if not in the eyes of others.*[47]

There is something in this form of expression that suggests it can be appropriate to recognise treatment as degrading by giving decisive weight to a person's subjective experience, regardless of public exposure. Logically this cannot be the case from a judicial perspective because the assessment of whether a particular situation falls within the meaning of a legal text has to be mediated by the judge. Yet the Strasbourg Court itself seems almost to confuse the issue in the post-*Tyrer* case of *Campbell and Cosans v. UK:*

> *It follows from [Tyrer] that 'treatment' itself will not be 'degrading' unless the person concerned has undergone – either in the eyes of others or in his own eyes ... – humiliation or debasement attaining a minimum level of severity.*[48]

On one reading this suggests that the Court can arrive at a finding of degrading treatment on the basis of humiliation as judged by the standards of a person's own perceptions. These forms of expression, which seem to privilege subjective experience, are misleading. This needs to be clarified because there is a strong likelihood that these expressions have bolstered negative, general perceptions of the scope of the right not to be subjected to degrading treatment as being broad and ambiguous. The feeling/state distinction should undermine concerns that relying on the idea of humiliation (and degradation) in legal decisions is too subjective,

46 E.g. Patrick Devlin, *The Enforcement of Morals, Maccabaean Lecture in Jurisprudence of the British Academy* (Oxford University Press 1959) 10–12, 15–16.

47 *Raninen v. Finland*, judgment of 16 December 1997, *Reports* 1997-VIII, para. 55. Also, *Tyrer v. UK*, judgment of 25 April 1978, Series A, no. 26, para. 32; *Berktay v. Turkey*, App no. 22493/93, 1 March 2001, para. 175.

48 *Campbell and Cosans v. UK*, judgment of 25 February 1982, Series A, no. 48, para. 28.

particularly because of a sense that humiliation is experienced differently by different people. Whether a person actually feels humiliated, and whether one person does while another does not, is not determinative of the existence of humiliation as a social fact. This approach does not deny the significance of actual emotional experience in a broader sense. It is surely the vividness of imagined experiences of *H*umiliation that drives judgments of whether humiliation has occurred in social fact. But actual personal experiences cannot be determinative in the application of the legal standard. This is seen in aspects of Article 3 jurisprudence (e.g. 'while the legal rules at issue probably present aspects which the applicants may feel to be humiliating, they do not constitute degrading treatment coming within the ambit of Article 3).[49] The emotional experience of humiliation will still be relevant, and those who claim with reference to Article 3 ECHR that they have suffered humiliation presumably will have felt humiliated.[50] In any event, from a judicial perspective, interpreters always only make judgments about whether humiliation has in social fact occurred when an applicant her- or himself invites this judgment. In those judgments, things cannot fall within the scope of meaning of humiliation only because a person identifies humiliation to have occurred in her or his own eyes. The principle that it is sufficient for a person to be humiliated in her or his own eyes, even if not in the eyes of others, does not give decisive weight to subjective experience when assessing the existence of humiliation.

Article 3 jurisprudence states that the intention behind particular treatment is relevant but not required to give rise to humiliation. We should understand this position as being about intention to place a person in a *state* of humiliation. The idea of a state of humiliation can coherently encompass the simultaneous relevance and non-necessity of intention. A person can be humiliated as a social fact *with* intention (as recognised in a case like *Iwańczuk v. Poland* concerning the conduct of a strip search),[51] *without* intention (such as in *Price v. UK* concerning the police detention of a severely disabled woman)[52] or even where there is an active attempt to *mitigate* (such as in *Farbtuhs v. Latvia* concerning detention of an elderly person in ill-health).[53] As a state of humiliation is a result of social norms, individual intention cannot be determinative. Intention can be relevant to our understanding of whether a person has suffered humiliation as an observable social fact, but it cannot be more than a relevant consideration. This is logical because the application of a legal norm like the right not to be subjected to degrading treatment demands a process of mediation, and this process would be nullified if the existence of degradation was rejected on the basis of a perpetrator's assurance that there had been no intention to cause humiliation.

49 *Marckx v. Belgium*, judgment of 13 June 1979, Series A, no. 31, para. 66. See also *Yankov v. Bulgaria*, para. 107.
50 Miller specifies that the feeling of humiliation seems to presuppose a personal belief that one is in a state of humiliation; Miller 151.
51 *Iwańczuk v. Poland*, no. 25196/94, 15 November 2001, para. 59.
52 *Price v. UK*, no. 33394/96, ECHR 2001-VII, para. 30.
53 *Farbtuhs v. Latvia*, no. 4672/02, 2 December 2004, paras 58 and 61.

In the same way that subjective perspectives of alleged perpetrators and victims are not determinative, the gaze of a public audience is not determinative of the existence of humiliation. Article 3 jurisprudence stipulates that if a situation is experienced in public this will weigh in the Court's judgment; at the same time it stipulates that an experience does not have to be public for it to give rise to degradation within the meaning of Article 3. This principle can be explained with reference to the social nature of humiliation. Onlookers are not necessary to create the (emotion or) social fact of humiliation because what we understand to be humiliation *already* depends on underlying social perceptions. Silver et al. call this the 'social base' of feeling and/or being humiliated. We identify humiliation on the basis of socially mandated standards of behaviour. What we consider to be humiliating is 'an inability to live up to' those standards considered appropriate by society.[54] The 'humiliation dynamic' is relational and derives from a social interplay.[55] Social perceptions and social standards are central to the (emotional and) social experience of humiliation.[56] This social dynamic is also why the presence of onlookers, whilst not being necessary, can be seen to reinforce the (feeling and/or) social fact of humiliation. Klein labels humiliation as *prototypical* when it involves the 'triangle of humiliation': a humiliator, a victim and a witness.[57] Silver et al., recognising that humiliation does not require an audience, attribute the relevance of one to its potential role in confirming a feeling of humiliation; in making an experience of humiliation harder to reinterpret as something less pernicious.[58] The presence or absence of a public audience is not determinative but 'merely' relevant to whether we understand humiliation to have occurred as a social fact.

Self-respect

In articulating the substance of humiliation I follow Margalit's conceptualisation, which accords a key place to the idea of self-respect. Margalit gives the idea of humiliation the central role in his study of what undermines the 'decency' of societies. He characterises humiliation as erosion of self-respect.[59] The usefulness of using the language of self-respect to explain the meaning of humiliation might be questioned. As a relatively familiar ordinary language term it might seem to confuse rather than clarify humiliation's meaning. As noted above in respect of the term 'humiliation' itself, the familiarity of the idea brings potential benefits but also risks. There must be accompanying clarity about its meaning in this specific context. Margalit's use of the term 'self-respect' is useful because it highlights the constitutive importance of self-perceptions and ties self-respect to an elemental,

54 Silver et al. 275–277.
55 Klein 101.
56 See Bernstein's account of torture and dignity, which is based on the idea of the social self; JM Bernstein, *Torture and Dignity: An Essay on Moral Injury* (University of Chicago Press 2015).
57 Klein 101.
58 Silver et al. 278–279.
59 Margalit 9.

basic status of persons as members of the human community (in line with the relevant meaning of dignity).

Margalit writes that 'self-respect is the honour persons bestow upon themselves by virtue of their own humanity'.[60] This is not about self-esteem. Dillon writes that the term 'self-respect' might seem more focused on personal merit and development of character than on anything inherent or fundamental.[61] Margalit briefly discusses the question of 'selfhood' when making the distinction between self-respect and self-esteem[62] and writes that both are about a process of valuing but self-esteem concerns achievements whilst self-respect concerns a fundamental status. Self-esteem concerns valuing oneself on the basis of one's achievements. Self-respect concerns valuing oneself on the basis of one's membership of the human community; one's status as a human person. Humiliation as a constituent of degrading treatment is not concerned with injury to self-esteem.

Self-respect is about a way of seeing oneself, but it is not a uniquely, internal regard. If it were, a state of humiliation could not be brought about by other persons or (institutions).[63] Its interactive dependence on external factors aligns with the social dimension of humiliation. Klein, writing about humiliation, recognises how this results from injury to one's 'identity and sense of self',[64] which I approximate to the idea of self-respect:

> *Our personal sense of self, self-worth, self-importance, and self-ideal are all internalized deposits of thousands upon thousands of interactions with real and imagined others.*[65]

Self-respect is a self-regarding attitude that is developed and sustained or undermined in the social environment. Isaiah Berlin captures this sociality when he writes:

> *[s]ome, perhaps all of my ideas about myself, in particular my sense of my own moral and social identity, are intelligible only in terms of the social network in which I am … an element.*[66]

These ideas about oneself can be negative as much as they can be positive. To maintain a respectful self-regard, others need to maintain it too. In Margalit's words: 'self-respect, although based on one's human worth in one's own eyes, implicitly assumes the need for other respectful human beings.'[67]

60 Margalit 24.
61 Robin S Dillon, 'Introduction' in Robin S Dillon (ed.), *Dignity, Character, and Self-respect* (Routledge 1995) 25–26.
62 Margalit 47.
63 Margalit 24.
64 Klein 97.
65 Klein 105.
66 Isaiah Berlin, *Four Essays on Liberty* (Oxford University Press 1969) 155.
67 Margalit 126. Honneth, commenting on Margalit's conceptualisation of self-respect, links it to a history of scholarship on the 'linguistic character of the human self-

The way that Margalit links self-respect to the basic status of human beings as members of the human community fits with the dignity-purpose behind the right not to be subjected to degrading treatment. Other scholarship on self-respect also supports this connection. Even approaches that characterise the idea of self-respect in broader terms, or differentiate between 'kinds' or 'senses' of self-respect,[68] include an understanding of self-respect as self-valuing on the basis of one's status as a human being.[69] Dillon, who describes self-respect as 'perceiving and valuing oneself as a being of genuine worth',[70] sees this as the core of the idea in the majority of contemporary conceptualisations.[71] Self-respect as self-valuing on the basis of one's status as a human being is in line with Article 3's purpose of respecting dignity, understood as an elemental status. This understanding of dignity should circumscribe the way that we understand the idea of self-respect.

Erosion of self-respect via loss of power and exclusion

Literature on humiliation, including Margalit's analysis, associates two key states with the experience and social fact of humiliation: powerlessness and exclusion. These are the experiences through which self-perceptions of basic status are eroded. They should be understood as profound experiences, linked as they are in this context to the diminution of a minimal kind of regard or capacity.

Silver et al. provide a rich justification for seeing 'profound' powerlessness as an inability to live up to social standards, or conduct oneself, in a way that is compatible with one's status as a human being. Powerlessness, in this very basic orientation, injures self-respect in a way that gives rise to humiliation. In illustrating the extremity of experiences of powerlessness, Silver et al. draw upon the example of what they call 'excremental assault' – when a human being is subjected to a situation in which physical contact with excrement is unavoidable. The example speaks to the jurisprudence of Article 3 in terms of the weight that it places on the relevance of sanitary and hygiene conditions. Silver et al. contrast narratives of concentration camp survivors with a hypothetical example of a surgeon carrying out an intestinal operation. They presume that the surgeon would be equally disgusted by the faecal contact but is inappropriately understood as

relation'; Axel Honneth, 'A Society Without Humiliation?' (1997) 5 *European Journal of Philosophy* 306, 311.

68 Rawls describes self-respect/self-esteem as having two aspects: a person's sense of his own worth (at 126), and a person's confidence in his ability to fulfil his worthy intentions (at 125); Rawls, John (1971), *A Theory of Justice*, Chapter VII, section 67, reprinted as John Rawls, 'Self-Respect, Excellences, and Shame' in Robin S Dillon (ed.), *Dignity, Character and Self-Respect* (Routledge 1995).

69 Stephen L Darwell, 'Two Kinds of Respect' in *ibid*; Thomas E Hill Jr, *Autonomy and Self-Respect* (Cambridge University Press 1991) (see, e.g., 134, footnote 6 referring to various senses in which Hill uses the term 'self-respect').

70 Dillon 18.

71 Dillon 19.

humiliated by it. The key distinguishing feature, they argue, is powerlessness to remove oneself from the situation. This is what induces humiliation[72]:

> *Faeces ... are the sort of thing that everyone would avoid if they could. Since this is the case, and we know that everyone knows that is the case, faecal contact is a powerful symbol for a profound, basic, powerlessness, i.e. '... If they lack control even over that what area could they control?'*[73]

Humiliation is linked to a lack of a basic ability to *maintain standards* that are socially deemed to befit human beings. This concerns lack of an ability to conduct oneself in a way that is compatible with being regarded, by oneself and others, as a human being. Something like deprivation of physical liberty is deprivation of physical freedom but it does not inherently seem to deprive a human being of the ability to conduct her- or himself in a way that is befitting of that human status. In this light, it makes sense that there should be a significant focus on *conditions* of detention in the application of Article 3; it is the nature of certain conditions (severe overcrowding, sharing cells with rodents, and of course something like faecal contact, and so on) that symbolises a more profound kind of powerlessness. Also in this light, I would argue that it is unhelpful to describe, as the ECtHR does, deprivation of liberty as inevitably 'humiliating' to some extent.[74] Margalit provides a more convincing explanation: that deprivation of liberty has the potential to *facilitate* basic loss of power.[75] The sort of powerlessness that gives rise to humiliation is an absence of ability to conduct oneself in a way that is befitting of one's status as a human being.

Social understandings of the basic interests that must be intact in order to maintain human status dictate the kinds of situations that we understand to symbolise powerlessness. The ability to prevent violation of personal boundaries is one such interest that stands out in the literature. Klein talks about 'invasion of the Self' (physical and/or symbolic).[76] Margalit talks about the invasion of 'private zones' being 'a sign of absolute helplessness in defending one's basic interests'[77]; it is loss of 'autarchy', which he understands as part of what it means to be a member of the human community.[78] Thus it is violation of personal boundaries that symbolises utter helplessness. It is powerlessness to protect one's ability to live a life worthy of a human being[79]; this is what can erode self-respect.

72 Silver et al. 270–272.
73 Silver et al. 272.
74 See, e.g., *Yankov v. Bulgaria*, para. 107; *Lindström and Mässeli v. Finland*, no. 24630/10, 14 January 2014, paras 39 and 41. John Vorhaus reminds us also of the obvious point that Article 3 prohibits not punishment, but *inhuman and degrading* punishment, clearly implying that there is a distinction; John Vorhaus, 'On Degradation. Part Two: Degrading Treatment and Punishment' (2003) 32 *Common Law World Review* 65, 67.
75 Margalit 268.
76 Klein 98.
77 Margalit 211.
78 Margalit 116.
79 Margalit 116, 122.

If it is not possible to maintain standards befitting a human being, if one cannot act in a way that maintains basic human status, the result may be symbolic exclusion from the human community. This is why the ideas of exclusion and rejection feature in Margalit's conceptualisation of humiliation. Symbolic rejection occurs when a human being is treated as if s/he were nonhuman or subhuman. The senses in which Margalit sees the possibility of humans being treated as if they were nonhuman concern seeing a human being as if s/he were an object, a machine, an animal, or as subhuman.[80] These are forms of rejection from the 'human commonwealth',[81] from the community of human beings. Others also make a link between exclusion from the community of human beings and humiliation, highlighting how exclusion is to be 'made less'[82] and characterising it as 'a deeply destructive and devastating experience'.[83]

We should understand degradation in Article 3 as concerned with a form of powerlessness so grave that it may result in symbolic exclusion from the human community. It is about a perceived loss of capacity to maintain one's status as a human being within a human community. This fits with the relevant meaning of dignity as an elemental status, which is diminished by experiences that undermine a minimal kind of regard or capacity.

The meaning of the idea of dignity that I have argued is relevant to the right not to be subjected to degrading treatment contributes to framing the meaning of the benchmark of humiliation (reinforced by the idea of debasement). This dignity meaning frames the interpretation I have put forward of humiliation as a perversion of the kind of humiliation that is more frequently used in common language. As such, this meaning limits the interpretive scope of the benchmark. It contributes to framing an understanding of humiliation as a socially rooted phenomenon, recognisable apart from individual emotional experiences. It directs an interpretation of humiliation as erosion of self-respect, limiting self-respect to a way of seeing one's basic status as a human being, also rooted in social norms. And it constrains our understanding of how erosion of self-respect is brought about, by profound loss of power resulting in symbolic exclusion from the community of human beings.

80 Margalit 89. Margalit discusses whether it is possible (other than in pathological cases) to see persons *as* animals, or machines, etc, and suggests that this is not possible: 'Treating persons *as if* they were not human is treating them *as if* they were objects or animals.' (emphasis added). The only sense in which it is possible to see a human *as* nonhuman is to see a human as subhuman – i.e. as an inferior human species; Margalit 108.

81 Margalit 112.

82 Klein 97.

83 Evelin Gerda Lindner, 'The Theory of Humiliation: A Summary', 25–26, available at: <www.humiliationstudies.org/documents/evelin/HumiliationTheorySummary.pdf> (accessed 7 March 2017).

Breaking of physical or moral resistance

The benchmark of the breaking of physical or moral resistance was introduced by *Ireland v. UK*.[84] This benchmark appears in the case-law often but not invariably. It tends to be absent from certain fields of application, notably detention conditions and expulsion cases,[85] but it does not tend to always be present in other fields of application. It has been present in cases from *Smith and Grady v. UK*, concerning a complaint based on expulsion of two homosexual members of the armed forces, to *Keenan v. UK*, concerning a lack of adequate medical care for a detainee who committed suicide.[86] It is sometimes present in certain fields of application and sometimes not, such as in cases concerning ill-treatment in detention.[87] So this benchmark seems potentially relevant across degrading treatment's fields of application, even if uncommon in some. Its roots are in the Commission Report in the *Ireland* case. Here the Commission referred to the will to resist interrogation, which it said had been broken by the ill-treatment suffered.[88] The Court picked up this idea in its judgment in the case, positioning it as a benchmark of degrading treatment. Unlike in respect of humiliation, the Court has not developed any further principles relating to the breaking of physical or moral resistance.

The idea of resistance is tied to the idea of strength – the strength or ability to resist or oppose some experience. It seems to encompass the idea of control, since to be able to resist something one must have the possibility of exercising some control over it. Resistance connects in this way to power and loss of power. Yet the idea of resistance is not easy to locate in social philosophical or psychological literature. It does seem relevant in some literature on humiliation, tying in to the idea of powerlessness. It is invoked in an observation by Silver et al.:

> *In so far as your history, your status, even your being a woman or a man offers you some point of pride, of comfort, and especially a source of standards for what you ought to do, what you must resist, persistent humiliation robs you of the vantage point for rebellion.*[89]

Resistance is linked here to the ability to conduct oneself in ways appropriate for a human being and to the impact of humiliation on one's self-perceptions in this

84 *Ireland v. UK*, para. 167.

85 See, e.g., *Dougoz v. Greece*, no. 40907/98, ECHR 2001-II; *Price v. UK*, no. 33394/96, ECHR 2001-VII; *Kalashnikov v. Russia*, no. 47095/99, ECHR 2002-VI; *Nevmerzhitsky v. Ukraine*, no. 54825/00, 5 April 2005; *Ahmed v. Austria*, judgment of 17 December 1996, *Reports* 1996-VI.

86 See also, e.g., *Soering v. UK*, judgment of 7 July 1989, Series A, no. 161, and *Peers v. Greece*, no. 28524/95, ECHR 2001-III.

87 E.g. *Büyükdağ v. Turkey*, no. 28340/95, 21 December 2000; *Ribitsch v. Austria*, judgment of 4 December 1995, Series A, no. 336.

88 *Ireland v. UK*, no. 5310/71, Commission Report of 25 January 1976, Series B, no. 23, p. 402.

89 Silver et al. 280.

respect. If resistance to certain forms of behaviour or states of being is not possible, it is as if one becomes less than human.[90] Resistance is necessary in order to maintain self-respect. Non-resistance, physically and/or mentally, is a symptom of loss of power and a facilitator of exclusion from the human community. In this sense, non-resistance is tied up with humiliation. Humiliation attacks the sources of those standards that influence how human beings should or should not conduct themselves. This is why, as Silver et al. neatly describe it, 'humiliation robs you of the vantage point for rebellion'; rebellion against being stripped of one's ability to act in a way that befits a human being.

The breaking of physical or moral resistance on this interpretation is a benchmark that finds a conceptually coherent place alongside humiliation and debasement. It reflects the relevant meaning of dignity that contributes to framing the scope of degrading treatment. The breaking of physical or moral resistance then, is best understood as the destruction of one's physical or moral strength to stand up against the stripping of human status.

Being driven to act against will or conscience

The Commission, in its Report in *Ireland v. UK*, suggests a link between the breaking of resistance and another benchmark of degrading treatment – the idea of being driven to act against will or conscience. It states, referring to the 'five techniques':

> *The will to resist or to give in cannot, under such conditions, be formed with any degree of independence. Those most firmly resistant might give in at an early stage when subjected to this sophisticated method to break or even eliminate the will.*[91]

Here, the Commission hints at how it understands the meaning of being driven to act against one's will or conscience, giving a rare example of how this benchmark is understood from the perspective of the jurisprudence. Such insight is rare despite the fact that this was the original benchmark of degrading treatment on which the Commission relied as early as 1969. This benchmark appears less frequently in the jurisprudence than humiliation and debasement but it is still present.[92] This idea has not been further unpacked. The Commission's statement in *Ireland v. UK* still provides the clearest insight through its reference to independence of the will. I interpret being driven to act against will or conscience as being rendered incapable of self-mastery.

Will and conscience have traditionally been understood to capture mental faculties and perspectives unique to human beings. The will can be understood as

90 Silver et al. 280.

91 *Ireland v. UK*, no. 5310/71, Commission Report of 25 January 1976, Series B, no. 23, p. 402.

92 *Keenan v. UK*, no. 27229/95, ECHR 2001-III, para. 110.

the mental faculty of choice and decision that directs our chosen actions.[93] It has long been a contentious and fraught idea, in particular when associated with the concept of freedom.[94] It has traditionally been identified as the core mental faculty that distinguishes humans from nonhuman animals and objects.[95] The idea of conscience is also relevant to this perception of human uniqueness. Its core concerns a sense of moral rectitude and moral wrong.[96] Conscience and will are faculties which inhabit the individual's internal world.

We should understand a concern with will and conscience to reflect a concern with personal autonomy but only in a very limited sense. If we associate degrading treatment, through its benchmarks, with an expansive and amorphous notion of autonomy, we assign to degrading treatment a potential breadth of meaning that it should not have. Autonomy is a broad and complex idea that we find in several contexts, from bioethics[97] to political philosophy,[98] and with different meanings.[99] Its different (though related) categories of meaning include political, social and moral autonomy, alongside personal autonomy. Political and social autonomy can be described as ideals of individual freedom to mould personal conceptions of the good life in society; conceptions not imposed by governments.[100] The idea of autonomy in these senses has come to be associated prominently with the liberal political principle of freedom of choice.[101] Moral autonomy can be summarised as the ideal ability to act on the basis of one's independently chosen moral code, in line with one's 'individual conscience' rather than on the basis of 'authority and tradition'.[102] This category encompasses the classic Kantian conception of autonomy; part of Kant's integrated metaphysical theory. Raz highlights this connection when he aligns moral autonomy with comprehensive moral doctrines.[103] I understand this sense of moral autonomy to be close to, but not constitutive of, the kind of

93 See Thomas Pink, 'Will' in E Craig (ed.), *The Shorter Routledge Encyclopaedia of Philosophy* (Routledge 2005) 1055–1056; Roy C Weatherford, 'Will' in T Honderich (ed.), *The Oxford Companion to Philosophy* (2nd edn, Oxford University Press 2005) 957–958.

94 Freedom is tied to the will since the will is understood to permit us to exercise control over our own choice of actions; Pink 1055. See also Berlin xi.

95 Weatherford 957; Pink 1055.

96 Thomas E Hill Jr, 'Four Conceptions of Conscience' in I Shapiro and R Adams (eds), *Integrity and Conscience* (New York University Press 1998) 13–52 (see Chapters 3 and 4 for an example of discussions of the idea of conscience); Philippa Foot, 'Conscience' in T Honderich (ed.), *The Oxford Companion to Philosophy* (2nd edn, Oxford University Press 2005) 160.

97 See, e.g., Onora O'Neill, *Autonomy and Trust in Bioethics* (Cambridge University Press 2002).

98 See, e.g., Joseph Raz, *The Morality of Freedom* (Clarendon Press 1986).

99 See, e.g., Gerald Dworkin, *The Theory and Practice of Autonomy* (Cambridge University Press 1988) 6–7.

100 Dworkin 10–11; Raz 369, 204.

101 Meir Dan-Cohen, 'Conceptions of Choice and Conceptions of Autonomy' (1992) 102 *Ethics* 221.

102 Dworkin 10–11.

103 Raz 370, footnote 2.

autonomy that is damaged by being driven to act against one's will or conscience. Even personal autonomy is too broad an association to make with the degrading treatment benchmark of being driven to act against will or conscience. Personal autonomy signals a desire to make life choices; to have personal autonomy is to have achieved to varying extents an autonomous life.[104] It signals opportunities – of family, community, work, arts, culture.[105] The meaning of being driven to act against will or conscience is informed at an even more basic level. This is what Raz understands as a preceding *capacity* for personal autonomy. It is the condition which permits us to achieve personal autonomy.[106] Raz understands the capacity for autonomy to have synergies with the idea of autarchy, in particular as conceptualised by SI Benn.[107] Benn sees the term 'autarchy' as expressing a basic capacity to self-govern:

> *The autonomous man is not merely capable of deciding for himself, he does so; he is not merely capable of considering reasons, he does consider them, and he acts on them. He is therefore the man who realizes what the autarchic man has merely in potentiality.*[108]

Margalit refers to autarchy also, linking it to loss of capacity for freedom and loss of control. In this sphere of the conditions of autonomy lies the meaning that should inform our interpretation of the 'being driven to act against will or conscience' benchmark. It is autonomy at a most basic level – 'the minimal status of being responsible, independent and able to speak for oneself.'[109] From whichever perspective the idea of autonomy is categorised, it maintains the same etymological roots (of self-rule)[110] and any of the categories we may articulate will be related. But within a formative interpretation framed by the protection of dignity as an elemental status the most relevant sense of autonomy is the foundational sense of a capacity for personal autonomy. Here, an individual's ability to act on the basis of will and conscience means her/his *capacity* to act on the basis of one's independent will and conscience.

The key cause of a lack of capacity to act on the basis of one's independent will and conscience in the degrading treatment context is signalled by the terminology of *being driven* to act in particular ways through subjection to an external force. Subjection to an external force that is capable of undermining a capacity to act in

104 Raz 369. See also Sarah Buss, 'Personal Autonomy' *Stanford Encyclopedia of Philosophy*, available at: <http://plato.stanford.edu/entries/personal-autonomy/> (accessed 1 May 2016).
105 Raz 247.
106 Raz 204.
107 Raz 371, in particular footnote 2.
108 SI Benn, 'Autonomy and the Concept of a Person' (1975) 76 *Proceedings of the Aristotelian Society* 109, 124; see also 112–113, 123.
109 John Christman, 'Autonomy in Moral and Political Philosophy' *Stanford Encyclopaedia of Philosophy*, section 1.1, available at: <http://plato.stanford.edu/entries/autonomy-moral/> (accessed 1 May 2016).
110 See, e.g., Dan-Cohen 232.

accordance with one's will or conscience, might come about in various ways.[111] One described by Raz derives from coercion of one person by another (he focuses particularly on coercive threats).[112] Coercive threats fail to respect the independence of another's will[113] (echoing the way that the Commission characterised the benchmark in *Ireland v. UK*). Coercion involves treating a human being as if she or he did not have the capacity for autonomy (e.g. as an animal or as an infant)[114]. These insights thus evoke a sense of rejection and denial of basic human status that is brought about by subjection to an external force.

In this unpacking of the meaning of being driven to act against will or conscience I intentionally refer to subjection to external forces rather than subjection to the will of another person. Raz's analysis in particular might seem to suggest that subjection to the will of another person is necessary to understand someone as having been *driven* to act against her/his will. The question is, must one act as the result of another's will? This question arises in relation to the 'being driven to act' benchmark more than in relation to humiliation simply because of the centrality of the idea of individual will, which might seem to presume the counter-presence of another's will dominating one's own. This is a possible but not sole source of external pressure. Other parts of the literature, including other parts of Raz's analysis, espouse the view that the driving force behind one's actions can stem from institutions (acting through individual agents) but also from societal conditions[115]; nowhere is this clearer than in Raz's acknowledgement that one can also be driven to act 'by circumstances that are of nobody's making'.[116] This is not coercion, but another form of external driver. From this perspective, being driven to act against will or conscience and humiliation align – intention on the part of another human being is not a requirement. What I do see as a requirement, also aligning with the interpretation of humiliation put forward above, is that one must be forced to act by a human source.[117] I understand 'circumstances of nobody's making' as 'circumstances of nobody in particular's making'. Being driven to act

111 Raz 154.
112 Raz 148.
113 Raz 378.
114 Raz 156.
115 Berlin 131.
116 Raz 154. See also p. 156:

> *Harsh natural conditions can reduce the degree of autonomy of a person to a bare minimum just as effectively as systematic coercive intervention. Moreover, non-coercive interferences with a person's life and fortunes may also reduce his autonomy in the same way as coercive interventions do. The only differences are that all coercive interventions invade autonomy and they do so intentionally, whereas only some non-coercive interventions do so and usually as a by-product of their intended results. They are not direct assaults on the autonomy of persons.*

117 Margalit 9–10. See also Berlin 122–123 where it is argued that coercion is deliberate interference; inability to do something is only a lack of freedom when you are prevented from doing it by other human beings: 'The criterion of oppression is the part that I believe to be played by other human beings, directly or indirectly in frustrating my wishes.'

by a natural source (such as extreme weather conditions) does not undermine the independence of one's will or conscience. This is because of the sociality that we should understand to permeate the idea of degradation, based on the above interpretation of humiliation and the breaking of physical or moral resistance. I interpret the idea of being driven to act against one's will or conscience then, as being driven to act by external forces (other human beings, institutions or societal conditions).

We should understand the idea of being driven to act against will or conscience from the perspective of the relevant dignity meaning, with its focus on a minimal kind of regard and on a vulnerable minimal capacity. We should understand it as a grave and devastating experience; as capable of degrading a human being. In Berlin's account of 'positive freedom',[118] he describes an individual's perception of her/his own capacity for autonomy:

> *I wish to be the instrument of my own, not of other men's, acts of will. I wish to be a subject, not an object; to be moved by reasons, conscious purposes, which are my own, not by causes which affect me, as it were, from outside. I wish to be somebody, not nobody; a doer – deciding, not being decided for, self-directed and not acted upon by external nature or by other men as if I were a thing, or an animal, or a slave incapable of playing a human role, that is, of conceiving goals and policies of my own and realizing them … I wish, above all, to be conscious of myself as a thinking, willing, active being, bearing responsibility for my choices and able to explain them by references to my own ideas and purposes. I feel free to the degree that I believe this to be true, and enslaved to the degree that I am made to realize that it is not.*[119]

I have quoted this elsewhere[120] but it deserves repetition here because it encapsulates with striking clarity why being driven to act against will or conscience fits with the present dignity-driven interpretation of the degrading treatment benchmarks. As Berlin also writes, to manipulate human beings, even with a beneficent motive, is to 'deny their human essence, to treat them as objects without wills of their own, and therefore to degrade them' – thus reinforcing the logic behind this benchmark.

The 'being driven to act against will or conscience' benchmark reflects a basic, limited aspect of autonomy. Different dimensions of the concept of autonomy likely find echo in the interpretation of other human rights, such as the right to

118 It should be clarified that it is not suggested, by pointing to similarities between the approaches of Berlin and Raz, that freedom and autonomy generally refer to the same quality, but Berlin's notion of positive freedom unquestionably resembles autonomy if autonomy is characterised in the sense of a basic capacity to lead an autonomous life. Referring to positive freedom, see Raz 408–409. The similarity between Berlin's characterisation of positive freedom and autonomy is also recognised by Christman section 1.1. (on divergences between the approaches of Raz and Berlin, see John Gray, *Isaiah Berlin* (HarperCollins 1995) 28–37).

119 Berlin 131.

120 Webster.

respect for one's private life. In the Article 3 context, being driven to act against will or conscience means being forced, by other human beings, institutions or societal conditions, to behave in ways that undermine one's capacity to independently direct one's own actions.

Adverse effect on personality

In determining whether an applicant has suffered degradation, the ECtHR also refers to the impact on that applicant's personality. It asks whether certain treatment results in an 'adverse' impact on personality[121]; an impact that is 'incompatible with Article 3'.[122] The Court has elaborated upon the idea of adverse impact on rare occasions, when it considered (once) whether treatment was aimed at 'debasement' of personality[123] and (again, once) whether certain treatment displayed 'contempt or lack of respect' for personality.[124] Although rarely used, these ideas of debasement of, and contempt or lack of respect for, personality can be integrated into a conceptually coherent interpretation of the benchmark.

It is the Court's use of the language of personality that is most intriguing. The term 'personality' has a commonly used meaning. In everyday language, 'personality' ordinarily refers to our behavioural tendencies. Goldie writes that '[p]oliteness, being fidgety, cheerfulness, irascibility, being quick-witted, being a book-lover, kindness, vanity: these examples bring out the diverse nature of personality traits.'[125] The Court itself uses it in this sense of characteristic tendencies, for example in the context of decisions about disciplinary measures imposed upon applicants in detention).[126] Personality as part of the degrading treatment benchmarks, and from the perspective of the relevant meaning of dignity that drives the present interpretation, must have a different meaning. We move closer to that meaning when we consider that personality also commonly denotes public image.[127] We know that a public-facing dimension can be relevant to the other benchmarks. But literature dealing with the concept of personality (in the discipline of psychology, prominently) points us beyond publicly facing traits to

121 *Iacov Stanciu v. Romania*, no. 35972/05, 24 July 2012, para. 165.

122 *Raninen v. Finland*, judgment of 16 December 1997, *Reports* 1997-VIII, para. 55. See also *Ahmet Özkan and Others v. Turkey*, no. 21689/93, 6 April 2004, para. 336; *Nazarenko v. Ukraine*, no. 39483/98, 29 April 2003, para. 125; *Rohde v. Denmark*, no. 69332/01, 21 July 2005, para. 90.

123 *Albert et Le Compte v. Belgium*, judgment of 10 February 1983, Series A, no. 58, para. 22.

124 *Abdulaziz, Cabales and Balkandali v. UK*, judgment of 28 May 1985, Series A, no. 94, para. 91; see also this phrase invoked on two occasions by Governments in *Raninen v. Finland*, judgment of 16 December 1997, *Reports* 1997-VIII, para. 54 and *Peers v. Greece*, no. 28524/95, ECHR 2001-III, para. 66.

125 Peter Goldie, *On Personality* (Routledge 2004) 16.

126 *Ramishvili and Kokhreidze v. Georgia*, no. 1704/06, 27 January 2009, para. 83.

127 Barbara Engler, *Personality Theories: An Introduction* (5th edn, Houghton Mifflin Company 1999) 2; Richard S Lazarus and Alan Monat, *Personality* (3rd edn, Prentice-Hall 1979) 1.

something more complex, yet in a sense more basic. It is recognised that the meaning of personality is the subject of longstanding debate.[128] Gordon W Allport, writing in the 1930s, at that time identified around 50 uses of the term 'persona' that included accepted meanings of 'personality'.[129] Allport's overview allows an interesting observation: there is, he argues, an essential concern across this range of meanings with individuals' external- *and* internal-facing aspects of persona. He situates the 50 meanings that he identifies along a continuum of meanings from external to internal self: 'This double and contradictory reference is the outstanding characteristic of the term 'persona', and of the contemporary term personality.'[130] Capturing perhaps the midpoint of a continuum of meanings, others have observed that at the heart of the idea of personality is 'recognition that all people are alike yet also uniquely individual'.[131] This points towards something more complex than different character traits and public image. In Allport's work we see 'personality' being used to signify a shared quality amongst human beings. In his 'biophysical' approach, personality is equal amongst human beings and encompasses physical as well as psychological dimensions.[132] He describes, as a commonly accepted idea in philosophical doctrines, personality as something with 'supreme value', which demands that 'persons are to be distinguished metaphysically from things'.[133] Psychology recognises this link to ideas of personhood: personality's meaning is tied up with different conceptualisations of persons.[134] On the continuum of meanings this is somewhere different to more popular parlance, in which personality is used as a mark of distinction.[135] An understanding of personality as being about some kind of basic, shared status of human beings might seem obvious to psychologists and philosophers of personality or personhood, but it is less obvious for the detainees, care-recipients, children, and so on, who might be potential victims of Article 3 violations, and not obvious to those who might criticise the scope of the right not to be subjected to degrading treatment partly on the basis of the scope of its constituent parts, including 'personality'. We should be clear about the meaning of the term 'personality' in this context and we should interpret it in a limited sense.

This is the meaning of personality that fits. This meaning does not exclude a 'public image' dimension. Rather it acknowledges that public witnessing can play a part in confirming the undermining of (or the 'adverse effect upon') one's personality, similar to the above understanding of humiliation. Maintaining this

128 Engler 2–3.
129 Gordon W Allport, *Personality: A Psychological Interpretation* (Henry Holt and Company 1937) Chapter 2.
130 Allport 29.
131 E Jerry Phares and William F Chaplin, *Introduction to Personality* (4th edn, Longman 1997) 3, 8.
132 Allport 41, 48.
133 Allport 33.
134 J Martin and M Bickhard (eds), *The Psychology of Personhood: Philosophical, Historical, Social-Developmental, and Narrative Perspectives* (Cambridge University Press 2012) Chapter 1.
135 Allport 41, 48.

public dimension allows us to see a coherent place for the ideas of debasement, contempt and lack of respect for one's personality – debasement, contempt and lack of respect might manifest themselves in practical actions but they can also be seen as attitudes, or forms of regard; they are ways of looking that gain symbolic power from the social context. So public witnessing can play a part but this is not tied to a public image-based understanding of the term 'personality'. The relevant, limited sense of the idea of personality pertains to something shared amongst human beings, which makes sense from the perspective of the present dignity frame, being focused on an elemental status.

Chapter summary

I have put forward interpretations of the degradation benchmarks that are directed by the framework laid out in Chapter 3. These interpretations respect the foundations of legal meaning, a purposive reading of the text that revolves around respect for human dignity as an elemental status diminished by experiences that undermine a minimal kind of regard or capacity, and the pragmatically motivated objective to resist re-inventing the existing jurisprudence. The interpretations of the benchmarks are internally and inter-connectedly coherent.

One core thread connects all of these interpretations – the social dimension of degradation. Within the interpretations put forward this social dimension brings sense and continuity. Across *all* of the benchmarks it allows us to make sense of the significance of self- and external-perceptions and the power of symbolic regards and interactions. Where there are feelings of fear, anguish, and/or inferiority these must be capable of causing the grave kinds of treatment captured by the right. Humiliation is erosion of self-respect as a result of profound loss of power and symbolic exclusion from the community of human beings. Its exclusionary action should be seen as reinforced by the 'downward' etymology of debasement, which can be seen to act as an anchor to the relevant dimension of humiliation. The breaking of physical or moral resistance is best understood as destruction of one's physical or moral strength to oppose the stripping of human status. Being driven to act against will or conscience is real or symbolic injury to one's capacity to independently direct one's own actions. Adverse effect on personality is injury to one's basic human status. Across these interpretations there is a convergence of ideas of loss of control and loss of self-mastery, impacting upon the way that we see ourselves and resulting in symbolic denial of one's basic status as a human being. These interpretations of the benchmarks reveal the essence of degradation, and thereby the substantive parameters of the prohibition of degrading treatment.

It might be objected that adding another layer of terminology and ideas to those already existing within the jurisprudence confuses rather than clarifies the meaning of degradation. This might reflect an abiding concern that it remains difficult to 'know' whether degradation has occurred in a particular situation; whether someone has been driven to act against will or conscience, and so on. It is inevitable that there cannot be only one possible outcome of such a judgment. The social dimension of all of the benchmarks means that their application will to some extent always depend on who is assessing the social norms at play. These judgments depend on how the interpreter (either in an authoritative judicial sense or in a looser sense of any interpreter making such a judgment) reads the social norms of the society in which that judgment/interpretation is being made. Therefore, in assessing the boundaries of degradation's scope of meaning and indeed in applying the degradation benchmarks to particular facts on the basis of these more developed interpretations, there is always a moment of interpretation when it comes to this step. Does detention of an elderly person in an unventilated cell with inadequate sanitary facilities for 20 hours per day entail that the individual has been degraded or not? Does detention of a young person in a ventilated cell with inadequate sanitary facilities, and overrun with vermin, for 16 hours per day entail that the individual has been degraded or not? In jurisprudential terms this is where the Strasbourg Court should be conducting its relative assessment of the minimum level of severity. In light of this relative assessment of all of the facts, it decides, with reference to 'community morality', whether a particular experience was, or is likely to fall, within one or more of the benchmarks; whether it was, or is likely to be, degrading. The act of labelling the experience is integrated with the making of a relative assessment of whether that experience crosses the threshold into the ambit of the right. This interpretative step is inevitable but does not undermine the importance and utility of more transparent and detailed interpretations of the benchmarks.

These interpretations contribute to our developing understanding of what degrading treatment should mean and how it should apply. The meaning of degradation is clearer now than it was before exploring the meanings of the benchmarks in the way that this chapter has done. The dignity idea makes an critical contribution because its contours contribute to framing (i.e. limiting as well as expanding) the conceptual substance of degrading treatment. This allows us to exclude related ideas from the ambit of degrading treatment, from ideas about everyday humiliation and embarrassment to the fulfilment of autonomous choices. It allows us to include, in a conceptually coherent and more transparent way, forms of treatment that undermine a minimal kind of regard towards, or capacity of, human beings. The conceptual boundaries of degradation do not stretch far, although its practical imprint might be differently conceived on the basis of a deeper, more transparent sense of what degradation is about in this context. The interpretations of the benchmarks should dispel any doubts about how efficiently the idea of degradation can 'defend' the somehow elevated gravity of the prohibition of torture as a whole; the degradation element of the right should not be seen to open the back door of the prohibition of torture to ill-defined or individually divergent, subjective experiences. At the degrading treatment end of the prohibition of torture spectrum are forms of treatment that are socially constituted and recognised, and that strike at the heart of elemental human status.

References

Allport, GW, *Personality: A Psychological Interpretation* (Henry Holt and Company, 1937)
Ben-Ze'ev, A, *The Subtlety of Emotions* (MIT Press, 2000)

Benn, SI, 1975 'Autonomy and the Concept of a Person' 76 *Proceedings of the Aristotelian Society* 109–130

Berlin, I, *Four Essays on Liberty* (Oxford University Press, 1969)

Bernstein, JM, *Torture and Dignity: An Essay on Moral Injury* (University of Chicago Press, 2015)

Buss, S, 'Personal Autonomy' *Stanford Encyclopedia of Philosophy*, available at: <http://plato.stanford.edu/entries/personal-autonomy/> (accessed 1 May 2016)

Christman, J, 'Autonomy in Moral and Political Philosophy' *Stanford Encyclopaedia of Philosophy*, available at: <http://plato.stanford.edu/entries/autonomy-moral/> (accessed 1 May 2016)

Dan-Cohen, M, 'Conceptions of Choice and Conceptions of Autonomy' (1992) 102 *Ethics* 221

Darwell, SL, 'Two Kinds of Respect' in Dillon, RS (ed.), *Dignity, Character and Self-Respect* (Routledge, 1995)

Deigh, J, 'Shame and Self-Esteem – A Critique' in Dillon, RS (ed.), *Dignity, Character and Self-Respect* (Routledge, 1995)

Devlin, P, *The Enforcement of Morals, Maccabaean Lecture in Jurisprudence of the British Academy* (Oxford University Press, 1959)

Dillon, RS, 'Introduction' in Dillon, RS (ed.), *Dignity, Character, and Self-Respect* (Routledge, 1995)

Dworkin, G, *The Theory and Practice of Autonomy* (Cambridge University Press, 1988)

Engler, B, *Personality Theories: An Introduction* (5th edn, Houghton Mifflin Company, 1999)

Foot, P, 'Conscience' in Honderich, T (ed.), *The Oxford Companion to Philosophy* (2nd edn, Oxford University Press, 2005)

Goldie, P, *On Personality* (Routledge, 2004)

Gray, J, *Isaiah Berlin* (HarperCollins, 1995)

Hill, J, Thomas, E, *Autonomy and Self-Respect* (Cambridge University Press, 1991)

Hill Jr, TE, 'Four Conceptions of Conscience' in Shapiro, I and Adams, R (eds), *Integrity and Conscience* (New York University Press, 1998)

Honneth, A, 'A Society Without Humiliation?' (1997) 5 *European Journal of Philosophy* 306

Klein, DC, 'The Humiliation Dynamic: An Overview' (1991) 12 *The Journal of Primary Prevention* 93

Lazarus, RS and Monat, A, *Personality* (3rd edn, Prentice-Hall, 1979)

Lindner, EG, 'The Theory of Humiliation: A Summary', available at: <www.humiliationstudies.org/documents/evelin/HumiliationTheorySummary.pdf> (accessed 7 March 2017)

Lindner, EG, 'Humiliation and the Human Condition: Mapping a Minefield' (2001) 2 *Human Rights Review* 46

Margalit, A, *The Decent Society* (Harvard University Press, 1996)

Martin, J and Bickhard, M (eds), *The Psychology of Personhood: Philosophical, Historical, Social-Developmental, and Narrative Perspectives* (Cambridge University Press, 2012)

McGuirk, C (ed.), *Robert Burns: Selected Poems* (Penguin, 1993)

Miller, WI, *Humiliation – and Other Essays on Honor, Social Discomfort and Violence* (Cornell University Press, 1993)

Nussbaum, MC, *Hiding from Humanity: Disgust, Shame and the Law* (Princeton University Press, 2004)

O'Neill, O, *Autonomy and Trust in Bioethics* (Cambridge University Press, 2002)

Phares, EJ and Chaplin, WF, *Introduction to Personality* (4th edn, Longman, 1997)
Pink, T, 'Will' in Craig, E (ed.), *The Shorter Routledge Encyclopaedia of Philosophy* (Routledge, 2005)
Quinton, A, 'Humiliation' (1997) 64 *Social Research* 77
Rawls, J, 'Self-Respect, Excellences, and Shame' in Dillon, RS (ed.), *Dignity, Character and Self-Respect* (Routledge, 1995)
Raz, J, *The Morality of Freedom* (Clarendon Press, 1986)
Silver, M et al., 'Humiliation: Feeling, Social Control and Construction of Identity' (1986) 16 *Journal for the Theory of Social Behaviour* 269
Vorhaus, J, 'On Degradation. Part Two: Degrading Treatment and Punishment' (2003) 32 *Common Law World Review* 65
Waldron, J, 'On Humiliation' (1995) 93 *Mich L Rev* 1787
Weatherford, RC, 'Will' in Honderich, T (ed.), *The Oxford Companion to Philosophy* (2nd edn, Oxford University Press, 2005)
Webster, E, 'Degradation: A Human Rights Law Perspective' in Kaufmann, P et al. (eds), *Humiliation, Degradation, Dehumanization: Human Dignity Violated* (Springer, 2011)
Webster, E and Flanigan, D, 'Localising Human Rights Law: A Case-study of Civil Society Interpretation of Rights in Scotland' (2018) 2 *International Journal of Human Rights* 22

5 The meaning of 'treatment'

The analysis in this chapter suggests that the term 'treatment' is the unassuming hub of Article 3's past and future scope of meaning. Within the ECHR system there have always been significantly more findings of inhuman and/or degrading *treatment* than torture. Therefore the idea of treatment essentially permeates the whole body of Article 3 jurisprudence. Understanding more clearly what it means allows us to look for a rationale behind that body of jurisprudence. This chapter deliberately singles out the term 'treatment' as an object of interpretation. To do so is not usual in the scholarship or the jurisprudence. Those with occasion to interpret the right not to be subjected to (inhuman and/or) degrading treatment seem to assume that the meaning of the term 'treatment' is obvious and straightforward. Human rights law literature generally glosses over it (e.g. 'it is particularly difficult to pinpoint the exact scope and meaning of the bans enshrined in Article 3 regarding the notion of "inhuman" and "degrading" treatment or punishment'[1]; '[d] egrading treatment is treatment that humiliates or debases'[2]). Commentaries state that treatment must display the established benchmarks of degradation and that treatment must reach a minimum level of severity[3]; they are generally concerned with what the ECtHR has said about the degrading or inhuman nature of the treatment, and not about treatment in its own right. This mirrors the lack of attention that the ECtHR has paid to the term 'treatment', which itself perhaps mirrors the lack of attention paid to the term in the drafters' initial formulation of

1 Antonio Cassese, 'Prohibition of Torture, Inhuman or Degrading Treatment or Punishment' in RSJ Macdonald, F Matscher and H Petzold (eds), *The European System for the Protection of Human Rights* (Martinus Nijhoff 1993) 225. See also Malcolm D Evans and Rod Morgan, *Preventing Torture – A Study of the European Convention for the Prevention of Torture and Inhuman or Degrading Treatment or Punishment* (Clarendon Press 1998) 73–98.

2 Richard Clayton and Hugh Tomlinson, *The Law of Human Rights* (Oxford University Press 2009), p. 502, para. 8.90; David J Harris, Michael O'Boyle and Colin Warbrick, *Law of the European Convention on Human Rights* (Butterworths 1995) 73–98; Karen Reid, *A Practioner's Guide to the European Convention on Human Rights* (3rd edn, Sweet and Maxwell 2008) 575, 577; Anthony P Lester, David Pannick and Javan Herberg, *Human Rights: Law and Practice* (LexisNexis 2009), 194, para. 4.3.12.

3 John Cooper, *Cruelty – An Analysis of Article 3* (Sweet and Maxwell 2003) 20, para. 1–31.

Article 3.[4] The Court has addressed the meaning of the term 'treatment' in the briefest way, and even more remarkably in only one amongst the hundreds of its Article 3 judgments. As a result, the impression seems to have been that the meaning of treatment is neither important nor impactful. But its interpretation equally shapes the scope of the right; treatment is the form that substantive degradation takes. In the ensuing interpretation, I argue that the scope of the term 'treatment' should be seen to play a pivotal role in shaping the contours of the right.

This chapter's interpretation of the term 'treatment' is guided by the answers to the epistemological, judicial and formative interpretive questions laid out in Chapter 3. Treatment has perhaps the most obvious common meaning of the Article 3 terms, which means that clarity about the foundations of *legal meaning* is all the more important. A key purpose of Article 3 is to protect an elemental status of human beings, which is diminished by, and demands freedom from, experiences that undermine a minimal kind of regard or capacity. This dignity-driven purpose encourages an understanding of treatment that is broad enough to permit the Court to realise respect for human dignity in this relevant sense. It also has an indirect effect on treatment's meaning via the social dimension that has emerged from interpretation of the degradation benchmarks. This chapter interprets the term 'treatment' in a way that progresses the existing authoritative interpretation. The authoritative interpretation, however, is only implicit in the jurisprudence. This opacity, combined with the deceptive simplicity of the term, makes the exercise of formative interpretation more difficult. The Court has examined an increasingly varied range of complaints under Article 3, which also complicates this exercise. In order to build on the existing 'chain novel' of interpretation, this chapter spends some time articulating the existing interpretation on the basis of case-law evidence. It identifies patterns and

4 The drafting history of the ECHR indicates no particular discussion about the term 'treatment'; Council of Europe, *Collected Edition of the 'Travaux Préparatoires' of the European Convention on Human Rights, vol. IV* (1977). In respect of the preceding Universal Declaration of Human Rights (UDHR), on which Article 3 is modelled, the drafting history indicates that the term 'treatment' was not included in early drafts of what became Article 5 UDHR (this early wording read: 'no one shall be subjected to torture, or to cruel or inhuman punishment or indignity'; *Report of the Drafting Committee [on an International Bill of Rights] to the Commission on Human Rights*, UN DOC E/CN.4/95, 21 May 1948, p. 6). The term 'treatment' appears to have been introduced in a communication from the French government: 'The horror inspired by crime shall never justify the use of cruel or degrading treatment, either for its discovery or for its punishment. Torture in all its forms shall be eliminated from modern law' (see *Comments from Governments on the Draft International Declaration on Human Rights, Draft International Covenant on Human Rights and the Question of Implementation*, UN DOC E/CN.4/82/ADD.8, 6 May 1948, Communication from the French Government, Article 7, para. 3). Belgium later introduced an amendment, referring to this French draft, which suggested rearranging the wording 'in a more logical sequence': 'no one shall be subjected to torture, or to cruel, inhuman or degrading treatment or punishment.' Commission on Human Rights, Third Session, 54th Meeting, UN DOC E/CN.4/SR.54, 1 June 1948, p. 15. This drafting history thereby indicates no discussion about the choice of the term 'treatment' in Article 5 UDHR, upon which the ECtHR might have drawn.

unpacks recurring themes. From this, it arrives at an umbrella meaning of treatment: treatment as social experience. Although the term 'treatment' may not have the same obvious conceptual substance as the term 'degrading', the framework of interpretation is the same and this chapter's main argument is that treatment has been and will remain a key anchor for interpretations that push the boundaries of the right.

Treatment's ordinary meaning

'Ordinary' meaning can encompass a term's everyday meaning or it may be a special meaning. Both are legitimate, in line with the foundations of legal meaning.[5] 'Treatment' is a commonly used word in everyday language. A prominent, common use of the term is treatment as an action. This is the most natural fit when we think about the meaning of treatment, in particular in this context of 'torture, inhuman or degrading treatment or punishment', which invokes a prototypical form of active ill-treatment. Treatment as an action, however, is only one of its everyday uses seen in the range of dictionary meanings, which include management of medical remedies, subjection to a chemical agent, and a way of representing a subject in literature or art.[6] Treatment's core is a sense of 'dealing with' or 'handling' something or someone. There is in the term 'treatment' an interesting duality of perspective. It is at once agent-centred and recipient-centred. It invokes an identifiable agent, acting towards or dealing with, and it invokes something or someone who is being dealt with. This duality of perspective is reflected in treatment's immediate Article 3 context – with the demand that 'no one shall *be subjected to* ... treatment' – and implies, thereby, some kind of relationship between agent and recipient. Treatment's everyday meaning, with its essence of 'dealing with/being dealt with', speaks to its Article 3 meaning.

Special meanings of treatment may still be found in the existing authoritative interpretations. Finding them requires interpretation of a body of case-law in which treatment's meanings are only implicit. It was more than 40 years into its existence before the Court explicitly referred to the scope of the term in a judgment on the merits, in 2002 in *Pretty v. UK*. The case of *Pretty*, which forced the Court to even minimally address the scope of the term, does not reveal a clear statement about its meaning. In *Pretty v. UK*, the Court, in an unhelpful turn of phrase, rejected the applicant's claim partly on the basis that it placed: 'a new and extended construction on the concept of treatment, which ... goes beyond the ordinary meaning of the word'.[7] It had been argued on the applicant's behalf that suffering as a result of a naturally occurring disease could constitute treatment. The applicant suffered from a progressive neuro-degenerative disease, which had resulted in paralysis and which would lead to death through a failure of the respiratory muscles. Her mental capacities were unaffected. The applicant argued that the UK state

5 See Chapter 3, pp. 47–48.

6 *The Compact Edition of the Oxford English Dictionary* (Clarendon Press 1991).

7 *Pretty v. UK*, no. 2346/02, ECHR 2002-III, para. 54. The Court also noted that Article 3 must be construed in harmony with protection of the right to life in Article 2. Accepting the argument of degrading treatment could have entailed a fundamental clash in this respect.

would be responsible for a violation of Article 3 if it failed to protect her from the suffering caused by the disease, and that the state could protect against the suffering by undertaking not to prosecute her husband if he assisted her to commit suicide. The significant point presently is the argument on behalf of the applicant that the *suffering* she faced as a result of her illness amounted to degrading treatment. When the Court rejected this argument on the basis that it went beyond the ordinary meaning of the word, the Court did not actually seem concerned with the ordinary meaning of the word as such; it seemed to be concerned that no-one was responsible for the naturally occurring suffering.[8] The Court's intuition was correct (in that naturally occurring suffering is not, in itself, coherently understood as degrading)[9], but its reasoning and justification was misleading. Therefore although the Court made its first explicit reference to the scope of meaning of the term 'treatment', it said little of substance in respect of treatment's ordinary (including special) meaning.

The scope of treatment's meaning is significant because as treatment's meaning is perceived to narrow, so too does the scope of protection offered by the right. And conversely, as treatment's meaning expands, so might that protection expand.

Treatment in Article 3 case-law

This section unpacks the Court's understanding of the term 'treatment' as a basis for how I think we should approach its interpretation and assess its consequent impact on Article 3's interpretive scope. This section draws on an analysis of both degrading treatment and inhuman treatment judgments, on the assumption that treatment possesses (or at least it should coherently possess) the same meanings whether qualified as degrading or as inhuman.[10] It gives an overview of the forms of treatment that can be drawn from the case-law and recognises that different forms of treatment often overlap within a single case.[11] What matters is having an understanding of treatment's meaning that can help to articulate a rationale for why the case-law has developed as it has, and that can guide judgments about the application of the right in new contexts where there is no obvious kind of treatment (such as in *Pretty v. UK*) as opposed to where there is an obvious instance of treatment. The analysis does not focus on how treatment is qualified (as degrading, or inhuman, or neither) but on making sense of the forms that treatment takes, and it does not focus on *who or what* inflicts inhuman or degrading treatment (e.g. police officers, prison officers, care home officials, family members, and so on; the source of prohibited treatment was discussed in Chapter 2). I am interested in the meaning of treatment itself.

8 *Pretty v. UK*, para. 55.
9 See Chapters 2 and 4, pp. 38–39, 81–82.
10 As with the analysis in Chapter 4, the interpretation is based on a comprehensive analysis of all inhuman and degrading treatment judgments on the merits to 1 January 2017.
11 For example, *Valasinas v. Lithuania*, no. 44558/98, ECHR 2001-VIII; *Ribitsch v. Austria*, judgment of 4 December 1995, Series A, no. 336.

The following briefly categorises the approaches to treatment's meaning in the Court's judgments.[12] It suggests three conceptual groupings, giving some examples of each in order to convey the breadth of the idea as manifested in the case-law. Three rough categories are listed: physical intrusion, conditions, and manners. Some manifestations of treatment, which show elements of more than one 'form', are difficult to place[13] but I have nevertheless placed them in one category; the principal intention is to make clear the *range* of forms of treatment. Across the three main conceptual categories treatment consists of distinct instances, overlapping and multi-factor environments and non-physical interactions – 'treatment' has a very broad meaning.

Physical intrusion

Physical (in the sense of not purely psychological) intrusion, reflects treatment's most obvious Article 3 meaning. Commonly, this takes the form of bodily intrusion, actively experienced through the victim's corporeality. The Court commonly examines physical violence[14] as a clear form of treatment. I include in this group of treatment's meanings forms of physical intrusion that might less obviously be understood as violence. The Court considered the conduct of a strip-search in detention in *Valasinas v. Lithuania*, in which the applicant had undergone a search in which he was forced to strip naked in front of a female officer and was subjected to intrusive searches by guards not wearing gloves. The Court understood the conduct of the search as the treatment (which was said to have demonstrated a clear lack of respect, etc).[15] The interrogation methods examined in *Ireland v. UK*, used during the period of internment of suspected terrorists in Northern Ireland, were a combination of 'techniques'[16] – of wall-standing, hooding, subjection to noise, deprivation of sleep, and deprivation of food and

12 These categories are based on judgments in which a violation of Article 3 was found. Some cases will suggest a particular interpretation of treatment and nevertheless arrive at a finding of no violation, but the present analysis errs on the side of caution by restricting the conclusions to cases in which the meaning of treatment is 'confirmed' by a finding of a violation.

13 An example of a multi-factor environment is the context of subjection to the death penalty. In *Al-Saadoon and Mufdhi v. UK* the Court found this to constitute a form of treatment (*Al-Saadoon and Mufdhi v. UK*, no. 61498/08, ECHR 2010). We might identify different forms of treatment involved in a case like this – the conditions of detention, bodily intrusion and maybe also the existence of the penalty itself as a form of legal intrusion.

14 Examples include *Barbu Anghelescu v. Romania*, no. 46430/99, 5 October 2004; *Z. and Others v. UK* [GC], no. 29392/95, ECHR 2001-V, para, 630; *E. and Others v. UK*, no. 33218/96, 26 November 2002, para. 89; *Ahmet Özkan and Others v. Turkey*, no. 21689/93, 6 April 2004; *Lakatoš and Others v. Serbia*, no. 3363/08, 7 January 2014; *Đorđević v. Croatia*, no. 41526/10, ECHR 2012; *O'Keeffe v. Ireland*, no. 35810/09, ECHR 2014 (extracts); *Bouyid v. Belgium* [GC], no. 23380/09, ECHR 2015.

15 *Valasinas v. Lithuania*, no. 44558/98, ECHR 2001-VIII, para. 117.

16 *Ireland v. UK*, judgment of 18 January 1978, Series A, no. 25, para. 167.

drink[17] – which the Court found to amount to inhuman and degrading treatment. The Court has accepted things like the shaving of a prisoner's hair as a form of treatment[18]; being used as a kind of prop in prison officer training exercises;[19] forms of physical restraint[20]; physical modes of transportation[21]; medical interventions[22]; and administration of medical drugs[23] or psychiatric treatment.[24]

Conditions

Treatment in the form of a set of conditions is most common within contexts of physical detention. Detention conditions do not reflect treatment's most obvious meaning, but constitute a frequent incarnation and make up a large group of the complaints under Article 3. Nonetheless, this is a form of treatment that might be overlooked because there is perhaps a tendency to see treatment here as reducible to the individual incidents that make up a set of conditions. This is particularly so when a particular incident within a context of physical detention has a strong symbolic impact, such as being placed in a cage during a court hearing.[25] However, some components of detention conditions are not easily understood as particular incidents to which someone is subjected; things like the presence of vermin, overcrowding, or lack of sanitary facilities, for example. The Court instead appears to understand treatment as the combined manifestation of such factors.[26]

The case-law indicates that the Court sees conditions of detention as a unit – as a culmination of factors that constitute treatment when taken together. The Court displayed this understanding of treatment when faced with the death row phenomenon in *Soering v. UK*. This was the first case in which the Court established the principle that a Contracting State could be responsible for a breach of Article 3 by sending an individual to another state in which there was a real risk that s/he would suffer torture, inhuman or degrading treatment or punishment. *Soering*, a German national who was detained in the UK pending extradition to the United States on murder charges, argued that there was a serious likelihood that he would be sentenced to death if extradited. The argument was that he would suffer

17 *Ireland v. UK*, para. 96.
18 *Yankov v. Bulgaria*, no. 39084/97, 11 December 2003; *Tarhan v. Turkey*, no. 9078/06, 17 July 2012.
19 *Davydov and Others v. Ukraine*, 17674/02, 39081/02, 1 July 2010.
20 For example, *Hénaf v. France*, no. 65436/01, ECHR 2003-XI; *Engel v. Hungary*, no. 46857/06, 20 May 2010; *Radkov and Sabev v. Bulgaria*, no. 18938/07, 36069/09, 27 May 2014.
21 *Engel v. Hungary*.
22 For example, *Ciorap v. The Republic of Moldova (No. 4)*, no. 14092/06, 8 July 2014.
23 *Jalloh v. Germany*, no. 54810/00, ECHR 2006-IX.
24 *Gorobet v. Moldova*, no. 30951/10, 11 October 2011; *Bataliny v. Russia*, no. 10060/07, 23 July 2015.
25 E.g. *Petyo Petkov v. Bulgaria*, no. 32130/03, 7 January 2010.
26 This understanding is also reflected in the work of the European Committee for the Prevention of Torture and Inhuman or Degrading Treatment or Punishment; see discussion in Evans and Morgan 241–245.

inhuman and degrading treatment and punishment on death row.[27] The Court accepted this way of locating the treatment:

> *The alleged breach derives from the applicant's exposure to the so-called 'death row phenomenon'. This phenomenon may be described as consisting in a combination of circumstances to which the applicant would be exposed ... The applicant likewise submitted that Article 3 ... not only prohibits the Contracting States from causing inhuman or degrading treatment or punishment to occur within their jurisdiction but also embodies an associated obligation not to put a person in a position where he will or may suffer such treatment or punishment at the hands of other States.*[28]

The conclusion of this landmark case is well-known: The Court concluded that it would be incompatible with the Convention's underlying values to surrender an individual to a state where there were grounds for believing that s/he would be subjected to torture, or to inhuman or degrading treatment or punishment.[29] It described the death row phenomenon as the 'source of the alleged inhuman and degrading treatment or punishment'[30] and stated that 'the applicant's extradition to the United States would expose him to a real risk of treatment going beyond the threshold set by Article 3'.[31] The detention conditions here are qualitatively different to most other detention conditions claims because of the connection with the death penalty, but the *form* of treatment is the same, i.e. an 'environmental' context. It is these contexts that the Court has understood as potentially inhuman or degrading; in *Peers v. Greece* the Court stated that:

> *The prison conditions complained of diminished the applicant's human dignity ... In sum, the Court considers that the conditions of the applicant's detention ... amounted to degrading treatment within the meaning of Article 3 of the Convention.*[32]

In *Dougoz v. Greece*, the Court stated that: 'conditions of detention may sometimes amount to inhuman or degrading treatment'.[33] This kind of statement shows an interpretation of treatment as a set of environmental conditions. Such conditions might also feature inappropriate medical care. The Court has commonly accepted that conditions of inadequate medical care in detention can amount to inhuman and/or degrading *treatment.* The Court in *Nevmerzhitsky v. Ukraine* for example, referred to the 'lack of adequate medical treatment and assistance provided to the applicant while he was detained, amounting to

27 *Soering v. UK*, judgment of 7 July 1989, Series A, no. 161, para. 76.
28 *Soering v. UK*, paras 81–82.
29 *Soering v. UK*, paras 87–88.
30 *Soering v. UK*, para. 92.
31 *Soering v. UK*, para. 111.
32 *Peers v. Greece*, no. 28524/95, ECHR 2001-III, para. 75.
33 *Dougoz v. Greece*, no. 40907/98, ECHR 2001-II, para. 46.

degrading treatment'.[34] I understand treatment in cases like these, which often involve a culmination of factors (structural factors, decisions, failures), as a set of conditions.[35] Treatment in detention cases then, is constituted by the conditions, or environment, that an applicant had to endure.

The Court brought this same meaning of treatment into play in the care home case of *Stanev v. Bulgaria*. It examined the applicant's 'physical living conditions'[36]:

> *It appears that the food was insufficient and of poor quality. The building was inadequately heated and in winter the applicant had to sleep in his coat. He was able to have a shower once a week in an unhygienic and dilapidated bathroom. The toilets were in an execrable state and access to them was dangerous.*[37]

The Court found that the applicant should not have been subjected to these conditions, which it qualified as degrading treatment. In a similar 2015 judgment, delivered in French, the Court stated: 'les conditions de vie auxquelles a été exposé le requérant … constituent un traitement dégradant', again referring to the 'living conditions' as a form of treatment.[38]

There are agents who have acted to place someone in those conditions, and this might be mistaken for the treatment itself, but the implication of those actors, who place individuals in such detention conditions, is in the *subjection* to the conditions (no one shall be subjected to) and also in their responsibility under international law for a Convention violation. Locating treatment as the conditions themselves does not detract from this role and responsibility. In other words, who or what caused those conditions can be conceptually separated from the conditions themselves. The Court has described, time and time again, conditions as treatment: 'The Court considers that conditions of detention may sometimes amount to inhuman or degrading treatment'[39]; 'the Court finds that the applicant's conditions of detention, in particular the overcrowded environment and the length of time the applicant was detained in such conditions, amounted to a degrading treatment'[40]; 'The Court concludes that the physical conditions of the applicant's detention caused him harm that exceeded the unavoidable level of suffering inherent in detention and have thus reached the minimum level of severity'.[41] The Court has instituted an understanding of treatment as a set of

34 *Nevmerzhitsky v. Ukraine*, no. 54825/00, 5 April 2005, 106.
35 This approach echoes that of Rodley and Pollard who refer to the 'conditions in which a person is detained or imprisoned (including the absence, inadequacy, or abusive imposition of medical treatment)'; Nigel Rodley and Matt Pollard, *The Treatment of Prisoners under International Law* (3rd edn, Oxford University Press 2009) 126.
36 *Stanev v. Bulgaria*, no. 36760/06, ECHR 2012, para. 209
37 *Stanev v. Bulgaria*, para. 209.
38 *Stefan Stankov v. Bulgaria*, no. 25820/07, 17 March 2015, para. 154.
39 *Dougoz v. Greece*, no. 40907/98, ECHR 2001-II, para. 46.
40 *Nevmerzhitsky v. Ukraine*, para. 87; *Mayzit v. Russia*, no. 63378/00, 20 January 2005, para. 42.
41 *Apostu v. Romania*, no. 22765/12, 3 February 2015, para. 84.

conditions; it is this 'environment' that is qualified or not, as inhuman and/or degrading.

The Court has recognised inhuman and/or degrading environments outside of contexts of detention. This has been the case for decades now, but for the reasons noted above concerning responsibility, treatment as a set of living conditions may not be an obvious meaning. The case of *D. v. UK* in 1997 was the first to hint at an interpretation of treatment as a set of social living conditions. This case concerned conditions of inadequate medical treatment and social care. The applicant, imprisoned in the UK after having been convicted of drug offences, was diagnosed as suffering from AIDS. The State authorities wanted to return him to his native St Kitts after his release but it was argued on the applicant's behalf that this would 'expose him to inhuman and degrading treatment'.[42] The UK Government urged the Court to reject the claim on the basis that the applicant 'would not be exposed in the receiving country to any form of treatment which breached the standards of Article 3.'[43] The Court acknowledged its previous expulsion case-law on a real risk of torture, inhuman or degrading treatment or punishment in a receiving state.[44] As noted in Chapter 2, I have written elsewhere about the Court's ambiguity in this leading case, which I have argued stemmed from its hesitancy in expanding the scope of positive state obligations and which has tainted its approach to subsequent medical-related expulsion claims.[45] The treatment in *D. v. UK* should be understood as a plurality of factors which together created a particular context. *D. v. UK* should be seen as accepting treatment as a form of context, similar to prison/institutional detention conditions cases.

Treatment in the form of living conditions has remained visible in the expulsion context. In the 2010 expulsion case of *N. v. Sweden*, it was argued on behalf of the applicant that she was at risk of suffering treatment prohibited by Article 3 if she was returned to her home country. The applicant and her husband had unsuccessfully made an application for asylum in Sweden on the basis of a risk of political persecution in Afghanistan. In the process of appealing against the refusal of asylum, the applicant made it known that she had separated from, and wished to divorce, her husband. As a result, she stated that her family had disowned her, that she risked reprisals from her husband's family and, as a divorced and childless women, she would be an outcast in Afghan society.[46] This appeal was rejected although a minority in the Swedish Migration Court 'wanted to grant the applicant leave to remain in Sweden on the ground that, since she did not have any

42 *D. v. UK*, judgment of 2 May 1997, *Reports* 1997-III, para. 39.
43 *D. v. UK*, para. 42.
44 *D. v. UK*, paras 46–48 and 50.
45 Elaine Webster, 'Medical-Related Expulsion and Interpretation of Article 3 of the European Convention on Human Rights' (2013) 6 *Inter-American and European Human Rights Journal* 36. The impact of *D. v. UK* is still negatively felt in medical-related cases although significant progress towards greater clarity has since been achieved, notably through the judgment in *Paposhvili* in 2016 (*Paposhvili v. Belgium*, no. 41738/10, ECHR 2016).
46 *N. v. Sweden*, no. 23505/09, 20 July 2010, paras 7–10.

children and had separated from her husband, she had shown that she would risk degrading treatment upon return to her home country.'[47] As part of further, ultimately unsuccessful appeals processes, a letter was presented from the UN High Commissioner for Refugees Regional Office, which referred to the 'situation' for potential female returnees in Afghanistan. This is cited in the Strasbourg Court's judgment:

> *In the context of Afghanistan, UNHCR would like to draw to your attention to the fact that an assessment of a refugee claim of an Afghan female asylum-seeker, should take into account the specifically vulnerable situation in which Afghan women are found, including pressure from within families, communities, and by the public to conform [to] behaviour in accordance with particular codes of behaviour. In this regard, a separation and/or divorce effected in the country of asylum, may indicate adoption of a Westernised way of life and be perceived as, or actually transgressing, prevailing social mores and thereby indicates a heightened risk of sur place persecution … UNHCR notes that Afghan female asylum-seekers' reliance for relative social, cultural and economic freedom is exclusively dependent on the existence of male protection (husband, father, brother or extended family member) and that lack of such networks may seriously undermine a returnee's personal physical, economic and emotional security.*[48]

The judgment goes on to cite several other sources discussing the general position of women in Afghanistan at that time relating to gender roles and social and religious norms, and the prevalence of domestic violence and lack of legal protection. Considering the applicant's personal situation, the Court stated:

> *In the special circumstances of the present case, the Court finds that there are substantial grounds for believing that if deported to Afghanistan, the applicant faces various cumulative risks of reprisals which fall under Article 3 of the Convention from her husband X, his family, her own family and from the Afghan society.*[49]

The Court thereby accepted that there would be a prospective violation of Article 3 if the applicant were to be deported because she faced a real risk of prohibited treatment in Afghanistan. She would face a set of cumulative social, living conditions and it is these conditions that would constitute inhuman and/or degrading 'treatment'.

Treatment as living conditions has also in recent years been seen in cases concerning destitution. In the well-known case of *M.S.S. v. Belgium and Greece*, the Grand Chamber appeared to understand the applicant's living conditions as a form of treatment:

47 *N. v. Sweden*, no. 23505/09, 20 July 2010, para. 13.
48 *N. v. Sweden*, para. 20.
49 *N. v. Sweden*, para. 62.

> *[The Court] considers that such living conditions, combined with the prolonged uncertainty in which [the applicant] has remained and the total lack of any prospects of his situation improving, have attained the level of severity required to fall within the scope of Article 3 of the Convention. It follows that, through the fault of the authorities, the applicant has found himself in a situation incompatible with Article 3 of the Convention.*[50]

A number of subsequent cases display the same meaning of treatment: in *F.H. v. Greece*, the applicant, an asylum seeker, was faced with homelessness after release from immigration detention. The Court described the applicant's living conditions as 'a degrading situation' ('une situation dégradante').[51] It repeated this in *AL.K. v. Greece.*[52] In *V.M. and Others v. Belgium*, after leaving a Belgian reception centre, a family was faced with a situation of destitution characterised by sleeping on the streets and at a train station. The judgment indicates that the treatment is, again, the living conditions faced by the family:

> *It finds that such living conditions, combined with the lack of any prospects of their situation improving, attained the level of severity required to fall within the scope of Article 3 of the Convention and amounted to degrading treatment.*[53]

The context of such cases concerning social conditions is very different to the context of detention cases, but treatment assumes the same form: a set of living conditions.

Manner

Treatment as a manner – as reaction or response – is perhaps the least tangible of all the examples of treatment, yet it is undoubtedly defensible. An early sense of the Court condemning authorities' reactions was in *Selçuk and Asker v. Turkey*, in which the applicants' homes and belongings were burned by state agents. The physical destruction of the property stands out but there is an underlying condemnation of the way in which the state agents ignored the applicants' pleas.[54] Later cases illustrate a clear focus on the manner of the authorities' response. Treatment in *Akkum and Others v. Turkey*, for example, emerges as an attitude of disrespect; it is a lack of concern that was callous to such a degree as to be considered degrading. The first applicant in this case alleged that his son had been killed by state security forces. The Strasbourg Court held that the Turkish authorities were responsible for the killing since they failed to account for the death of the applicant's son (and the death of the relatives of the two other applicants)

50 *M.S.S. v. Belgium and Greece* [GC], no. 30696/09, ECHR 2011, paras 263–264.
51 *F.H. v. Greece*, no. 78456/11, 31 July 2014, para. 111.
52 *AL.K. v. Greece*, no. 63542/11, 11 December 2014, para. 62.
53 *V.M. and Others v. Belgium*, no. 60125/11, 7 July 2015, para. 162.
54 *Selçuk and Asker v. Turkey*, judgment of 24 April 1998, *Reports* 1998-II, paras 74 and 77.

within an area under the security forces' control. The first applicant made a specific complaint under Article 3 on the basis that his son's body had also been mutilated, arguing that:

> *The mutilation of his son Mehmet Akkum represented inhuman treatment contrary to Article 3 of the Convention in relation to him, and that the mutilation of a body was offensive to a Muslim, given that he had had to bury an incomplete and mutilated body.*[55]

The Turkish Government did not address this complaint. This 'treatment' derives from the attitudes and reactions of the authorities and it is in this sense that a relative can be a direct victim. The Court found the treatment – the authorities' 'conduct'[56] – to be degrading within the meaning of Article 3. It referred to the 'anguish caused' to the father.[57] The Court understood this complaint to be 'in the same vein'[58] as previously examined cases in which it was possible for a family member of a disappeared person to be 'a victim of treatment contrary to Article 3'.[59] In an earlier case, it had referred to a mother requesting information about her disappeared son as a victim of the 'complacency' of state authorities in response to her anguish and distress.[60] In another case it found authorities' 'callous disregard for the applicant's concerns', a father trying to ascertain what had happened to his son, to constitute treatment.[61] In *Uçar v. Turkey*, the Court referred to the manner of the authorities' responses in coming to a finding of no violation; it found there was 'nothing in the content or tone of the authorities' replies to the enquiries made by the applicant that could be described as inhuman or degrading treatment.'[62] In the same case, it also reiterated that:

> *The essence of such a violation does not so much lie in the fact of the 'disappearance' of the family member but rather concerns the authorities' reactions and attitudes to the situation when it is brought to their attention.*[63]

The Court has thereby understood treatment as 'silence'.[64] Such claims have become increasingly common beyond the context of disappearances in Turkey and

55 *Akkum and Others v. Turkey*, no. 21894/93, 24 March 2005, para. 253.
56 *Akkum and Others v. Turkey*, para. 258.
57 *Akkum and Others v. Turkey*, para. 259.
58 *Akkum and Others v. Turkey*, para. 259.
59 *Akkum and Others v. Turkey*, para. 258.
60 *Kurt v. Turkey*, judgment of 25 May 1998, *Reports* 1998-III, paras 130–134.
61 *Timurtaş v. Turkey*, no. 23531/94, ECHR 2000-VI, para, 97.
62 *Uçar v. Turkey*, no. 52392/99, 11 April 2006, para. 110.
63 *Uçar v. Turkey*, para. 109.
64 *Janowiec and Others v. Russia*, no. 55508/07; 29520/09, ECHR 2012, para. 163. Later cases include *Pitsayeva and Others v. Russia*, no. 53036/08, 9 January 2014; *Malika Yusupova and Others v. Russia*, no. 14705/09, 15 January 2015.

in Russia. Claims concerning the 'indifference'[65] of state authorities have been brought in cases concerning responses to requests for medical intervention (such as after a violent street attack by private persons[66]) and access to genetic testing.[67] In a different context, the case of *Elberte v. Latvia* concerned that state's non-responsiveness to the applicant's anguish surrounding removal of tissue from her deceased husband's body in the absence of her knowledge and consent. The Court referred to: 'the manner in which the domestic authorities dealt with the complaints brought to their attention and their disregard vis-à-vis the victims of these acts and their close relatives, including the applicant.'[68] As such complaints have increasingly been examined by the Court, the meaning of treatment as a manner has become increasingly established. Manners of reaction or response are characterised by omissions as much as by actions. It is very clearly a manner of being 'dealt with' and 'dealing with', which expresses the essence of treatment's ordinary meaning.

Treatment as social experience

This overview portrays a broad understanding that I describe, at the most general level, as treatment as a *social experience*. This section clarifies the way in which this meaning of treatment developed from two key turning points in treatment's jurisprudential development noted above – the Court's approach to cases concerning prison conditions and, later, responses to families of disappeared persons. It suggests that these turning points have led to a broadening of treatment's meaning such that the key characteristic of treatment is less the form that it takes and more its expression of a relationship between agent and recipient.

The Court by including 'conditions' within the meaning of treatment, instituted a pivotal development in this term's interpretation. The Convention drafters, in approving the language of inhuman and degrading 'treatment', likely had in mind ill-treatment of an individual by an identifiable individual or group. If they held such a perception it was probably influenced by how they viewed torture within the right. This first and most rhetorically striking of the right's elements would likely have been accompanied by imaginings of physical containment and powerlessness, and so ill-treatment by other concrete individuals. But the Court was faced with complaints about conditions of detention. This led it to subsume the idea of 'conditions' or 'circumstances' – essentially living conditions in detention – within Article 3 as a species of treatment. As a result, the Court accepted, in effect, that the legal meaning of treatment would be more than treatment in its most common meaning of action towards one person by another person. Instead

65 *Hristozov and Others v. Bulgaria*, no. 47039/11; 358/12, ECHR 2012 (extracts), para. 112.
66 *Denis Vasilyev v. Russia*, no. 32704/04, 17 December 2009.
67 *R.R. v. Poland*, no. 27617/04, 26 May 2011.
68 *Elberte v. Latvia*, no. 61243/08, ECHR 2015, para. 140.

it was to include a living environment (at that time brought about by identifiable agents towards an applicant).

The Court instituted another major development in the interpretation of treatment when it was faced with a context in which an environment did not result in direct physical stress (in the way that overcrowding, lack of hygiene or lack of exercise might) but in something less physically tangible. This context was the suffering of relatives of disappeared persons. The form of suffering here was non-physical and, correspondingly, the form that 'treatment' took was non-physical – it was a way of being dealt with but not physically; it was 'merely' a way of being *looked at.* It was a form of regard rather than a physically tangible incident. The Court accepted that this should fall within the meaning of the term 'treatment'.

Through both of these developments, towards treatment as an environment and as a form of regard, the Court actually moved treatment's meaning away from its most obvious everyday meaning. It accepted that treatment should not only be seen as an action and in doing so reduced focus on what particular agents *did.* It moved closer to seeing treatment from the perspective of treatment's recipient and not its agent. I noted above the duality of perspective inherent in treatment's ordinary meaning beyond its most common everyday meaning – that it is at once an agent-centred *and* recipient-centred idea. The Court's approach to treatment has moved along that scale, away from a focus on the agent of the treatment towards a focus on the victim's experience. This approach fits the surrounding text with its reference to being 'subjected to' inhuman and/or degrading treatment. The 'subjection' must be present but so too must some form of relationship. The Court's approach encourages us to understand treatment as 'a way of being looked at or dealt with' and not only as 'a way of looking at or dealing with'. In this sense, the Court foregrounds the victim's perspective but maintains treatment's inherent sociality.

We should see the dimension of social experience as the key limit on treatment's meaning. As such, it is conceptually coherent to understand treatment as capable of assuming many forms – whether that is an incident, a context, a series of overlapping omissions, a way of being looked at; as something that can last for minutes or for years. The categories outlined above, based on the case-law to date, are few in number yet are capable of encompassing a vast range of forms of treatment. They are capable of encompassing things that the Court has hinted at as falling within the scope of treatment but in cases where no violation of Article 3 has been found, for example threats,[69] or polluted

69 In *Campbell and Cosans v. UK*, two mothers argued that the use of corporal punishment in their sons' schools amounted to a violation of their children's rights under Article 3. The applicants complained of the *threat* of prohibited treatment (The Court examined treatment rather than punishment as no punishment had actually been inflicted upon the children); *Campbell and Cosans v. UK*, judgment of 25 February 1982, Series A, no. 48, para. 28). In relation to one of the children, the Court's view was that he: 'may well have experienced feelings of apprehension or disquiet when he came close to an infliction of the tawse [a type of leather implement used for belting] but such feelings are not sufficient to amount to degrading treatment', para. 30. The

living conditions.[70] And they are likewise capable of encompassing other forms of treatment that might arise in future.

The essence of treatment's interpretation is not that it must take a particular form, but that it must express some kind of social relationship that impacts upon an applicant. This is more significant than whether it is of a certain scale or duration (which instead speaks to the way that treatment is qualified as crossing, or failing to cross, a threshold to become inhuman and/or degrading). The dignity-driven purpose of the right not to be subjected to degrading treatment impacts more on this qualificatory exercise than on the form of treatment but it too supports an interpretation of treatment as social experience. There is nothing in the dignity-driven purpose (dignity as an elemental status, which is diminished by, and demands freedom from, experiences that undermine a minimal kind of regard or capacity) that restricts the meaning of treatment. On the contrary, the interpretation of degradation to which this purpose gives rise (summarised as symbolic denial of one's basic status as a human being) also foregrounds a social context. Treatment should be seen then as capable of taking different forms and different combinations of forms. In new contexts we should question the existence of treatment from the perspective of the applicant's experience and we should be able to identify a social interaction within this experience. This approach will enable us to conceive, as clearly as possible, the boundaries of the prohibition of degrading treatment.

Conclusion

There might be an objection that the exercise undertaken in this chapter takes the term 'treatment' almost too seriously; that the essence of the right is that 'something' is inhuman or degrading, and not whether it amounts to treatment. To some extent the way that the Court has applied Article 3 has encouraged this perception because it has so rarely stopped to indicate how it understands treatment. The Court has not been intentional in its development of the scope of the term, which remains surprising given the breadth of the meaning that we can deduce from the body of case-law. This should not detract from the fact that the right expressed in Article 3 (and indeed wherever this right is expressed) is a legal text that must be interpreted; i.e. there is no reason to see the word 'treatment' as redundant. It can have a very broad meaning, but as long as it is there it should mean something. The meaning of a text is, and should be, determined by the meaning of the words that make up that text.[71] We should insist, therefore, on

Court hints that being subjected to a threat would be a valid way of understanding treatment; para. 26.

70 The applicant in *López Ostra v. Spain* claimed that she had been subjected to degrading treatment caused by pollution; *López Ostra v. Spain*, judgment of 9 December 1994, Series A, no. 303-C, para. 59. The Court rejected the Article 3 claim on the basis that the minimum level of severity had not been reached (para. 60) but had the minimum level of severity been reached, the judgment indicates that treatment would have been the living conditions of the applicant.

71 Brian Bix, *Law, Language, and Legal Determinacy* (Clarendon Press 1993) 19.

articulating the meaning of the term 'treatment'. What we find is that 'treatment' within Article 3 can be understood to have a broad meaning, which goes beyond the word's most commonly used everyday meaning.

The combination of expansions in meaning and a recipient-centred perspective leads us to an interpretation of the term 'treatment' that significantly contributes to broadening the application of Article 3. There are different ways in which we could conceptually segment what is ultimately an extremely broad legal meaning, and we could articulate the meaning of treatment at different levels of generality. But understanding 'treatment' as social experience can encompass a range of more concrete manifestations while maintaining a broad umbrella meaning, within which the interpretation of treatment can, and will, continue to evolve. I have aimed to show an interpretation of treatment that reflects the ordinary meaning of the word (on the spectrum from everyday meaning to special meaning) in context and that aligns with the purposes of the right. It is an interpretation of treatment that progresses in the spirit of the authoritative interpreter's approach, although a key feature is that this interpretation is more recipient- than agent-centered. It is the victim focus that leads to an *experiental* understanding of treatment in the context of the broader right, accompanied by the idea of subjection. The importance of this exercise has been to articulate treatment's meaning in a way that can guide our judgments about the application of the right in new contexts, including where there is no obvious kind of treatment. Understanding treatment as social experience achieves this. Interpreting treatment is a crucial step towards a richer appreciation of the boundaries of the right.

References

Bix, B, *Law, Language, and Legal Determinacy* (Clarendon Press, 1993)

Cassese, A, 'Prohibition of Torture, Inhuman or Degrading Treatment or Punishment' in Macdonald, RSJ, Matscher, F and Petzold, H (eds), *The European System for the Protection of Human Rights* (Martinus Nijhoff, 1993)

Clayton, R and Tomlinson, H, *The Law of Human Rights* (Oxford University Press, 2009)

Cooper, J, *Cruelty – An Analysis of Article 3* (Sweet and Maxwell, 2003)

Council of Europe, *Collected Edition of the 'Travaux Préparatoires' of the European Convention on Human Rights, Vol. IV* (1977)

Evans, MD and Morgan, R, *Preventing Torture – A Study of the European Convention for the Prevention of Torture and Inhuman or Degrading Treatment or Punishment* (Clarendon Press, 1998)

Harris, DJ, O'Boyle, M and Warbrick, C, *Law of the European Convention on Human Rights* (Butterworths, 1995)

Lester, AP, Pannick, D and Herberg, J, *Human Rights: Law and Practice* (LexisNexis, 2009)

Reid, K, *A Practioner's Guide to the European Convention on Human Rights* (3rd edn, Sweet and Maxwell, 2008)

Rodley, N and Pollard, M, *The Treatment of Prisoners under International Law* (3rd edn, Oxford University Press, 2009)

Webster, E, 'Medical-Related Expulsion and Interpretation of Article 3 of the European Convention on Human Rights' (2013) 6 *Inter-American and European Human Rights Journal* 36

6 The ends of Article 3

The protection of human dignity and the limits of state responsibility

I have argued for an interpretation of degrading treatment as a social experience characterised by profound powerlessness and symbolic exclusion from the community of human beings, or by destruction of a minimal capacity to oppose the undermining of one's human status or to direct one's own actions. This interpretation rests on the foundations of legal meaning, the Strasbourg Court's purposive system of interpretation, and a constructive approach to forming the meaning of degrading treatment. It is a layered interpretation that has aimed to distil all that the text of the Convention and the case-law contains[1] in respect of this right. The current chapter seeks to consider its implications in practice: where might this meaning lead, and what can we subsequently deduce about the boundaries of the right's application? It explores these questions in order to support reflection in the next chapter on what the scope of degrading treatment should tell us about the interpretive boundaries of the broader right not to be subjected to torture.

To explore the limits of the right not to be subjected to degrading treatment, this chapter contextualises its interpretation through an example. A juxtaposition between the right and an apparently extreme circumstance is a simple route into wide-ranging questions about that right's scope of meaning and application and I use that approach here. The discussion below considers an experience of socio-economic deprivation in which an individual plays an active role. It considers whether a situation like this could fall within the interpretation of degrading treatment and examines the implications thereof for understanding the scope of meaning and application of the right not to be subjected to degrading treatment. The discussion is rooted in an application that was found by the Strasbourg Court to be manifestly unfounded. This is a useful approach because it provides a context that is not improbable. It begins from a factual claim and allows space for imagining the details of that context, since we only have limited insight into what actually occurred. The circumstances in this case, *O'Rourke v. UK*, concerned a form of socio-economic deprivation to which the applicant's active choices appeared to significantly contribute. The role played by the individual applicant himself was at the forefront of the Court's decision that the Article 3 claim was

1 Aharon Barak, *Purposive Interpretation* (Princeton University Press 2005) 57.

inadmissible. It is an example that encapsulates questions about dignity and responsibility. It encapsulates questions about the impact of the idea of dignity in understanding the reach of the idea of degrading treatment, and about when a state should be held responsible for a particular situation. This chapter demonstrates that the outer limits of the right's scope of meaning and application revolve around the axes of dignity and responsibility, which are both understood in socially embedded, context-dependent ways, and which simultaneously expand and restrain the right's boundaries.

Socio-economic deprivation and active individual 'choice'

With reference to the Strasbourg Court's admissibility decision in the case of *O'Rourke v. UK*, this section imagines a situation of socio-economic deprivation that apparently results from an individual's choices. The prominence of an individual's choices might suggest that this situation is self-inflicted, yet the individual nevertheless claims that it should be condemned within a human rights law framework. This kind of scenario could potentially arise wherever someone chooses to put themselves in a particular situation and at the same time argues that it constitutes degrading treatment for which the state should be held responsible; for example, it could conceivably form the basis of a complaint in a context of undertaking particular forms of work.[2] On the one hand, the prospect of degrading treatment which is apparently 'self-inflicted' might be, at best, fanciful, and at worst, damaging to states' political willingness to protect Article 3 because it seems to go too far. On the other hand, a significant consensus has developed that socio-economic deprivation can entail degradation. In the 1990 admissibility decision of *Van Volsem v. Belgium* before the European Commission on Human Rights, the restriction of electricity supply to a single parent household for non-payment of bills was argued to amount to inhuman or degrading treatment. The Commission indicated then that socio-economic hardship could potentially fall within the interpretation of Article 3.[3] Responding to *Van Volsem*, Antonio Cassese noted that Strasbourg was open to the prohibition of inhuman and degrading treatment encompassing socio-economic harm as early as the 1970s.[4] The Strasbourg institutions have not, however, given a rationale for why socio-economic deprivation might be captured by the specific text of Article 3 and its related case-law. This section explores how socio-economic deprivation, in which the applicant plays an active role, might be argued to entail a violation of the right not to be subjected to degrading treatment.

The questions asked are: What is it about socio-economic deprivation that is apt to bring it within the scope of meaning of degrading treatment? What are the implications of seemingly voluntary choices on the process of interpreting and

2 See, e.g., *Tremblay v. France*, no. 37194/02, 11 December 2007.
3 *Van Volsem v. Belgium*, no. 14641/89, Commission Decision of 9 May 1990.
4 Antonio Cassese, 'Can the Notion of Inhuman and Degrading Treatment be applied to Socio-economic Conditions?' (1991) 2 *Eur J Int'l L* 141, 143, note 8.

applying the right not to be subjected to degrading treatment? To reiterate: the purpose of this exercise is to apply the meaning of degrading treatment at the same time as exploring the outer limits of this right's scope of application.

O'Rourke v. UK

Peter O'Rourke, 56 years old at the time of the application to the ECtHR and a UK national, had applied to a London local authority for housing. He had served a prison sentence after conviction on charges of attempted rape and indecent assault. The local authority, having (eventually) accepted that Mr O'Rourke had a priority need in light of respiratory health problems, provided him with hotel accommodation as a temporary measure. Before more permanent arrangements could be made the applicant was evicted from the hotel 'following complaints about his behaviour there, including allegations of nuisance and assault on female residents.'[5] Then began a series of refusals made by Mr O'Rourke that would be a key factor in the Court's dismissal of his claim under Article 3 (and Article 8 ECHR, the right to respect for one's home). The narrative in the decision is one of failure to follow advice and unwillingness to accept compromise. For example, it is noted that 'the applicant refused an offer of permanent bed-sit accommodation because it shared a bathroom and a toilet', and that he later 'decided' to accept temporary accommodation. In the midst of a protracted process, Mr O'Rourke's respiratory health condition deteriorated, as confirmed by a doctor, after he spent around 14 months sleeping on the streets.

The Article 3 complaint was that the applicant's eviction from the hotel in April 1991, which led to street homelessness, 'constituted a breach of Article 3'. The Court found that the Article 3 claim was manifestly unfounded and so inadmissible. It asserted that the 'applicant's suffering following his eviction' did not cross the minimum severity threshold. It did not explain this further. It did, however, go on to highlight one point: *even if* the minimum threshold for engaging Article 3 had been reached:

> *The Court notes that the applicant failed to attend a night shelter pending a decision on permanent housing, contrary to the advice he was given by [the local authority] following his eviction. He also indicated an unwillingness to accept temporary accommodation and refused two specific offers of accommodation prior to his acceptance of temporary accommodation in June 1992. The applicant was therefore largely responsible for his own deterioration following his eviction.*

There is one dominant narrative in this decision, but also a less prominent underlying narrative. Clearest is a narrative of 'undeserving-ness'. This echoes a now well-known narrative of the 'undeserving poor'.[6] There is a sense that the

5 *O'Rourke v. UK* (dec.), no. 39022/97, 26 June 2001.
6 James D Wright, 'The worthy and unworthy homeless' (1988) 25 *Society* 64.

applicant's refusals, for example to accept accommodation with a shared toilet, were unreasonable and demonstrated ingratitude whilst the local authority's response had been reasonable since it had made significant efforts to identify suitable accommodation. This narrative firmly places responsibility for the 'suffering' on the applicant. His own actions brought about the situation. *Even if* this suffering could be seen to amount to prohibited treatment (presumably degrading treatment, since it would certainly have been seen by the Court to fall at the lowest end of the perceived severity spectrum), his own actions displaced any responsibility that might otherwise have been placed on the local authority. There is another underlying narrative – the applicant's perspective. In the overview of circumstances, it is noted that the local authority tried to respond to the applicant's requirements, which were 'designed to minimise his exposure to women'. It is not entirely clear where this narrative came from, but the text indicates that it was at the behest of the applicant. The decision recounts that the applicant wanted to be settled somewhere permanently where the community did not know about his criminal history and where he would not be threatened because of it. The decision narrates these claims as ungrounded rather than as potentially reasonable demands by a holder of human rights for state assistance.

The narratives that are present in the decision point towards a tension between what is required in order to cross the severity threshold and what is required to impute responsibility to the state. Judgments and decisions like *M.S.S. v. Belgium and Greece*,[7] *Budina v. Russia*,[8] and *Shioshvili and Others v. Russia*[9] confirm that the Court continues to accept that contexts of socio-economic deprivation are capable of crossing the severity threshold. At the same time, the *O'Rourke* decision obviously does not demonstrate a favourable approach to a claim which reveals an individual apparently bringing about his misfortune by his own actions. It demonstrates the opposite. The Court foregrounds the responsibility of the applicant for his own suffering as one reason for the claim being manifestly unfounded. In this decision we glimpse a tension between the nature of the suffering that would be required to cross the threshold to activate Article 3 protection, and the reach of the obligations and responsibility of the state authorities for this suffering. Exploring this tension, spurred by the circumstances of this claim, reveals some useful insights for understanding the scope of the prohibition of degrading treatment.

Degrading treatment?

Chapters 4 and 5 demonstrated that the conceptual boundaries of degradation do not stretch far, whilst the conceptual boundaries of treatment stretch further. I have argued for an interpretation of the term 'treatment', on the basis of its manifestation in Article 3 case-law (in physical intrusion, sets of conditions, and non-responsive

7 *M.S.S. v. Belgium and Greece* [GC], no. 30696/09, ECHR 2011.
8 *Budina v. Russia*, no. 45603/05, 18 June 2009.
9 *Shioshvili and Others v. Russia*, no. 19356/07, 20 December 2016.

attitudes) as a social experience. I have argued for an interpretation of degradation as characterised by feelings of fear, anguish or inferiority capable of eroding self-respect as a result of profound powerlessness and symbolic exclusion from the human community (bringing about humiliation or debasement), eroding one's strength to oppose the stripping of one's human status (the breaking of physical or moral resistance), the breakdown of one's capacity to independently direct one's own actions (being driven to act against will or conscience), and/or characterised by injury to one's basic human status (adverse effect on personality). The bench-marks are all conceptually connected – degrading treatment has been interpreted as a social experience that results in symbolic denial of one's basic status as a human being. This is a meaning that is substantiated *and* limited by an under-standing of human dignity as an elemental status, which is diminished by, and demands freedom from, experiences that undermine a minimal kind of regard or capacity.

I will apply this interpretation alongside consideration of the relative assessment of the minimum level of severity and in light of the Court's other Article 3 prin-ciples. Whether a situation will be considered to fall within the scope of meaning of degrading treatment should depend on all the circumstances of the case, including the sex, age, and state of health of the applicant. I bear in mind the Court's affirmation that the meaning and scope of application of the right not to be subjected to degrading treatment, like the whole of Article 3, has an inherent capacity for evolution. Article 3's aim is to achieve practical and effective protection of individuals in a way that reflects evolving conditions.[10]

In *O'Rourke*, the Court characterises the potential Article 3 harm as 'the appli-cant's suffering following his eviction', i.e. a 14-month-long experience of street homelessness. It was the applicant's 'suffering following his eviction' that the Court did not accept to have crossed the minimum severity threshold. Treatment here must be understood as a set of living conditions, one of the forms of social experience encompassed by the term 'treatment's very broad meaning.[11] (The treatment could alternatively have been located as the eviction, argued to be degrading for X reasons.[12]) The Court did not accept, therefore, that this 14-month-long experience of street homelessness (by a middle-aged man with a recognised health condition, newly released from prison) revealed degrading treatment. As noted earlier, it now seems widely accepted that contexts of social deprivation *can* fall within the scope of Article 3 prohibited treatment. What is the rationale for making a link to experiences of socio-economic deprivation? If we further imagine the characteristics of circumstances like those in *O'Rourke*, the question becomes, in which sense might an experience of street homelessness involve symbolic denial of one's basic status as a human being?

10 Chapter 2, pp. 28–29.

11 See Chapter 5.

12 The way that the alleged degrading treatment is situated is critical for the maintenance of clarity about interpretive scope; see Elaine Webster, 'Medical-Related Expulsion and Interpretation of Article 3 of the European Convention on Human Rights' (2013) 6 *Inter-American and European Human Rights Journal* 36.

The focus of the degrading treatment claim in *O'Rourke* was the 'applicant's suffering following his eviction'[13] from temporary accommodation; on the experience of being without accommodation. Street homelessness is only one narrow category within the range of recognised forms of homelessness. Homelessness has been defined at a general level as 'lacking access to minimally adequate housing'.[14] Street homelessness is often referred to as 'rough sleeping' or as being 'without' accommodation (as opposed to, for example, having temporary accommodation; another form of homelessness).[15] The situation of Mr O'Rourke, including when in temporary accommodation, would, as a whole, be considered as homelessness. Homelessness in this sense could have been the focus of the degrading treatment claim but the Court addressed the problem differently. It focused on the 'applicant's suffering following his eviction'[16] so on the applicant's experience of rough sleeping. A different potential focus in a situation like Mr O'Rourke's could be on legislative responses to rough sleeping. In recent times, political responses to rough sleeping have often been marked by punitive public order approaches and many countries have criminalised rough sleeping.[17] Criminalisation, writes Waldron, can preclude persons who have no private spaces from satisfying essential human needs, and as such can have the effect of making it impossible to exist at all by restricting the use of public space.[18] It would be very difficult for the Strasbourg Court to reject a claim that a homeless applicant, who had been legally barred from sleeping in a public place, had been subjected to degrading treatment (at least in light of the interpretation of degrading treatment that I have put forward). Waldron's argument is convincing. The symbolic denial of human status in such a context is incontrovertible, as is the presence of 'treatment' in the form of a legislative regime. Yet another focus could be on other forms of 'treatment' that might be associated with rough sleeping. For example, interactions with service providers, which have been described in some research as engendering misrecognition, and as 'infantilising'

13 *O'Rourke v. UK.*

14 Volker Busch-Geertsema, Dennis Culhane and Suzanne Fitzpatrick, 'Developing a Global Framework for Conceptualising and Measuring Homelessness' (2016) 55 *Habitat International* 124, 125.

15 See Volker Busch-Geertsema, 'Defining and Measuring Homelessness ' in Eoin O'Sullivan et al. (eds), *Homelessness Research in Europe: Fetschrift for Bill Edgar and Joe Doherty* (FEANTSA (European Observatory on Homelessness) 2010) for an overview of ETHOS – the European Typology on Homelessness and Housing Exclusion, which includes four 'conceptual' and 13 'operational' categories. This typology is reflected in more recent global models – see Busch-Geertsema, Culhane and Fitzpatrick.

16 *O'Rourke v. UK.*

17 On the U.S. context, see., e.g., Maria Foscarinis, 'Homelessness and Human Rights: Towards an Integrated Strategy' (2000) 19 *Louis U Pub L Rev* 327; Leonard C Feldman, *Citizens without Shelter: Homelessness, Democracy, and Political Exclusion* (Cornell University Press 2004), 2–4.

18 Jeremy Waldron, 'Homelessness and the Issue of Freedom' (1991) 39 *UCLA L Rev* 295.

and 'objectifying'.[19] Experiences of criminalisation or personal interactions that the individual believes have been 'infantilising' and so on could go hand-in-hand with experiences of rough sleeping. The approach in *O'Rourke*, with a focus on the experience of rough sleeping itself, is perhaps even more challenging. I will suggest that there is equally potential to make a strong argument on behalf of an individual like Mr O'Rourke that the experience of rough sleeping could be accepted as a social experience that results in symbolic denial of an individual's basic human status.

Before exploring this further, I address a potential objection: Some might fundamentally object that considering a link between rough sleeping and degrading treatment implies that rough sleeping is inherently or somehow inescapably degrading and reinforces problematic perceptions of those who are street homeless as 'victims'.[20] I do not intend to make any generalisable claims that rough sleeping is a universally negative experience.[21] It is not in fact possible to make generalisable claims from a human rights *law* perspective – claims about what does or does not amount to degrading treatment should always be individualised. Individualisation is inherent in the framework of human rights law.[22] At the same time, I agree with Foscarinis' observation that describing homelessness, in certain circumstances, 'as "involuntary" does not need to be interpreted as diminishing anyone's capacity for self-determination.'[23] Further, for a rights-holder to challenge the action/inaction of state authorities in a human rights claim is an

19 Lisa Hoffman and Brian Coffey, 'Dignity and Indignation: How People Experiencing Homelessness View Services and Providers' (2008) 45 *The Social Science Journal* 207 (research carried out in the U.S.).

20 Research on homelessness has found victimisation to be a common perspective, including amongst the press (for example, Henk Meert et al., *Homelessness in the Written Press: A Discourse Analysis* (Addressing Homelessness in Europe, 2004)) and welfare advocates (for example, Justeen Hyde, 'From Home to Street: Understanding Young People's Transitions into Homelessness' (2005) 28 *Journal of Adolescence* 171, 172).

21 Research has shown that the nature of the experience differs from person-to-person, and has evidenced positive manifestations of individuals' relationships. Megan Ravenhill, *The Culture of Homelessness* (Ashgate 2008) 161 and (narrative and practical) agency (e.g. Katherine M Boydell, Paula Goering and Tammy L Morrell-Bellai, 'Narratives of Identity: Re-presentation of Self in People Who Are Homeless' (2000) 10 *Qualitative Health Research* 26, 36; Alan Radley, Darrin Hodgetts and Andrea Cullen, 'Visualizing Homelessness: A Study in Photography and Estrangement' (2005) 15 *Journal of Community & Applied Social Psychology* 273).

22 The Strasbourg Court explicitly states this in, for example, *Hristozov and Others v. Bulgaria*, no. 47039/11; 358/12, ECHR 2012 (extracts). Individualisation within human rights law has indeed been a source of critique; see, e.g., Suzanne Fitzpatrick, Bo Bengtsson and Beth Watts, 'Rights to Housing: Reviewing the Terrain and Exploring a Way Forward' (2014) 31 *Housing, Theory and Society* 447. Other homelessness researchers, however, have argued that *a lack of individualised perspectives* in homelessness research is also problematic; see Radley, Hodgetts and Cullen, and Ravenhill, who raise a similar point as a critique of structuralist approaches to understanding homelessness (Ravenhill 30).

23 Foscarinis 334.

example of agency, not a denigration of it.[24] All human rights arguments portray the individual involved as a victim – that is the whole point. The present discussion is not an argument to see rough sleeping in general (or, of course, socio-economic deprivation in general) as degrading treatment.

A link between rough sleeping and degrading treatment emerges from an understanding of rough sleeping as a set of living conditions characterised by socially symbolic dynamics of exclusion. I note three related aspects recognised in homelessness research that evoke particularly strong associations with the interpretation of degradation that I have put forward: the inherently public nature of rough sleeping, the link between social- and self-perceptions, and the potential for symbolic exclusion from the human community. All of these points could be relevant in the further-imagined circumstances of the *O'Rourke* claim. The meaning of degradation's interconnected benchmarks and the meaning of the term 'treatment' reflect a social dimension – of socially based standards and socially constituted perceptions of when those standards are or are not being met. Rough sleeping has a strong social dimension because it is inherently public. It is (at least potentially) always publicly visible because it takes place in a space that is not private to the individual.[25] Feldman refers to the 'face-to-face' encounters[26] that are often experienced by those who are without homes, in public spaces. Such encounters might be argued to have particular symbolic power in that they might involve a very immediate communication of judgment about one's ability to live up to standards deemed fitting for human beings. Ravenhill cites the views of a research participant who was new to living on the streets:

> *Most people walk straight by, as if you're nothing, as if you don't exist. Some look down their noses at you. Some are really horrible and call you names. Kids are the worst because they come up and kick you when you're lying down. They can give you a right kicking.*[27]

An experience does not have to be actually publicly witnessed to be judged as degrading, but the presence of onlookers can cement feelings of humiliation (recall the idea of the 'humiliation dynamic').[28] In such encounters, the idea of 'regard' or 'ways of looking' is close-up and real as well as symbolic. It has been observed in homelessness research that negative *social* perceptions might sustain negative *self*-perceptions.[29] Several studies have also shown that homelessness impacts upon self-identity.[30] This echoes Klein's point about the social-embeddedness of

24 Just as experiences of rough sleeping have been shown to reveal agency not passivity on the part of individuals, the claiming of rights also displays agency; see Waldron in particular, 324; Hyde; Radley, Hodgetts and Cullen; Hoffman and Coffey.
25 Waldron.
26 Feldman 93.
27 A research participant named Tommy, cited in Ravenhill 157.
28 Chapter 4, p. 72.
29 Boydell, Goering and Morrell-Bellai 32.
30 Boydell, Goering and Morrell-Bellai 26.

one's 'sense of self'.[31] The term 'self-respect' was used in Chapter 4 to describe a form of self-regard that acknowledges one's elemental status as a member of the human community, and which can be undermined by experiences of grave humiliation. It was argued that erosion of self-respect occurs through experiences of profound powerlessness. The visibility and 'publicness' of rough sleeping are capable of reinforcing a social perception that an individual is powerless to protect vital interests in fulfilling basic needs; a basic need for shelter, most obviously, but also related abilities to live up to socially appropriate standards. Notable in homelessness research is individuals' concerns to maintain standards of personal hygiene and cleanliness.[32] We can imagine that the circumstances in *O'Rourke* could justify invoking also the 'will or conscience' benchmark. Chapter 4 described being driven to act against will or conscience as being forced by one or more external forces (other human beings, human institutions, human-made societal conditions) to behave in ways that actually or symbolically undermine one's capacity to direct one's behaviour such that this is understood to be socially inappropriate for a human being. We could also point to connections between being driven to act against will or conscience and an inability to resist the experience, which might itself be understood as a symptom of profound powerlessness. As argued in Chapter 4, profound powerlessness to protect vital interests is problematic in Margalit's view because it can result in symbolic exclusion from the community of human beings on the basis of a perception that an individual is less than human. Feldman foregrounds the grave impact of a lack of acknowledgement of personality (in the sense discussed in Chapter 4) of those who are without a home. He draws upon the language of misrecognition as a mode of denial of basic human status, specifically in the context of homelessness:

> *The extent to which homelessness is an injustice of both distribution and recognition is manifest strikingly in the double meaning attached to the word 'address', which indicates both a spatial location and a mode of intersubjective recognition. To have an address means to have a place of residence, and to be addressed means to be spoken to, recognized as a human subject in dialogue. To be homeless is to risk being addressless in both senses.*[33]

A woman named Jean who had experienced sleeping rough, interviewed in Radley et al., says: 'There are a lot of times when you think, I am not human anymore.'[34]

If it was argued on behalf of an individual, like Mr O'Rourke, that s/he had suffered degrading treatment, the idea of a relative assessment would come into play. The Strasbourg Court has continually affirmed the appropriateness of a relative assessment of all the circumstances of a particular case. The requirement for a

31 Donald C Klein, 'The Humiliation Dynamic: An Overview' (1991) 12 *The Journal of Primary Prevention* 93, 96.

32 E.g. Radley, Hodgetts and Cullen 281, 293.

33 Feldman 91.

34 Radley, Hodgetts and Cullen 291.

relative assessment might sometimes seem like a get-out clause, justifying 'only' an individualised focus. The Strasbourg Court has asserted that states do not have a general duty to house the homeless, under any of the Convention's provisions, including Article 3.[35] Morris portrays this perspective at play in the context of an Article 3-based decision in the UK: in her examination of a line of cases concerning the destitution of asylum seekers, Morris highlights how the judges deliberately interpreted 'treatment' in a way which clearly excluded 'the indigenous homeless'; they were not intended to be commented upon in any way.[36] The whole structure of the ECHR complaints system is a judicialised, individualised one (see point above regarding non-generalisable conclusions) and as such, the Strasbourg Court's insistence on a non-generalised, relative perspective should be unsurprising. However, a different question might be raised about a relative assessment. A requirement to take into account things like an individual's age and state of heath might seem incoherent in light of an interpretation of degrading treatment that draws attention to a most basic – shared – human status. 'Relativity' can nevertheless be accepted. It can be explained by the power of symbolism within the process of labelling certain experiences as degrading. The Court might judge certain things to have particular symbolic resonance. This would be a consideration when deciding, for example, whether a minor who is subjected to physical violence whilst detained in a room with two adults exercising power on behalf of the state represents a diminution of a minimal kind of regard or capacity; or, for example, whether an elderly person left alone in a hospital room wearing a nappy for 24 hours represents a diminution of a minimal kind of regard or capacity. The age of the individual and the degree of powerlessness in such examples might be judged to have a socially symbolic resonance that moves the experience 'over the threshold'. This makes sense in relation to the particular characteristics of an individual and also in relation to the factual peculiarities of a situation. For example, temporary accommodation with a shared toilet which is otherwise clean and adequate might not evoke degrading treatment, whereas temporary accommodation with a toilet that was not only shared but not enclosed, and which was used for several months, might evoke degrading treatment. On this view it makes sense that the special characteristics of a whole situation will be taken into account in judgments as to whether an experience should be considered as degrading in social fact.

I argue then, that Article 3's benchmarks of degradation can be identified through the prism of the public nature of rough sleeping, the link between social- and self-perceptions, and the potential for symbolic exclusion from the human community. This is an argument concerning the interpretation of one legal standard. For example, that it was a social experience (in the form of living conditions) that led to erosion of self-respect as a result of profound powerlessness (humiliation), and/or as a result of being driven to act in ways that undermine one's

35 *M.S.S. v. Belgium and Greece*, para. 249; *Shioshvili and Others v. Russia*, para. 80.
36 Lydia Morris, *Asylum, Welfare and the Cosmopolitan Ideal: A Sociology of Rights* (Routledge 2010) 55, 105.

capacity to independently direct one's own actions. It might be objected that the focus so far, essentially on the symbolic denial of human status, is likely, or least possibly, far more 'dramatic' than what Mr O'Rourke may actually have experienced sleeping rough on the streets of London – this really is the nub of this exercise, because imagining what experiences might have been stressed in a more developed argument on Mr O'Rourke's behalf provokes consideration of the right's interpretive boundaries.

From state obligations to state responsibility?

Even if we imagine that a convincing argument could be made on behalf of an individual that an experience of rough sleeping amounted to degrading treatment, what of the role of the individual, like in *O'Rourke*? To what extent is apparent voluntariness of the individual a barrier to a situation of rough sleeping triggering the protection of the right? In *O'Rourke*, the Court notes that *even if* the minimum threshold for engaging Article 3 had been reached, the State could not be held responsible because of the role played by the applicant himself in bringing about the complained-of suffering. In this section, I explore why social/legal/bureaucratic norms about individual responsibility are likely to overcome even the expansive scope of state obligations.

Chapter 2 gave an overview of state obligations applicable to Article 3, describing three forms of positive obligation. The form of state obligation that reflects the circumstances in *O'Rourke* is the third form of positive obligation: the obligation to take positive measures to protect individuals from suffering degrading treatment that stems from 'other' sources, *beyond* the state authorities. This obligation developed progressively out of an obligation to protect individuals from prohibited harm by the state's authorities. Chapter 2 described it as an obligation that has been pivotal to the development of Article 3's scope of application. The idea of 'sources' refers to who or what can inflict or bring about treatment.

This form of positive obligation to protect individuals from sources beyond the institutions of the state is often associated with the actions of third parties – other individuals or other states[37] – whereas Chapter 2 gave case-law evidence of the Strasbourg Court's acceptance that treatment does not have to be traceable to a particular active, identifiable inflictor of harm.[38] The 'other source' in a context like *O'Rourke* would be this kind of indeterminate source, rather than an identifiable third party. Treatment is located as 'living conditions'. Degrading treatment could be argued to stem from no one identifiable actor or group of actors.[39] This manifestation of the third form of positive obligation does not contradict the idea of 'subjection', which is an integral part of Article 3's text ('no one shall be subjected to ...'). The idea of subjection need not suggest the presence of a coercive

37 E.g. see the references to positive obligations in Ellie Palmer, *Judicial Review, Socio-economic Rights and the Human Rights Act* (Bloomsbury Publishing 2007) 58.

38 Chapter 2, pp. 38–40.

39 Webster 44–45.

will of another identifiable person. As I concluded from the interpretation of the benchmarks in Chapter 4, one can be driven to act by 'circumstances of nobody in particular's making'[40]; in the same way, one can be subjected to degrading treatment by external forces that lead to circumstances that are nobody in particular's making. The same caveat applies as it did in interpretation of the benchmarks: these circumstances should have a human, not natural, source to be understood as *degrading*. In other words, circumstances can be of nobody in particular's making, but they must be of somebody's making. The degrading character of a set of conditions derives from *social* interactions. This is recognised by scholars like Margalit, Raz and Berlin, cited in Chapter 4. Therefore, the idea of subjection in the text of Article 3 should be seen as compatible with recognising that degrading treatment, as the Strasbourg case-law suggests, can be understood to stem from an indeterminate source. The idea of degrading treatment being bought about by an indeterminate, amorphous source fits with what research tells us about the causes of homelessness, including street homelessness – they are multiply complex social causes; often not directly attributable to one time-circumscribed action/decision/incident.[41] The key point is that the breadth of this third form of positive obligation is such that it could encompass a situation like that in *O'Rourke*.

In respect of this form of positive obligation, the state will only be held responsible if it had specific knowledge of, or, judged reasonably, should have had knowledge of, the living conditions in question. This is an important limitation from a human rights law perspective. Further, on the basis of the '*Osman* test', as discussed in Chapter 2, the Court will ask whether the authorities did all that could be *reasonably expected* of them. This is a factual evaluation which asks whether a lack of action on the part of state authorities could be judged unreasonable at particular points in the sequence of events. The Court has acknowledged the need to avoid imposing an impossible burden upon the state when taking practical preventative action to protect particular individuals. The question is, could the state authorities reasonably have been expected to do more? For states, this removes the possibility of being held responsible for a violation of Article 3 if an individual suddenly appears and argues that s/he has experienced degrading treatment for which the state should be held responsible, when the state authorities had no specific knowledge of the circumstances. The human rights law analysis will look for a robust chain of events that points towards a lack of reasonable intervention on the part of the state authorities. Otherwise, there will be no link to state responsibility for a rights violation. This is not an easy test for an applicant to satisfy. In the context of circumstances like those in *O'Rourke*, and in the context of a claimed obligation to take positive measures to protect against degrading treatment that stems from an indeterminate source, the crucial link to state responsibility would derive from the nature of the relationship between a particular individual and particular authorities/institutional actors. Things that we know to be key contributory factors in causing homelessness, including rough

40 Chapter 4, pp. 81–82.
41 Ravenhill 95–143.

sleeping, could coherently be seen as part of an indeterminate source of degrading treatment. In the United Kingdom, homeless persons have for decades been understood as 'casualties of the welfare state'[42] and recent research has documented the impact of welfare benefit sanctions[43] and noted increases in all forms of homelessness, including rough sleeping, in the post-2010 age of austerity.[44] But these kinds of macro-level manifestations of state responsibility would not be enough to satisfy the '*Osman* test'; instead, an argument would have to be made about the particular chain of events and the reasonable implication of state actors in those events in order to make a relevant argument for state responsibility.

Therefore, the third form of positive obligation can be seen as broad enough to encompass a situation like that in *O'Rourke* but the success of an argument like this would be reliant not only upon the way that the experience itself is judged by the Court, but also on the strength of an applicant's argument that state authorities did not do all that could reasonably have been expected of them to intervene preventatively. This latter step, of making the link to state responsibility, would itself depend on overcoming the 'problem' of the apparent voluntariness of the individual.

The pull towards recognising *individual responsibility* is strong. It is the default position. Social norms suggest a default understanding of an individual's choices as free, and of free choice as mitigating the responsibility of others for one's own circumstances. That is, holding other actors responsible for one's own actions does not conform to modern conceptualisations of the individual as free agent. The individual as an autonomous agent exercising free will is at the heart of the way we see the modern world, of which human rights are a part. This is not a reflection of how individuals actually live or act in society; it is, as Douzinas recounts, a conceptualisation of the individual sovereign agent that is at the very foundations of modernity. Douzinas describes this conceptualisation as the characteristic feature of the modern age. In historical perspective, he traces how the individual free agent came to be the epicentre of a changed vision of the world.[45] He describes human rights as an aspect of legal rights within modern positive law systems and the legal person as the 'metaphysical companion of the subject of modernity'[46]:

> *Our whole anthropocentric universe has been built on the assumption that the subject is morally responsible for his freedom and legally liable for his actions. The law must disregard motives and circumstances, which introduce external*

42 Peter Robson and Paul Watchman, *Homelessness and the Law in Britain* (2nd edn, The Planning Exchange 1989) 8.
43 Homelesswatch, *A High Cost to Pay: The Impact of Benefit Sanctions on Homeless People* (2013).
44 See overview in Suzanne Fitzpatrick and Hal Pawson, 'Fifty Years Since Cathy Come Home: Critical Reflections on the UK Homelessness Safety Net' (2016) 16 *International Journal of Housing Policy* 543, 548–552.
45 C Douzinas, *The End of Human Rights: Critical Legal Thought at the Turn of the Century* (Hart Pub. 2000) 74.
46 Douzinas 239–240.

> *determinations, in order to support the foundation stone of our epoch, the claim that free will is the dominant principle and the subject the master of his fate and the world.*[47]

The Subject of law, including human rights law, is responsible for her actions. This foundational building block is revealed in the Court's statement in *O'Rourke*, that the applicant was 'largely responsible for his own deterioration following his eviction.'[48] When the applicant essentially argued that he had suffered degrading treatment by being subjected to 14 months of rough sleeping, the Court observed that he had brought this upon himself; he chose to put himself in this harmful situation that was now argued to constitute prohibited treatment and the state authorities could not be seen as responsible for his suffering of this (admittedly unfortunate) situation. The Court resisted the attribution of responsibility to the state for a situation that the applicant had apparently chosen to engage in. It resisted the attribution of state responsibility by resisting the denial of the applicant's individual responsibility.

These kinds of foundational dispositions around individual responsibility are not purely abstract. They are expressed in practical moral/political/legal judgments. They seem to colour in a particular way judgments pertaining to socio-economic deprivation.[49] They are visible in what I described above as the dominant narrative in *O'Rourke* and its concern with voluntariness and intention. And we see their outworking in the legal regulation of homelessness. Despite some accommodation in law of the impact of external factors on individual choices,[50] Watchman and Robson's 1980s study of homelessness and the law in Britain picks up on a long-standing concern of the authorities with 'intentional' homelessness.[51] They argue that historical hostility towards the homeless (including conceptualisation of homelessness as a criminal matter) shaped the pre-welfare state approach to homelessness in Great Britain and lingered more subtly in post-welfare state public policy models.[52] For example, they note how this hostility is reflected in 'moral censorship'[53] by local authorities. These authorities were reluctant to provide temporary accommodation to those whose need was foreseeably the result of 'rent arrears or anti-social behaviour,'[54] who were seen as undeserving of assistance. Despite progress in state responses to homelessness in 1970s and 1980s Britain, one group left behind were the 'intentional' homeless,[55] as a result of concerns

47 Douzinas 240.
48 *O'Rourke v. UK.*
49 Didier Fassin, in research on social humanitarianism in France, illustrates how social perceptions of poverty and the poor play out in political and bureaucratic interactions; see Didier Fassin, *Humanitarian Reason: A Moral History of the Present* (Universty of California Press 2011).
50 See footnote 42.
51 Robson and Watchman 10, 23.
52 Robson and Watchman 26–35.
53 Robson and Watchman 29.
54 Robson and Watchman 30.
55 Robson and Watchman 48.

about potentially deceitful or exploitative individuals.[56] The presence of intentionality restricted the duties of state authorities towards those requesting accommodation. The authors discuss 1980s legislation stating that a person would be intentionally homeless if s/he became homeless as a result of doing, or failing to do, something 'deliberately'; for example, as opined by a domestic judge, acts or omissions would be deliberate if a 'fair-minded bystander can say of the person evicted, "Well, I'm very sorry but he asked for it."'[57] The Strasbourg Court would not use such colourful language, but its decisions, in *O'Rourke* and in later admissibility decisions referring to *O'Rourke*, reveal similar perceptions around desert, intention, and individual responsibility for socio-economic deprivation. In *Budina v. Russia*, summarising the approach in *O'Rourke*, the Court confirmed the view that Mr O'Rourke's suffering had:

> *In any event, not been the result of State action rather than his own volition as he had been eligible for public support but had been unwilling to accept temporary accommodation and had refused two offers of permanent accommodation ...*[58]

The Court reiterates embedded moral/political/legal judgments pertaining to socio-economic deprivation.

By 'upholding' the individual's responsibility in this context, the Court risks implementing a simplistic view of *legal responsibility* practices. Legal responsibility – a 'product of a complex set of social practices'[59] – acknowledges a freedom of individual choice, but also acknowledges that freedom of choice is limited; the position differs depending on the function of the area of law in question.[60] According to Cane, it is 'readily conceded' that factors that render choice 'less than fully free' may weaken the case for holding a person responsible.[61] The Strasbourg Court, without contradicting the pre-eminence of individual responsibility, could concede that, in Raz's words, '[n]ot everything we willingly embrace is something we have freely or deliberately chosen from among various alternatives open to us.'[62] Indeed acceptance of a more complex model of individual responsibility is arguably implicit in the Court's Article 3 jurisprudence. The Court would not hold an individual responsible for suffering torture because s/he played a role in bringing it about; it would not say that the individual, for whatever reason, 'deserved' this treatment. It has continuously affirmed that an individual's own behaviour is not determinative of its assessment of whether prohibited

56 Robson and Watchman 103.
57 *Robinson v. Torbay Borough Council* [1982] 1 All ER 726 at 730, cited in Robson and Watchman 134.
58 *Budina v. Russia*, no. 45603/05, 18 June 2009.
59 Peter Cane, *Responsibility in Law and Morality* (Hart 2002) 56.
60 Cane 66–70.
61 Cane 100.
62 Joseph Raz, *The Morality of Freedom* (Clarendon Press 1986) 369.

treatment has occurred or will occur, including degrading treatment.[63] The idea of involuntariness on the part of the individual can indeed be seen as one part of what it means to be *driven to act* in particular ways; to be 'subjected' to degrading treatment. This view fits with the way that scholars have linked the wrongness of torture to an individual's *active* implication, highlighting the impact of the individual's role as, effectively, an accomplice in her or his own suffering.[64] At the very least, the Court can coherently recognise that not all choices are free. In a situation like in *O'Rourke*, if an individual wished to put forward an argument that her or his choices and actions were not 'willingly embraced' from 'among various alternatives', the Court should, at the very least, be able to accept this. Homelessness research and housing law both reflect the possibility of such 'choices'.[65] (Further, the individual could argue that her or his choices were only one element of multiply complex causes of the complained-of living conditions, in addition to, for example, changes to a system of welfare benefit sanctions).[66] An understanding of human rights law as operating on the basis of a conceptual paradigm of individual responsibility need not restrict the implementation of a more complex picture of such responsibility.

However, even if the Convention system is capable of accepting that an individual's choices do not undermine the possibility of degrading treatment or indeed can be part of the essence of degrading treatment, the default position of acknowledging individual responsibility seems difficult to overcome. This is not only because of perceptions of homelessness, but because of the nature of the Article 3 positive obligation and the indeterminate source of the alleged degrading treatment. That is, a simplistic view of legal responsibility practices may be avoidable but avoidance is not facilitated by the circumstances of the rough sleeping example. The example of rough sleeping is characterised by a combination of the individual's immediate and obvious choices *and* the state's more distant implication. This is crucial. The choices of the individual would be foregrounded in the application of the '*Osman* test' in examining a practical sequence of events, and would undermine an argument that state authorities could reasonably have been expected to intervene. The individual's own active responsibility would be prominent in a situation in which there is already a significant distance between that situation and the attribution of state responsibility. In the context of a positive obligation to take measures to protect against suffering that is *not* inflicted by state

63 See Chapter 2, p. 30.

64 See, e.g., David Sussman, 'What's wrong with torture?' (2005) 33 *Philosophy & Public Affairs* 1.

65 For example, in relation to young people who become homeless, research has acknowledged the lack of options, other than leaving than home, open to young people to remove themselves from harmful relationships; see Hyde 171–172. In the UK, domestic legislation has for decades instructed housing authorities to take into account personal factors and the condition of housing when they determine whether individuals have made themselves homeless 'intentionally'; see Robson and Watchman 107–112.

66 Homelesswatch.

agents, the prominent responsibility of the individual stands in the way of attributing responsibility to the state.

Chapter summary

This chapter has built upon the *O'Rourke* example as a way of contextualising and testing the interpretation of degrading treatment. This example provokes reflection on the boundaries of the right's meaning and scope of application. The discussion has focused on exploring the contributory elements as well as the barriers to an argument that living conditions in the form of rough sleeping, which the individual played an active role in bringing about, should amount to a violation of the right not to be subjected to degrading treatment. This is not the only kind of argument that could be made about rough sleeping in respect of Article 3[67] (or, of course, other rights) but it is the one that emerges from the claim in *O'Rourke* in which I chose to anchor this discussion. The discussion has looked at the example of rough sleeping within a legal human rights framework from the perspective of a rights-holder, and does not undermine the possibility of individuals experiencing rough sleeping in different and unique ways, as social science research evidences. I have stressed that recognising the possibility of a rights-holder's claim based on degrading treatment is as important, from the perspective of respecting individual agency, as recognising that generalised conclusions should not be drawn about individual experiences. The example suggests that the scope of meaning of degrading treatment is wide, on the basis of a conceptually narrow understanding of degradation but a conceptually broad understanding of treatment. Further, while the now significant breadth of positive obligations corresponds to an expansion in the right's scope of application, limits are placed on this by the reach of a state's responsibility. The scope of meaning *and* application of the right depends on socially embedded, context-dependent judgments about dignity violation and the attribution of responsibility.

In light of the relevant meaning of dignity in this context, if an individual like Mr O'Rourke wished to make a claim a strong argument could be made that an experience of rough sleeping should fall within the *meaning* of degrading treatment. The strength of such an argument would depend on the particular circumstances of the individual and the particular circumstances of the experience. In making or judging an argument, the guiding questions to ask are embedded in the benchmarks of degradation and in the meaning of treatment. The tipping point, or 'threshold' in Strasbourg terminology, is when the experience can be judged as a social one characterised by erosion of self-respect as a result of profound powerlessness and symbolic exclusion from the human community, the destruction of physical or moral strength to oppose the stripping of one's human status, the

67 It could be argued on behalf of an individual that the state inflicted degrading treatment by non-responsiveness to requests for assistance (see *Budina v. Russia*, no. 45603/05, 18 June 2009), which led to erosion of self-respect, exclusion from the human community, and so on.

breakdown of one's capacity to independently direct one's own actions, and/or injury to one's basic human status. This is the result of a limited meaning of degradation combined with a wide meaning of treatment. It is the result of a judgment about 'social facts', to use the terminology employed earlier in discussion of the benchmarks, which are inherently socially embedded and context-dependent.

The key determinant of success in a claim like *O'Rourke* is less likely to be the nature of the harm and more likely to be the nature of the state's involvement. Judgments about the reach of state responsibility are also socially embedded. This has been illustrated through one example of homelessness; an experience which has often been stigmatised on the basis of it having been 'self-induced'.[68] In this context, foundational social perceptions of individual responsibility seem likely to act as a strong counterpoint to the attribution of state responsibility. At the same time, judgments about the reach of state responsibility are also context-dependent. This is seen clearly in the discussion of the *Osman* test, applicable to states' obligation to protect individuals from degrading treatment that stems from non-state sources. This context-dependency suggests that even a tension between state responsibility and individual responsibility *could* be overcome on the basis of particular facts. Article 3's 'landmark' cases have emerged from combinations of either state control that is obvious and dignity violations that are less clearly defined (think *Ireland v. UK*), or strong perceptions of a dignity violation alongside less clear state control (think *D. v. UK*). A claim based on actively constituted socio-economic deprivation would similarly follow this pattern. A compelling dignity violation, perceived by the Court to be incontrovertible, would be required to overcome the powerful influence of foundational ideas of individual responsibility in favour of expanding state responsibility. It is the nature of the context-specific inhibitors or indicators of state responsibility that will determine a claim's success.

The example exposes questions at the extremes of degrading treatment's meaning and potential scope of application because it forces interpreters to confront the impact of the ideas of dignity and responsibility. When this impact is foregrounded, we can see the imprint of these ideas in those claims under Article 3 that have proved most contentious (from various perspectives) in recent decades: the Court's approach to the treatment of non-nationals suffering from serious health conditions,[69] and its approach to diplomatic assurances in expulsion cases.[70] Arguably, these limited contexts sparked intense criticism because they exposed points of tension around the threshold of state responsibility, and/or the threshold of dignity's meaning and influence. We can understand them to reflect an undercurrent of unanswered questions: What *should* be the influence of the apparently subjective and ambiguous dignity idea? What *should* states be held responsible for? The example considered in this chapter illustrates the need to understand what dignity means in the Article 3 context and to understand

68 Peter Robson, 'The House of Lords and Homeless People's Rights' (2000) 22 *The Journal of Social Welfare & Family Law* 415, 430.
69 *N. v. United Kingdom*, no. 26565/05, ECHR 2008.
70 *Saadi v. Italy* [GC], no. 37201/06, ECHR 2008.

judgments about dignity to be socially embedded. It illustrates also that the boundaries of the right not to be subjected to degrading treatment are the same as the boundaries of any other right and the boundaries of human rights law itself – the limits of state responsibility. Attribution of responsibility, whether in the sense of territorial, regulatory, physical, or knowledge-based control, is the 'red line' in any human rights claim; this becomes clear in contexts, like the example of rough sleeping, in which the site of responsibility is not obvious. The link to state responsibility is the inherent 'limitation' of the human rights law framework. In that sense, the example based in *O'Rourke* captures not only competing sites of responsibility but shared sites of incapacity, of individuals, of the Court, and perhaps even of states, to remedy violations of fundamental human dignity. In summary, the example in this chapter indicates that questions of dignity and responsibility are the key axes which determine the interpretive boundaries of the right not to be subjected to degrading treatment. These two ideas have a simultaneous expansionary and exclusionary impact, and they are inherently dependent on instances of socially embedded judgment.

References

Barak, A, *Purposive Interpretation* (Princeton University Press, 2005)

Boydell, KM, Goering, P and Morrell-Bellai, TL, 'Narratives of Identity: Re-presentation of Self in People who are Homeless' (2000) 10 *Qualitative Health Research* 26

Busch-Geertsema, V, 'Defining and Measuring Homelessness' in O'Sullivan, E et al. (eds), *Homelessness Research in Europe: Fetschrift for Bill Edgar and Joe Doherty* (FEANTSA (European Observatory on Homelessness) 2010)

Busch-Geertsema, V, Culhane, D and Fitzpatrick, S, 'Developing a Global Framework for Conceptualising and Measuring Homelessness' (2016) 55 *Habitat International* 124

Cane, P, *Responsibility in Law and Morality* (Hart, 2002)

Cassese, A, 'Can the Notion of Inhuman and Degrading Treatment be Applied to Socio-economic Conditions?' (1991) 2 *Eur J Int'l L* 141

Douzinas, C, *The End of Human Rights: Critical Legal Thought at the Turn of the Century* (Hart Publishing, 2000)

Fassin, D, *Humanitarian Reason: A Moral History of the Present* (University of California Press, 2011)

Feldman, LC, *Citizens Without Shelter: Homelessness, Democracy, and Political Exclusion* (Cornell University Press, 2004)

Fitzpatrick, S and Pawson, H, 'Fifty Years since Cathy Come Home: Critical Reflections on the UK Homelessness Safety Net' (2016) 16 *International Journal of Housing Policy* 543

Fitzpatrick, S, Bengtsson, B and Watts, B, 'Rights to Housing: Reviewing the Terrain and Exploring a Way Forward' (2014) 31 *Housing, Theory and Society* 447

Foscarinis, M, 'Homelessness and Human Rights: Towards an Integrated Strategy' (2000) 19 *Louis U Pub L Rev* 327

Hoffman, L and Coffey, B, 'Dignity and Indignation: How People Experiencing Homelessness View Services and Providers' (2008) 45 *The Social Science Journal* 207

Homelesswatch, *A High Cost to Pay: The Impact of Benefit Sanctions on Homeless People* (HomelessLink, 2013)

Hyde, J, 'From Home to Street: Understanding Young People's Transitions into Homelessness' (2005) 28 *Journal of Adolescence* 171

Klein, DC, 'The Humiliation Dynamic: An Overview' (1991) 12 *The Journal of Primary Prevention* 93

Meert, H et al., *Homelessness in the Written Press: A Discourse Analysis* (Addressing Homelessness in Europe, 2004)

Morris, L, *Asylum, Welfare and the Cosmopolitan Ideal: A Sociology of Rights* (Routledge, 2010)

Palmer, E, *Judicial Review, Socio-economic Rights and the Human Rights Act* (Bloomsbury Publishing, 2007)

Radley, A, Hodgetts, D and Cullen, A, 'Visualizing Homelessness: A Study in Photography and Estrangement' (2005) 15 *Journal of Community & Applied Social Psychology* 273

Ravenhill, M, *The Culture of Homelessness* (Ashgate, 2008)

Raz, J, *The Morality of Freedom* (Clarendon Press, 1986)

Robson, P, 'The House of Lords and Homeless People's Rights' (2000) 22 *The Journal of Social Welfare & Family Law* 415

Robson, P and Watchman, P, *Homelessness and the Law in Britain* (2nd edn, The Planning Exchange, 1989)

Sussman, D, 'What's Wrong with Torture?' (2005) 33 *Philosophy & Public Affairs* 1

Waldron, J, 'Homelessness and the Issue of Freedom' (1991) 39 *UCLA L Rev* 295

Webster, E, 'Medical-Related Expulsion and Interpretation of Article 3 of the European Convention on Human Rights' (2013) 6 *Inter-American and European Human Rights Journal* 36

Wright, JD, 'The Worthy and Unworthy Homeless' (1988) 25 *Society* 64

7 From degrading treatment to torture, cruel and inhuman treatment

I suggested in Chapter 1 that the interpretive scope of degrading treatment was relevant for thinking more broadly about the interpretive scope of the right not to be subjected to torture. I suggested that degrading treatment was of particular interest because it is often perceived to be closest to the boundary between harm that is absolutely prohibited under human rights law and harm that is not, and because it linguistically evokes most immediately the idea of human dignity. Having formed an interpretation of degrading treatment, this section offers reflections on what this interpretation implies for the interpretive scope of the other constitutive elements of the right not to be subjected to torture and the relationship between those elements. The interpretive scope of each element, and the relationships between them, are important because each element of the text should be understood individually *and* within the context of the right in order to optimise (i.e. facilitate in a transparent way) interpretations about which experiences should or should not be captured by the text in any given situation.

Existing literature is a patchwork of law, philosophy and psychology perspectives. Sometimes these perspectives come together and sometimes they do not. They *should* come together to illuminate each of the forms of harm within the right. The most substantial aspect of this literature focuses on the meaning of torture. There is in-depth legal literature. One branch of this literature is doctrinal and focuses on torture in contexts of deprivation of liberty[1] or physical control,[2] and another branch is critical and brings a feminist challenge, primarily to the 'acquiescence of a public official' requirement in supranational human rights law.[3] There is in-depth philosophy and psychology literature focusing on the impact of

1 For example, Malcolm D Evans and Rod Morgan, *Preventing Torture – A Study of the European Convention for the Prevention of Torture and Inhuman or Degrading Treatment or Punishment* (Clarendon Press 1998), and Nigel Rodley and Matt Pollard, *The Treatment of Prisoners under International Law* (3rd Edition edn, Oxford University Press 2009).

2 Dewulf refers to contexts in which a perpetrator exercises 'factual control' over a victim; Steven Dewulf, *The Signature of Evil: (Re)Defining Torture in International Law* (Intersentia 2011) 535–551.

3 See Chapter 1, footnote 2.

torture on the individual and its moral wrongness.[4] In respect of cruel and inhuman treatment, there is very little dedicated literature.[5] From a human rights law perspective, most insight about the meaning of these elements of the right comes indirectly from discussions of torture and what marks it out from the other elements. If the interpretations of, in particular cruel and inhuman treatment are not fully developed, our understanding of the relationships cannot be fully developed. The existing sources then, present a disjointed picture.

This chapter references some of this literature in touching upon questions of the meaning, impact and wrongness of torture, cruel, and inhuman treatment. It starts from the meaning of torture and its relationship to degrading treatment, and goes on to consider how cruel and inhuman treatment might conceptually fit into this picture in terms of their specific meanings and their relationships with torture and degrading treatment. The aim of this chapter is to begin to draw out implications of the interpretation of degrading treatment for understanding the broader right. The discussion will only make sense in light of the interpretation of degrading treatment that I have put forward. It does not make detailed arguments. Each element of the text should be subject to its own multi-perspective, in-depth interpretation as this book has aimed to do in respect of degrading treatment. Instead, this chapter aims to make the point that the interpretation of each element should sit coherently within the conceptual umbrella of the right, and that a richer understanding of each element leads to a richer understanding of the interpretive scope of the whole.

Torture

The most prominent legal articulation of torture is found in Article 1 UNCAT.[6] As is well-known, Article 1 describes torture as the intentional infliction of severe physical or mental pain or suffering for a purpose, and the responsibility of the state under the Convention derives from the implication of a public official:

> *For the purposes of this Convention, the term 'torture' means any act by which severe pain or suffering, whether physical or mental, is intentionally inflicted on a person for such purposes as obtaining from him or a third person information or a confession, punishing him for an act he or a third person has committed or is suspected of having committed, or intimidating or coercing him or a third person, or for any reason based on discrimination of any kind, when such pain or*

4 For example, David Sussman, 'What's wrong with torture?' (2005) 33 *Philosophy & Public Affairs* 1, and Andreas Maier, 'Torture: how denying moral standing violates human dignity' in P Kaufman et al. (eds), *Humiliation, Degradation, Dehumanization: Human Dignity Violated* (Springer 2010).

5 Examples of work that does discuss cruel treatment or inhuman treatment are Colin Dayan, *The Story of Cruel and Unusual* (MIT Press 2007), and Kevin J Murtagh, 'What is Inhuman Treatment?' (2011) 6 *Criminal Law and Philosophy* 21.

6 Rodley and Pollard 85.

> *suffering is inflicted by or at the instigation of or with the consent or acquiescence of a public official or other person acting in an official capacity.*[7]

Article 2 of the Inter-American Convention to Prevent and Punish Torture (IACPPT), however, articulates torture differently.[8] There is a similar public acquiescence/non-intervention dimension required in order to invoke the state's responsibility for a violation but Article 2 of this Convention states:

> *For the purposes of this Convention, torture shall be understood to be any act intentionally performed whereby physical or mental pain or suffering is inflicted on a person for purposes of criminal investigation, as a means of intimidation, as personal punishment, as a preventive measure, as a penalty, or for any other purpose. Torture shall also be understood to be the use of methods upon a person intended to obliterate the personality of the victim or to diminish his physical or mental capacities, even if they do not cause physical pain or mental anguish.*[9]

This first paragraph of Article 2 does not refer to the severity of pain or suffering and it adds an additional element. It describes torture as the intentional infliction of physical or mental pain or suffering for a purpose, including in ways that aim to 'obliterate the personality of the victim or to diminish his physical or mental capacities, even if they do not cause physical pain or mental anguish'.[10] It encompasses this additional reference to the personality of the victim and the diminution of the victim's physical or mental capacities and removes the reference to severity of suffering.

This approach also differs from the existing prominent approaches in the legal literature. This literature combines a focus on meanings and relationships (although the focus is on the meaning and distinctiveness of torture and its relationship to cruel/inhuman and *not* degrading treatment). One prominent approach highlights *purpose* as the key feature that distinguishes torture from cruel/inhuman treatment[11] (not degrading treatment). Torture and cruel/inhuman treatment inflict equally 'severe' suffering and degrading treatment is at the

7 United Nations General Assembly, *Convention Against Torture and Other Cruel, Inhuman or Degrading Treatment or Punishment* (adopted 10 December 1984, entered into force 26 June 1987) 1465 UNTS 85. Rodney and Pollard observe that the understanding of torture as causing 'severe' pain and suffering is common across the different arms of international and regional human rights law (and international criminal law); Rodley and Pollard 144.

8 See Dewulf 203–205 discussing the approach of the IACPPT to the definition of torture.

9 Organisation of American States, *Inter-American Convention to Prevent and Punish Torture* (adopted 9 December 1985, entered into force 28 February 1987), 67 OASTS.

10 *Inter-American Convention to Prevent and Punish Torture*, Article 2.

11 See Rodley and Pollard 100. See also their analysis of the approach in some aspects of international criminal law, in which purpose and not severity of pain or suffering distinguishes torture from cruel and inhuman treatment; at 116–117.

other end of what then seems to be a two-point severity threshold.[12] Another prominent approach additionally highlights the *powerlessness* of the victim. Nowak and McArthur point to physical powerlessness as a result of physical control in detention as a key distinguishing feature of torture.[13] Nowak has described cruel/inhuman treatment as involving the 'infliction of severe pain or suffering' and he marks out degrading treatment as essentially different, not on the basis of lowest-severity but because it has a special focus on humiliation. Degrading treatment, he writes, is the intentional infliction of any 'humiliation' even if the pain or suffering is not severe.[14] (Note that Nowak is concerned with a restricted context of law-enforcement, which is significantly narrower than the ECHR-based interpretation of degrading treatment). The advantage of the IACPPT approach to the meaning of torture is that it foregrounds a *coherent conceptual connection* between torture and degrading treatment, and arguably then between all of the elements of the right.

A conceptual connection is reflected in Article 2 IACPPT's additional reference to the personality and physical or mental capacities of the victim and the omission of a severity dimension. The first aspect is significant because it echoes the benchmarks of degrading treatment. This in turn allows us to see torture and degrading treatment as *essentially* the same kind of harm. The second is important because it reinforces this view of torture and degrading treatment as essentially the same kind of harm by removing the temptation to mark torture out on the basis of severity of pain and suffering of the victim. By doing so, it simultaneously removes the temptation to perceive cruel, inhuman and especially degrading treatment as less severe. The conceptual connections to degrading treatment that I have begun to explore here – from injury to personality and minimal capacities to social relationships, human status, powerlessness, and exclusion – show that degrading treatment and torture are coherently conceptually linked by the text of the right. Opening these doors is an advantage of the IACPPT approach over the UNCAT approach to the legal meaning of the term 'torture'.

Torture can still be seen as different but it can be seen as contextually, not essentially, different. Torture can be seen as different on the basis of its more *intense communication of the perpetrator's intention to destroy the victim's personality in pursuit of some goal (purpose) and the victim's close-up experience of that intention.* From the perspective of a conceptual connection between torture and degrading treatment, an explanation for the distinctiveness of contexts of torture would seem to be found in a victim's inescapable experience of a perpetrator's intense intention to 'obliterate' her or his human status. The proximity of the intention of other human beings seems significant. Degrading treatment is also

12 Rodley and Pollard 124–125.

13 Manfred Nowak and Elizabeth McArthur, 'The Distinction between Torture and Cruel, Inhuman or Degrading Treatment' (2006) 16 *Torture* 147.

14 Manfred Nowak, 'What Practices Constitute Torture? US and UN Standards' (2006) 28 *Hum Rts Q* 809, 839–840. Nowak understands cruel/inhuman treatment as treatment that occurs in detention but lacks other elements of torture, or that occurs outside of detention and is not proportional.

something that has a human source,[15] but the difference in contexts of torture can be seen as the close proximity of intention to undermine another's human status. The intention refers to the perpetrator's intent to undermine another's human status; the purpose refers to the reason for doing so. Human rights law and some human rights scholars have understood the pursuit of a goal to be part of the meaning of torture but they have also recognised that the pursuit of a goal (a purpose) is not unique to torture. It can also be found in cruel, inhuman and degrading treatment. The relevance of purpose is perhaps more in the intention that it engenders. It is the intensity of intention to destroy the victim's basic human status in pursuit of a goal that can be seen as unique. And it is the intensity of this intention *on the part of other human beings* that should also be seen as constitutive of torture.[16] The presence of a clear intention on the part of other human beings recalls the explanation given by Silver et al. of the significance of an audience in humiliation – the context makes it impossible for the victim to reinterpret the treatment as something else[17]; as something other than an intention to 'obliterate' her or his basic status as a human being and member of the human community. Oliver, discussing dehumanisation, refers to torture as a magnification of a 'logic of dehumanisation'[18] – torture as 'magnification' is a helpful idea. If exclusion is magnified it is more difficult not to see, or as Silver et al. say, to reinterpret. Such magnification might be seen as the rationale for understanding torture to give rise to a 'special stigma', as has been the rhetoric of the ECtHR.[19] From the way that the ECtHR has used this label it is not wholly clear whether it understands this special stigma to derive from the nature of the harm itself or from a heightened blameworthiness when public officials are directly or indirectly involved, or perhaps a combination of both. Arguably, we should understand any special stigma to derive from the nature of the harm as an archetypal experience of symbolic exclusion, which is inherently expressed in the singling out of torture within the text of the broader right. We should understand a special stigma to derive from torture as a social experience in which human beings demonstrate, often in a strikingly immediate way, to other human beings that they are profoundly powerless to protect vital interests.[20] This is how I understand the significance of powerlessness as constitutive of torture. Powerlessness as physical inescapability through detention/restraint is a key element, as Nowak suggests,

15 See Chapter 4, pp. 81–82.
16 See Maier's 'relational account' of the moral wrongness of torture; Maier.
17 See Chapter 4, p. 72.
18 Sophie Oliver, 'Dehumanization: Perceiving the Body as (In)human' in P Kaufman et al. (eds), *Humiliation, Degradation, Dehumanization: Human Dignity Violated* (Springer 2010) 93.
19 *Ireland v. UK*, judgment of 18 January 1978, Series A, no. 25, para. 167; and more recently *Al Nashiri v. Poland*, no. 28761/11, 24 July 2014, para. 508.
20 I suggest that torture can be seen as the archetype of harm within the legal right as opposed to suggesting anything beyond this context. See Bernstein who forcefully argues that rape has the same essence of moral injury as torture, and considers why this has been the case in law; JM Bernstein, *Torture and Dignity: An Essay on Moral Injury* (University of Chicago Press 2015) Chapter 3.

but it is key *because* it is so strongly symbolic of powerlessness in the more profound sense of inability to protect vital interests.[21] As Kuch writes, all humiliation is symbolic.[22] In the case of torture, the *demonstration* to the victim of profound powerlessness symbolises exclusion.[23] For these reasons, torture can be described as an archetype of symbolic exclusion from the human community.

This approach to understanding torture is a departure from prominent legal approaches. This includes the approaches of Rodley and Pollard and Nowak and McArthur, who highlight key distinguishing features of purpose and powerless. It is also a departure from the more detailed analysis of the meaning of torture (as opposed to the other forms of harm) offered by Dewulf, although it shares several similar elements. Both approaches maintain the place of torture as an 'epitome' of harm within the right.[24] They share a similar focus on victim-perpetrator relationships, the presence of intent on the part of a perpetrator, and the pursuit of some goal by a perpetrator.[25] The understanding that I have outlined differs in the emphasis that it places on the intensity of communication of a perpetrator's intent to destroy the victim's basic human status, and in the meaning that it gives to the idea of powerlessness. This understanding has synergies with other, non-legal, accounts of torture. Notably, the account given by JM Bernstein, whose approach gives rich substance to some of the points that I have drawn from current legal approaches and the interpretation of degrading treatment. His account, to which I cannot do justice here, includes extreme helplessness as one characteristic of torture,[26] and on torture's effect of breaking, or devastating, the victim: 'whatever its final purpose, torture is a process of devastation'[27]; an '*active* non-recognition of the sufferer's humanity'.[28] Fundamentally, the point of the present reflections on the meaning of torture is not to propose a detailed alternative definition; Dewulf correctly observes the difficulties inherent in this task and the inadequacy of the range of international law approaches.[29] The point of the present reflections is to show that the interpretation of degrading treatment can help to rethink the interpretation of torture, and the other forms of harm.

This way of thinking about torture, rooted in conceptual connections to degrading treatment, implies that torture is singled out as *one form* of cruel/inhuman/degrading treatment. As suggested above, it is essentially the same kind of harm, singled out because it is an archetype of symbolic exclusion, and so an archetype of injury to dignity as an elemental status. Referring to cruel, inhuman

21 See Chapter 4, pp. 74–76.
22 Hannes Kuch, 'The Rituality of Humiliation: Exploring Symbolic Vulnerability' in P Kaufman et al. (eds), *Humiliation, Degradation, Dehumanization: Human Dignity Violated* (Springer 2010) 47–48.
23 Kuch 52–53.
24 Dewulf 469.
25 Dewulf 535–551.
26 Bernstein 109.
27 Bernstein 77.
28 Bernstein 104.
29 Dewulf 449.

or degrading treatment as the *'other'* forms of harm should not imply some kind of lesser status, but torture's status as an archetypal example of them. The UDHR and ICCPR do not use the term 'other' in their formulation of the right, but 'other' is used in the UNCAT.[30] Some authoritative interpreters have suggested that torture is one type of cruel, inhuman or degrading treatment[31] as have some authors. Nowak has described torture as a 'particularly serious and reprehensible form' of cruel, inhuman and degrading treatment; as an 'aggravated form'.[32] Perhaps the idea of torture as 'aggravated' remains useful. Rodley and Pollard discuss the drafting process leading up to the UN General Assembly's Declaration on the Protection of All Persons from Being Subjected to Torture or Other Cruel, Inhuman or Degrading Treatment or Punishment. The first draft of the Declaration put forward in 1975 defined torture as 'an aggravated form of cruel, inhuman or degrading treatment or punishment'.[33] Rodney and Pollard observe that the idea of torture as an aggravated form of inhuman treatment has mostly fallen away, except in the ECHR case-law.[34] 'Aggravation' is unhelpful if it is linked to severity, but it seems otherwise conceptually coherent if it captures the idea that torture is an example of cruel/inhuman/degrading treatment.

Cruel and inhuman treatment

This way of thinking about torture and its place within the text also has implications for our understanding of the legal meanings of the terms 'cruel' and 'inhuman', although these meanings are less easily circumscribed than the meaning of torture. The key implication is that the meaning of these forms of harm should be seen as coherently conceptually linked into the whole. The introductory chapter noted that as early as 1969 the EComHR stated that all torture was necessarily inhuman and degrading, and all inhuman treatment was degrading. The idea that all torture is cruel, inhuman and degrading makes sense but it should not automatically follow that all cruel treatment is inhuman and degrading, and so on and so forth. The question needs to be asked by exploring the legal meaning of each term individually within context. We should insist that the words 'cruel', 'inhuman' and 'degrading' mean unique if obviously related things.[35] *Legal* interpretations at least, which are ultimately constrained by the text, should take seriously the meaning of each word.

30 United Nations General Assembly, *Universal Declaration of Human Rights* (10 December 1948) 217 A (III), Article 5; United Nations General Assembly, *International Covenant on Civil and Political Rights* (adopted 16 December 1966, entered into force 23 March 2976) 999 UNTS 171, Article 7; UNCAT, Article 16.
31 For example, the Inter-American Court of Human Rights as noted in Rodley and Pollard 113.
32 Nowak 818 and 839 respectively.
33 Rodley and Pollard 30.
34 Rodley and Pollard 87.
35 See Jeremy Waldron, 'Inhuman and Degrading Treatment: The Words Themselves' (2010) 23 *Canadian Journal of Law and Jurisprudence* 269.

It is conceptually coherent to associate cruel treatment with inhuman treatment. The words 'cruel' and 'inhuman' invoke an agent; a 'someone' who acts in a cruel or inhuman way. Waldron observes this when he notes that 'inhuman' is often understood as an 'agent-centred' idea.[36] I think the same can be said of the idea of cruelty. In Radin's discussion of cruelty, which she addresses in light of the United States' constitutional prohibition of cruel and unusual punishment, the attitudes and actions of the 'inflictor' of cruelty are prominent.[37] This agent-centred perspective on the idea of cruelty is reflected in the United States' Eighth Amendment jurisprudence and its focus on intent of those responsible.[38] Human rights case-law gives little insight. Cruel treatment has not tended to stand alone in the way that torture, inhuman treatment and degrading treatment have in human rights case-law.[39] The principal insight given by the case-law is interpreters' perception that it has more affinity with inhuman treatment than degrading treatment. The ECtHR, although Article 3 ECHR does not include the term 'cruel', associates it with inhuman treatment, principally as a way of explaining what it understands by 'torture'. It continues to refer back to *Ireland v. UK* and to describe torture as 'deliberate inhuman treatment causing very serious and cruel suffering'.[40] It used the term in a different context in the case of *Salakhov and Islyamova v. Ukraine* concerning the attitudes of the state authorities in the face of the applicant's pleas for assistance. The Court condemned the authorities' 'cynical, indifferent and cruel attitude'[41] and arrived at a finding of inhuman treatment. The idea of a 'cruel attitude' as an element of inhuman treatment brings us back to the idea of a perpetrator's perspective, which I understand as a key element of cruel and inhuman treatment.

The ECHR case-law foregrounds another element that is useful for understanding cruel and inhuman treatment – *indifference*. This is seen in cases in which the Court clearly identifies inhuman treatment specifically, standing apart from torture or from degrading treatment. The ECtHR has commonly linked inhuman treatment to experiences of physical violence,[42] but its early cases also arrived at findings of inhuman treatment in contexts that seem to specifically

36 Waldron 279.

37 Margaret Jane Radin, 'The Jurisprudence of Death: Evolving Standards for the Cruel and Unusual Punishments Clause' (1978) 126 *U Pa L Rev* 989, 1043.

38 See, e.g., Dayan 27–33.

39 See Chapter 1, pp. 2–4.

40 E.g. *Gafgen v. Germany*, no. 22978/05, ECHR 2010, paras 90 and 108; *Taylan v. Turkey*, no. 32051/09, 3 July 2012, para. 39; *El-Masri v. The Former Yugoslav Republic of Macedonia*, no. 39630/09, 13 December 2012, para. 197.

41 *Salakhov and Islyamova v. Ukraine*, no. 28005/08, 14 March 2013, para. 204. 'Cruel' was used in this context in a Partly Dissenting Opinion in the earlier case of *Çakıcı v. Turkey* [GC], 8 July 1999, Reports of Judgments and Decisions 1999-IV, Partly Dissenting Opinion of Judge Thomassen Joined by Judges Jungwiert and Fischbach.

42 E.g. *Rehbock v. Slovenia*, no. 29462/95, ECHR 2000-XII; *Ognyanova and Choban v. Bulgaria*, no. 46317/99, 23 February 2006; *Gafgen v. Germany*; *Subaşı and Çoban v. Turkey*, no. 20129/07, 9 July 2013.

condemn an attitude of indifference on the part of state agents. In *Selçuk and Asker v. Turkey* the Court reached a finding of inhuman treatment, contrary to the Commission's finding of inhuman and degrading treatment. The Court condemned State security agents' premeditation and their attitudes of ignoring the protests of the applicants as they watched their homes and belongings being burned to the ground.[43] The Court has arrived at a finding of inhuman treatment in subsequent similar cases.[44] Inhuman treatment has been found very often in cases concerning the experiences of relatives of disappeared persons; again a context in which the Court condemns the attitudes and manners of the authorities. This category of case is the second largest in terms of number of findings of inhuman treatment after physical violence.[45] This category has now expanded to include attitudes and responses of the authorities in other contexts, as in *Salakhov and Islyamova v. Ukraine*, in which a mother had witnessed what the Court described as the 'slow death'[46] of her son in detention, deprived of necessary medical care, in the face of the authorities' indifference:

> *The Court notes that, as soon as the second applicant became aware of the disease of her son, who was in detention, she took every effort to save his life, appealing to the hospitals, prosecution authorities and courts involved. Nonetheless, the first applicant continued to be detained even after the prosecution had agreed to his release given the gravity of his health condition … Neither was he released after the verdict had been pronounced in his case with the penalty being limited to a fine and not providing for any custodial sentence … His mother, the second applicant, could only passively witness this in a state of complete helplessness. Furthermore, her complaints about the underestimation of the seriousness of her son's condition were disregarded, even though later they were found to be well-grounded … Lastly, the Court observes that even after the death of the first applicant, the authorities manifested an equally unacceptable attitude towards the second applicant, in particular, by ignoring her requests to get access to her son's medical file.*[47]

In cases like these there is a theme of condemning the culpability of identifiable individual or institutional agents who showed such indifference towards individuals seeking their assistance. Culpability (as something different to intention and something more than simply state responsibility under the Convention) permeate

43 *Selçuk and Asker v. Turkey*, judgment of 24 April 1998, *Reports* 1998-II, paras 77–78.
44 E.g. *Bİlgİn v. Turkey*, no. 23819/94, 16 November 2000; *Dulaş v. Turkey*, no. 25801/94, 30 January 2001; *Yöyler v. Turkey*, no. 26973/95, 24 July 2003; *Altun v. Turkey*, no. 24561/94, 1 June 2004; *Benzer and Others v. Turkey*, no. 23502/06, 12 November 2013.
45 E.g. *Orhan v. Turkey*, no. 25656/94, 18 June 2002; *Akdeniz v. Turkey*, no. 25165/94, 31 May 2005; *Janowiec and Others v. Russia*, no. 55508/07; 29520/09, ECHR 2012; *Sultygov and Others v. Russia*, no. 42575/07, 9 December 2014.
46 *Salakhov and Islyamova v. Ukraine*, no. 28005/08, 14 March 2013, para. 204.
47 *Salakhov and Islyamova v. Ukraine*, para. 203.

the ECtHR's findings of inhuman treatment across the range of contexts in which it has featured: *Mubilanzila Mayeka and Kaniki Mitunga v. Belgium* concerning detention and deportation of a five-year-old non-national child, in which the Court emphasises the attitudes of the authorities, whose actions 'demonstrated such a total lack of humanity towards someone of her age'[48]; *Gorodnitchev v. Russia* (an early case to arrive at a finding of inhuman treatment in respect of detention conditions) concerning a complete failure to ensure medical care and a prescribed diet to the applicant (including serious lack of proper records being kept) and his detention in solitary confinement[49]; and *Denis Vasilyev v. Russia* in a non-detention context concerning the authorities' 'vicious circle of shifted responsibility and multiple failings.'[50] Such cases highlight asymmetric power relationships characterised by indifference on the part of the actors holding power.

I understand an expression of indifference within a dependent relationship as central to what links cruel and inhuman treatment and what makes them both distinctive in relation to degrading treatment. As noted above, our understanding of these other terms would benefit from in-depth interpretation and so I only indicate here where I think such interpretations might go on the basis of the interpretation of degrading treatment that I have put forward. Cruel and inhuman treatment can be seen as linked by the relevance of an agent-centred perspective and a context of dependency also seems significant. It need not be physical dependency (as in detention contexts), but dependency in the sense of practical dependency upon other human beings to allow one to protect some vital interest (in Margalit's sense).[51] The combination of agent-centredness and contexts of dependency could help to make sense of a dimension of culpability that I noted in the ECHR case-law. Cruel and inhuman treatment can be seen to convey something about *a relationship between individual human actors that is characterised by immediately experienced power asymmetry and indifference as to the human status of the powerless individual(s)*. This direction of understanding is conceptually coherent from the point of view of understanding how torture might be seen as a kind of progression from cruel and inhuman treatment – as an archetype of cruel, inhuman and degrading treatment on the basis of its intense communication, not only of indifference but of the perpetrator's intention to destroy the victim's personality in pursuit of some goal (purpose), and not only of the victim's experience of a relationship with other human beings but the proximity of the victim's experience of an intention to destroy her or his personality within that relationship. This direction of understanding is also conceptually coherent from the point of view of understanding how degrading treatment might be seen to relate to cruel and

48 *Mubilanzila Mayeka and Kaniki Mitunga v. Belgium*, no. 13178/03, *Reports* 2006-XI, para. 69. See also *Ghorbanov and Others v. Turkey*, no. 28127/09, 3 December 2013.

49 *Gorodnitchev v. Russia*, no. 52058/99, 24 May 2007, in particular paras 95–96. An example of a more recent inhuman treatment detention conditions case is found in, e.g., *Mircea Dumitrescu v. Romania*, no. 14609/10, 30 July 2013.

50 *Denis Vasilyev v. Russia*, no. 32704/04, 17 December 2009, para. 121.

51 See Chapter 4, pp. 74–76.

inhuman treatment – as different but connected through the experience of profound powerlessness to protect vital interests and an experience of symbolic exclusion from the human community. Cruel and inhuman treatment can be understood as different from degrading treatment because of a prominent indifferent regard on the part of identifiable actors towards the victim. The relationship between the parties is in closer proximity; it is a relationship between individual human actors that is characterised by immediately experienced power asymmetry. At the same time, cruel and inhuman treatment can be understood as connected to degrading treatment because, if the protection of vital interests is at stake, an experience of callous indifference from other human beings upon whom one is dependent can lead to an experience of symbolic exclusion. Oliver's analysis of dehumanisation (which I understand as a process of moving towards the inhuman) includes a strong focus on the idea of exclusion.[52] Discussing Haslem's understanding of dehumanisation from a psychology perspective, she refers to dehumanisation as a process of animalisation or mechanisation.[53] A similar perspective is found in Margalit's brief reference to 'nonhuman' treatment (which he argues can include treating humans as if they were objects, machines, animals or subhuman (the latter 'includes treating adults as children')).[54] We see here a conceptual connection to degrading treatment. Note that these forms of nonhuman treatment are associated with *degradation* in Waldron's discussion of that term; he notes some similarities to Margalit's approach[55] to nonhuman treatment. I understand cruel and inhuman treatment therefore, as simply different to degrading treatment rather than as more severe or more serious, and as conceptually threaded together and so as likely to often co-exist. Further research should tell us more about what cruel and inhuman treatment mean but these reflections being to point towards a coherent way of understanding the distinctiveness of experiences of cruel and inhuman treatment and how they fit within the broader right.

Chapter summary

The point I have sought to make is that these reflections on the meaning of torture, cruel and inhuman treatment indicate ways in which the interpretation of degrading treatment can be used to inform interpretation of the right as a whole. This book's interpretation of degrading treatment points towards an understanding of the broader right not to be subjected to torture, cruel, inhuman or degrading treatment or punishment as connected by a unified conceptual core. It points towards an understanding of the broader right as expressing a conceptually-unified kind of harm, of which torture is an archetypal expression. Cruel, inhuman and degrading treatment can all be seen as social experiences[56] but they are

52 Oliver 86–87.
53 Oliver 88–89.
54 Avishai Margalit, *The Decent Society* (Harvard University Press 1996) 89.
55 Waldron 282–283.
56 The term 'punishment' can also be readily understood as a social experience.

distinctive in different ways. It makes sense then that particular experiences can but need not involve more than one form of harm. In terms of the parameters of the right as a whole, these reflections on the basis of degrading treatment's interpretation indicate why the 'other' forms of harm are at the heart of the right, and not peripheral as is sometimes the impression. It is right that there should be no difference in terms of legal consequences of a finding of one form or the other. The future interpretive scope of the right as a whole, as with degrading treatment specifically, will turn upon the axes of dignity and responsibility.

This discussion, and this book in general, has been motivated by the claim that a more developed and reasoned idea of the relationship between the forms of harm matters. More in-depth interpretations will emerge not only from human rights jurisprudence (although authoritative interpreters have an important role to play because they should be very clear about where a particular form of harm is located in any claim based on the prohibition of torture, cruel, inhuman or degrading treatment).[57] Richer interpretations should emerge primarily from other international fora (notable options are the mechanism of the Special Rapporteur on Torture and Other Cruel, Inhuman or Degrading Treatment or Punishment and the General Comments of the UN Human Rights Committee on interpretation of the ICCPR) as well as human rights interpreters (through scholarship like the present study and civil society advocacy) outside of the judicial sphere. More developed and reasoned interpretations matter because the text of the right is limited, in whichever regional or international sphere in which it is present, and because the question of what fits within the limited interpretive scope of the right is high-stakes for all involved. This is the bottom line. I do not suggest, of course, that greater clarity about interpretive scope, the rationale behind it and how interpretive decisions are made, can singlehandedly support the ongoing battle against torture, cruel, inhuman and degrading treatment or punishment but these are relevant factors. A lack of clarity has been shown to have a negative impact on the right's sphere of protection to date, from states showing hesitancy in the process leading to the UNCAT, resulting in differentiated obligations,[58] to the ECtHR seeming to attach different rules for the admissibility of evidence based on a distinction between forms of harm.[59] The interpretations of each of the

57 I make this point in the context of discussing the ECHR line of case-law on medical-related expulsion of non-nationals from Council of Europe states in Elaine Webster, 'Medical-Related Expulsion and Interpretation of Article 3 of the European Convention on Human Rights' (2013) 6 *Inter-American and European Human Rights Journal* 36.

58 Rodley and Pollard detail how concern from state representatives about the 'undefined concept' of cruel, inhuman or degrading treatment or punishment led to a differentiation in applicable obligations in respect of torture on the one hand and cruel, inhuman or degrading treatment or punishment on the other hand in the Declaration which preceded the UNCAT; Rodley and Pollard 84–85 and 111. See also Nowak, who observes the same concern in discussions that preceded Article 7 of the ICCPR; Manfred Nowak, *U.N. Covenant on Civil and Political Rights: CCPR Commentary* (NP Engel 1993) 128.

59 See dissenting opinion in *Gafgen v. Germany,* in which dissenting judges criticised what they saw as the Court's acceptance that different consequences attached to the

elements of the right, and their interrelations, impact on what states are required to do and on the extent to which individuals are protected.

References

Bernstein, JM, *Torture and Dignity: An Essay on Moral Injury* (University of Chicago Press, 2015)
Dayan, C, *The Story of Cruel and Unusual* (MIT Press, 2007)
Dewulf, S, *The Signature of Evil: (Re)Defining Torture in International Law* (Intersentia, 2011)
Douzinas, C, *The End of Human Rights: Critical Legal Thought at the Turn of the Century* (Hart Pub., 2000)
Evans, MD and Morgan, R, *Preventing Torture – A Study of the European Convention for the Prevention of Torture and Inhuman or Degrading Treatment or Punishment* (Clarendon Press, 1998)
Kuch, H, 'The Rituality of Humiliation: Exploring Symbolic Vulnerability' in Kaufman, P et al. (eds), *Humiliation, Degradation, Dehumanization: Human Dignity Violated* (Springer, 2010)
Maier, A, 'Torture: How Denying Moral Standing Violates Human Dignity' in Kaufman, P et al. (eds), *Humiliation, Degradation, Dehumanization: Human Dignity Violated* (Springer, 2010)
Margalit, A, *The Decent Society* (Harvard University Press, 1996)
Murtagh, KJ, 'What is Inhuman Treatment?' (2011) 6 *Criminal Law and Philosophy* 21
Nowak, M, *U.N. Covenant on Civil and Political Rights: CCPR Commentary* (NP Engel, 1993)
Nowak, M, 'What Practices Constitute Torture? US and UN Standards' (2006) 28 *Hum Rts Q* 809
Nowak, M and McArthur, E, 'The Distinction between Torture and Cruel, Inhuman or Degrading Treatment' (2006) 16 *Torture* 147
Oliver, S, 'Dehumanization: Perceiving the Body as (In)Human' in Kaufman, P et al. (eds), *Humiliation, Degradation, Dehumanization: Human Dignity Violated* (Springer, 2010)
Radin, MJ, 'The Jurisprudence of Death: Evolving Standards for the Cruel and Unusual Punishments Clause' (1978) 126 *U Pa L Rev* 989
Rodley, N and Pollard, M, *The Treatment of Prisoners under International Law* (3rd edn, Oxford University Press, 2009)
Sussman, D, 'What's Wrong with Torture?' (2005) 33 *Philosophy & Public Affairs* 1
Waldron, J, 'Inhuman and Degrading Treatment: The Words Themselves' (2010) 23 *Canadian Journal of Law and Jurisprudence* 269
Webster, E, 'Medical-Related Expulsion and Interpretation of Article 3 of the European Convention on Human Rights' (2013) 6 *Inter-American and European Human Rights Journal* 36

categorisation of the experience: if torture, this would lead to inadmissibility of evidence but the standard was lower if inhuman treatment, which was the majority's finding in this case; *Gafgen v. Germany,* Joint Partly Dissenting Opinion of Judges Rozakis, Tulkens, Jebens, Ziemele, Bianku and Power, paras 9–10.

8 Conclusion

The scope of human rights standards is determined on several levels through processes of interpretation. The interpretive limits of the right not to be subjected to torture, cruel, inhuman or degrading treatment or punishment are symbolic of the limits of human rights protection; symbolic of the boundary between protecting the dignity of rights-holders and attributing responsibility to states. As such, the question of this right's limits has particular symbolic as well as practical force. In practice, the limits of this right are of special importance because claims that it has been violated are always high-stakes for human rights duty-bearers who are faced with an absolute prohibition, and high-stakes for individuals who claim to have suffered injury to their minimal status as human beings. It matters, therefore, to try to understand as clearly as possible where the limits lie between experiences that fall within and experiences that fall outside the text of the right. Understanding the interpretive scope of the right not to be subjected to torture, cruel, inhuman or degrading treatment or punishment means addressing the interpretive scope of its constituent parts. The premise of this book has been that a critical aspect of this understanding centres on the meaning of degrading treatment.

The idea of degrading treatment seems often to be perceived as a gateway to trivialisation of the broader right not to be subjected to torture. This perceived risk can be seen to derive from degrading treatment's location within the text, at its outer edge. It can also be seen to derive from the familiar-yet-vague idea of degradation. Part of the difficulty with degrading treatment's meaning is undoubtedly a concern about the ambiguity of the idea of human dignity. This idea is not only intuitively tied to degradation but explicit in human rights jurisprudence. In the 2015 judgment in *Bouyid v. Belgium*, concerning an applicant in custody who was slapped on the face by a police officer, the dissenting judges raised important questions about the meaning of the dignity idea that should be seen to inform the scope of the meaning of degrading treatment.[1] This recent judgment illustrates the on-going need to seek greater insight into a rationale behind degrading treatment's scope of meaning. And it is not only judges or other authoritative interpreters who ask questions about where the right's

1 *Bouyid v. Belgium* [GC], no. 23380/09, ECHR 2015, Joint Partly Dissenting Opinion of Judges De Gaetano, Lemmens and Mahoney.

protection should begin and end, but anyone, from scholars to activists to legal advisors, with a stake in the way that the right's interpretation is understood in law. This book has aimed to show how processes of interpretation can coalesce into a rationale behind the scope of meaning and application of the right not to be subjected to degrading treatment and how this rationale might impact on our understanding of the interpretive scope of the broader right not to be subjected to torture, cruel, inhuman or degrading treatment.

Addressing the interpretive scope of degrading treatment means addressing a series of overlapping interpretative questions. The focus on interpretative questions that permeates the book reflects the nature of its methodological approach as neither doctrinal nor normative; its interpretive perspective seeks an understanding that remains within, but is not restricted by, the law's current 'range of hearing'.[2] The ECtHR retains a leading voice on the interpretation of degrading treatment across the interconnected regional and international human rights protection systems and its existing interpretive approach has been central to forming a richer understanding of degrading treatment's scope of meaning and application. Its approach is one in which degrading treatment is a distinct yet integrated element, characterised by several benchmarks, and understood as flexible and context-specific. The Court has upheld the absolute nature of the prohibition, whichever form of harm is at stake, thereby making especially strong demands for Article 3's protection and redress. The Court has continued to interpret the prohibition as absolute in nature even as it has significantly enlarged the scope of applicable positive obligations. The answers given by the Court to date, when it has been asked to pass judgment on the scope of protection offered by the right not to be subjected to degrading treatment in individual cases, form a significant body of doctrine. These answers could be expanded by the Court in some areas but they can only ever take us so far – they are inherently limited by the nature of the Court as an authoritative legal interpreter. It falls to others with a stake in the right's interpretation to ask and answer further interpretive questions, and to do so in a way that takes seriously the authoritative approach. This gives rise to an interpretation of degrading treatment that has added value; it progresses the current interpretation whilst resonating within the current practical landscape.

The framework for forming a more developed interpretation of degrading treatment has rested on foundations of legal meaning and acknowledgement of the purposive nature of the ECtHR's interpretive approach. A key element of the Court's purposive interpretation of Article 3 is the idea of human dignity in the form of a fundamental value. The Court has positioned respect for dignity as a core goal of the right. For interpreters to fruitfully work with the dignity idea it must have some circumscribed meaning; otherwise, the complexity that has threatened to undermine the idea's utility outside of, and elsewhere within, human rights discourse will also undermine any possibility of it providing positive

2 Chapter 1, pp. 11–12.

interpretive direction here. The meaning of dignity that can anchor the framework for interpreting degrading treatment has been described as dignity as an elemental status, which is diminished by, and demands freedom from, experiences that undermine a minimal kind of regard or capacity. Reflecting this dignity frame, the essence of degrading treatment's meaning is in its social and symbolic dimension. The ECtHR's degradation benchmarks have been interpreted as: erosion of self-respect through profound loss of power and symbolic exclusion from the community of human beings; destruction of one's physical or moral strength to oppose the stripping of one's human status; real or symbolic injury to one's capacity to independently direct one's own actions causing injury to one's basic human status. These interpretations are coherent in themselves and fit coherently together. The sociality of degradation carries through to the meaning of treatment, which is the form that degradation must take. Treatment has been interpreted as a way of being looked at or dealt with within a social interaction. Treatment has taken a number of forms in the ECHR case-law (described as physical intrusion, sets of conditions, and manners), but these forms are less important than recognising that its meaning expresses a relationship between agent and recipient where the focus has come to be on the experience of the recipient. *Within* these meanings of degrading and treatment, there is an inherent openness that is imported by the sociality of the relevant meaning of dignity. There is always some potential for disagreement because judgment depends upon what an interpreter accepts as a social fact. This kind of openness is standard. That is, it is a space in which interpreters can put forward potentially persuadable arguments, not a space of interminable contestation. It is when a judgment could only be satisfactorily made by addressing dimensions of dignity's meaning that are *not* encompassed within the Article 3 meaning of dignity that interpretation could move into a space of deep contestation. This is likely to occur around questions of the source of dignity in human beings.[3] The possibility of questions like these indicates that the frame of degrading treatment's meaning is not impermeable; it has blurred edges at which judgments about dignity's relevant meaning may stray into aspects of dignity's non-relevant meaning. However, whilst there are blurred edges at the boundaries of dignity's meaning, and so degrading treatment's meaning, most judgments about the interpretation of the right will not stray this far. Overall, while the presence of the dignity idea opens up the right's meaning to disagreement at these blurred edges (reflective of the impact of the dignity idea in human rights discourse more broadly), its presence also elevates the right. Its presence is what makes this right so fundamental in the first place and its meaning permeates concentric and overlapping layers within the right's interpretation. The substantive dignity core of the interpretive framework for addressing degrading treatment's meaning, along with this framework's 'epistemological' and 'formative' dimensions focusing respectively on the foundations of legal meaning and on balancing

3 Such questions are most likely to arise in Article 3 claims concerning the beginning and end of life, in which there are pronounced questions about the basis on which we ascribe dignity to human beings in the first place.

conservation and innovation going forward, permeate conclusions about the scope of the right on multiple levels.

A central conclusion about the meaning of degrading treatment is that the term 'degrading' should be understood to have a narrow conceptual core and the term 'treatment' should be understood to have a wide conceptual core. I evaluate the Strasbourg case-law, which has been central within this analysis, as largely positive. The body of Article 3 case-law reveals the underpinnings of a unified, conceptually coherent meaning. The Court has, on the whole, been restrained in its interpretation of the idea of degradation. This restrained approach underpins the interpretation of degradation as concerned with injury to an individual's elemental human status. Having a transparent understanding of this narrow conceptual core should dispel scepticism about degrading treatment's ability to guard a high threshold for gaining entry to the text of the right not to be subjected to torture; Degradation is not a gateway to ill-defined subjective experiences touching upon any sense of dignity violation. The partly dissenting judges in *Bouyid* were right to be sceptical about whether degrading treatment could be seen to arise from *any* interference with human dignity.[4] It should not. Indeed, interpreters as well as states who might be concerned with an over-generous stretching of the meaning of degrading treatment have more reason to be concerned with the meaning of treatment than with the meaning of degradation. It is not clear that the Court is fully cognisant of the way that the meaning of the term 'treatment' can be seen to have implicitly evolved in its case-law. This is one aspect of the case-law that is unsatisfactory. The term 'treatment' is an integral part of the text of Article 3, it has been the vehicle for important interpretive moves by the Court, and yet its meaning has more or less clandestinely developed over decades now on a case-by-case basis. Despite this criticism, however, the case-law approach makes sense, and I have used it to underpin an interpretation of treatment that has a convincing conceptual core, which fits with the meaning of degradation and reflects the relevant meaning of dignity. Taken together then, the Strasbourg Court's approach to the meaning of the words 'degrading' and 'treatment' within the text has largely been coherent. There is only one particular direction in the case-law that seems out of step – the Court's acceptance of naturally occurring sources of degrading treatment. Accepting that degrading treatment can coherently stem from non-human sources is problematic from the perspective of the present interpretive framework, which centralises the human sociality of experiences of degradation via the relevant meaning of dignity. From this perspective, accepting that degrading treatment can stem from naturally occurring, non-human sources goes too far and is arguably a wrong turning in an otherwise largely coherent and consistent body of case-law. The present interpretive framework then, allows us to articulate a richer interpretation of the term 'degrading' as narrowly construed, and 'treatment' as widely construed, and to see the rationale behind the case-law in a new light.

4 *Bouyid v. Belgium*, Joint Partly Dissenting Opinion of Judges De Gaetano, Lemmens and Mahoney.

This rationale provides a new perspective for thinking about the future trajectory of the right not to be subjected to degrading treatment. Exploring the example of *O'Rourke v. UK*, I argued that there are no inherent limitations in terms of practical contexts or fields of application for the right, but that its limits of meaning and scope of application turn on the limits of dignity and responsibility. While socio-economic deprivation in the form of street homelessness was argued to be capable of falling within the meaning of the degradation benchmarks (with a focus on the public dimension, the link between social-perceptions and self-perceptions, and the potential for symbolic exclusion) *and* the meaning of treatment (as a social experience in the form of a set of living conditions), the barrier to a potential finding of a violation of Article 3 was found in the displacement of state responsibility by perceptions of individual responsibility. In other words, while this context could be captured by degrading treatment's scope of meaning, and characterised therefore as an experience that could undermine a minimal kind of regard towards or capacity of the individual, I suggested that it was not likely to be captured by the right's scope of application, despite the broad nature of the relevant positive state obligation to protect. This example of street homelessness was an extreme challenge to the interpretive scope of the right because it confronted questions about degrading treatment's meaning in a non-classic environment with questions about choice and responsibility. This example showed how the interpretive boundaries of the right not to be subjected to degrading treatment expand and contract simultaneously along the axes of dignity and responsibility. It also showed that judgments about the reach of dignity protection and the limits of state responsibility are inherently context-dependent and socially embedded. The future trajectory of the right not to be subjected to degrading treatment will mirror these tensions. The best chance of understanding the right's future trajectory comes from having a rich sense of why certain things should fall within its scope of meaning and an understanding of how an authoritative assessment about its scope of application is likely to be made. We can make claims about certain new directions – significant future directions may be, for example, socio-economic deprivation for nationals of the state in contexts in which age and extreme poor health of the individual are key, or the experience of elderly persons relating to personal care and the actions of relatives or private care home staff – but the limitations on degrading treatment's scope of meaning and application are not field-based, but conceptual and practical in the form of the axes of dignity and responsibility. There is potential for degrading treatment to be recognised in almost any field.

This book's approach to understanding, and its conclusions about, the interpretive scope of degrading treatment urge a different way of thinking about the interpretive scope of the prohibition of torture, cruel, inhuman or degrading treatment or punishment as a whole. It demonstrates how the idea of human dignity can, in practice, shape a unified conceptual core across all of the elements of the right and how this can, in practice, influence the way we see the distinctiveness of each element. Starting from the interpretation of degrading treatment, the right as a whole has been seen to reflect a concern with profound powerlessness through experiences leading to symbolic exclusion from the human community. Cruel and inhuman treatment have been seen to capture something distinctive about expressions of indifference within relationships of power asymmetry and practical dependency, and torture has been seen as a magnified form of symbolic exclusion characterised by its intense communication of an intention to destroy the victim's human status. Cruel and inhuman treatment are seen as *different* to, rather than simply more serious or severe than degrading treatment, and torture is seen as *not different* to degrading treatment in terms of the essence of the experience, but different on the basis of its context. The point I have aimed to make is that the interpretation of degrading treatment can make a significant contribution to rethinking the broader right, and that rethinking the right on this basis can potentially lead to better informed, more nuanced and ultimately more successful claims that the right not to be subjected to torture, cruel, inhuman or degrading treatment should do more or indeed should do less. The right might indeed be 'cheapened' by 'overuse'[5] but it can also be cheapened by underuse. A clearer rationale behind the whole right's interpretive scope is in the interest of all interpreters.

In summary, processes of interpretation on several overlapping levels validly feed into perceptions and decisions about what should or should not fall within any legal human rights standard. Interpretations by scholars, by civil society actors, by rights holders themselves and their legal advisors, by government actors and their legal advisors, by experts in quasi-judicial bodies, by lawyers and judges in courts, can all permeate, in sometimes subtle long-term ways, the legal meaning of a human rights standard. The legal meaning of the text may absorb and manifest some interpretations and ignore others but it is constrained by interpretation on a more basic level, by the semantic meaning that the text can bear. It must also reflect the motivations that its authoritative interpreters draw upon to direct their decisions about why particular interpretations should succeed and others not. Interpretation on multiple levels determines the effectiveness of human rights law: it determines how effective it is in offering protection and redress to rights-holders, in avoiding placing impossible burdens on states that would carry a risk of political disengagement, and in respecting the need to interpret the text in line with international law requirements for the interpretation of treaties. These processes are common across human rights law but they are brought into sharp relief when applied to the right not to be subjected to torture, cruel, inhuman or degrading treatment or punishment. This is so because the practical consequences of interpretive claims and decisions are high-stakes for states who find themselves faced with an absolute prohibition, and for individuals who are seeking recognition of injury to their most elemental status as human beings. For this reason, the boundaries around, and space within, the text of this right have special significance. In delineating these limits over time, every element of the legal text has

5 *McGlinchey and Others v. UK*, no. 50390/99, ECHR 2003-V, Concurring Opinion of Judge Costa, para. 2.

played, will play, and should play a part. The 'other' forms of harm should not be seen as peripheral to the right not to be subjected to torture, cruel, inhuman or degrading treatment or punishment – they should be seen as carrying the conceptual core of the right. Arguably, the degrading treatment element of the right encapsulates more than any of the other elements of the text the overlapping interpretive questions noted above because it is perceived to be closest to the outer reaches of the right's protection and because of the intuitive pull that comes from its implicit linguistic referencing of the idea of dignity. This book has interpreted degrading treatment as a socially constituted and socially recognised experience that strikes at the heart of elemental human status. As such, the interpretive scope of degrading treatment matters in and of itself. It also matters because it should influence understandings of torture, cruel, and inhuman treatment or punishment, which as a whole is symbolic of the commitment of human rights law, within the limits of state responsibility, to protect individuals' human dignity.

Index

For Product Safety Concerns and Information please contact our EU representative GPSR@taylorandfrancis.com
Taylor & Francis Verlag GmbH, Kaufingerstraße 24, 80331 München, Germany

www.ingramcontent.com/pod-product-compliance
Ingram Content Group UK Ltd.
Pitfield, Milton Keynes, MK11 3LW, UK
UKHW011018180926
475701UK00004B/807
9780367894290